고등학교 영어로 다시 읽는 세계명작

무기여 잘 있거라

Ernest Miller Hemingway 원작
넥서스콘텐츠개발팀 엮음

넥서스

고등학교 영어로 다시 읽는 세계명작
New Collection 11
무기여 잘 있거라

원　작 Ernest Miller Hemingway
엮은이 넥서스콘텐츠개발팀
펴낸이 안용백
펴낸곳 (주)넥서스

초판 1쇄 인쇄 2012년 8월 25일
초판 1쇄 발행 2012년 8월 30일

출판신고 1992년 4월 3일 제311-2002-2호
121-840 서울시 마포구 서교동 394-2
Tel (02)330-5500 Fax (02)330-5555

ISBN 978-89-5994-426-2 14740
978-89-5797-462-9 14740 (세트)

www.nexusbook.com

머 리 말

어릴 적 즐겨 읽었던 『이상한 나라의 앨리스』나 『작은 아씨들』을 이제 영어로 만나 보세요. 지난날 우리들을 설레게 했던 명작들을 영어로 읽어봄으로써, 우리말로는 느끼지 못했던 또 다른 재미와 감동을 느낄 수 있습니다. 또한 친숙한 이야기를 영어로 바꿔 읽는 것은 그 어느 학습 자료보다도 효과적입니다. 자신이 알고 있는 이야기를 떠올리며 앞으로 전개될 내용을 상상하며 읽어 나가면, 낯선 내용을 읽을 때만큼 어렵거나 부담스럽지 않기 때문입니다.

『중학교 · 고등학교 영어로 다시 읽는 세계명작 시리즈 New Collection』은 기존에 나와 있는 명작 시리즈와는 달리, 소설책을 읽듯 추억과 감동에 빠져들 수 있도록 원서의 느낌을 최대한 살렸습니다. 또한, 영한 대역 스타일을 탈피하여 우리말 번역을 권말에 배치함으로써 독자 여러분이 스스로 이야기를 이해하는 연습을 할 수 있도록 하였습니다. 더불어 원어민 성우들이 정확한 발음과 풍부한 감성으로 녹음한 MP3 파일은 눈과 귀로 벅찬 감동을 동시에 경험하며, 최대의 학습 효과를 얻을 수 있도록 제작되었습니다.

'순수하고 가슴 뭉클한 그 무엇'이 절실한 요즘, 주옥같은 세계명작을 다시금 읽으며 잠시나마 마음의 여유를 갖고 영어소설이 주는 감동에 빠져 보세요.

넥서스콘텐츠개발팀

이 시리즈의 특징

1 읽기 쉬운 영어로 Rewriting

한국인이 가장 좋아하는 세계명작만을 엄선하여, 원문을 최대한 살리면서 중고등학교 수준의 쉬운 영어로 각색하였다. 『중학교 영어로 다시 읽는 세계명작 시리즈 New Collection』은 1,000단어, 『고등학교 영어로 다시 읽는 세계명작 시리즈 New Collection』은 2,000단어 수준으로 각색하고, 어려운 어휘는 별도로 설명하여 사전 없이도 읽을 수 있다.

2 학습 효과를 배가시키는 Summary

각 STORY 및 SCENE이 시작될 때마다 우리말 요약을 제시하여 내용을 추측하면서 읽을 수 있기 때문에, 원서의 부담을 덜면서 더 큰 학습 효과를 얻을 수 있다.

3 학습용 MP3 파일

전문 원어민 성우들의 실감나는 연기가 담긴 MP3 파일을 들으면서, 읽기와 함께 듣기 및 말하기까지 연습할 수 있다.

4 독자를 고려한 최적의 디자인

한 손에 쏙 들어오는 판형, 읽기 편한 서체와 크기 등 독자가 언제 어디서나 오랜 시간 즐겁게 읽을 수 있도록 최상의 편집 체제와 세련된 디자인으로 가독성을 높였다.

추 천 리 딩 가 이 드

step 1 **청해** 들으면서 의미 추측하기

책을 읽기에 앞서 MP3 파일을 들으며 이야기의 내용을 추측해 본다.

step 2 **속독** 빨리 읽으면서 의미 추측하기

STORY 및 SCENE의 영문 제목과 우리말 요약을 읽은 다음, 본문을 읽으면서 혼자 힘으로 뜻을 파악해 본다. 모르는 단어나 문장이 나와도 멈추지 말고 전체적인 흐름을 파악하는 데 주력한다.

step 3 **정독** 정확히 읽으면서 의미 파악하기

어구 풀이와 권말 번역을 참고하면서 정확한 의미를 파악한다.

step 4 **낭독** 소리 내어 읽으면서 소리와 친해지기

단어와 단어가 연결될 때 나타나는 발음 현상과 속도 등에 유의하면서 큰 소리로 또박또박 읽어 본다.

step 5 **섀도잉** 따라 말하면서 회화 연습하기

MP3 파일을 들으며 원어민의 말을 한 박자 늦게 돌림노래 부르듯 따라 말하면서, 속도감과 발음 등 회화에 효과적인 훈련을 한다.

이 시리즈의 구성

우리말 Summary

이야기를 읽기 전에 내용을 짐작해 봄으로써, 편안한 마음으로 읽을 수 있도록 우리말 요약문을 제시하였다. 이를 힌트 삼아 보다 효과적인 내용 이해가 가능할 것이다.

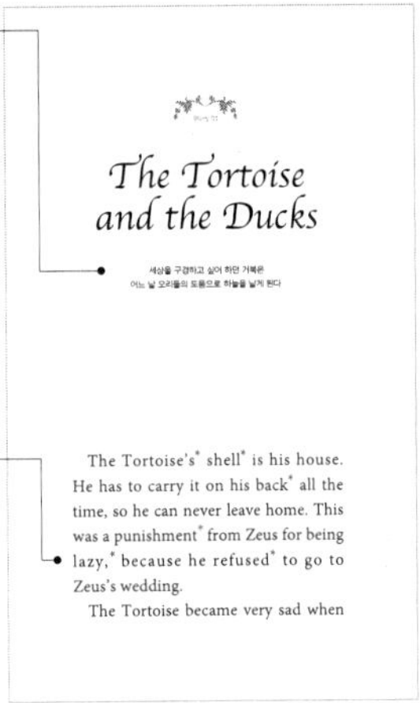
The Tortoise and the Ducks

세상을 구경하고 싶어 하던 거북은
어느 날 오리들의 도움으로 하늘을 날게 된다

영문

부담스러워 보이지 않고 편안하게 술술 읽히도록 서체와 크기, 간격 등을 최적의 체제로 편집하였다.

The Tortoise's* shell* is his house. He has to carry it on his back* all the time, so he can never leave home. This was a punishment* from Zeus for being lazy,* because he refused* to go to Zeus's wedding.

The Tortoise became very sad when

어구 풀이

이야기를 이해하는 데 도움이 되도록 어려운 어구를 순서대로 정리하였다. 이야기에 사용되는 의미를 우선순위로 하였으나, 2차적 의미가 중요하거나 불규칙 활용을 하는 경우도 함께 다뤄주어, 보다 풍부한 어구 학습이 되도록 배려하였다.

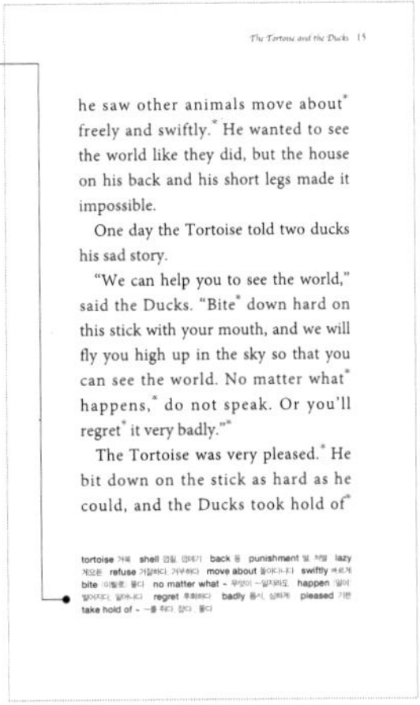
The Tortoise and the Ducks 15

he saw other animals move about* freely and swiftly.* He wanted to see the world like they did, but the house on his back and his short legs made it impossible.

One day the Tortoise told two ducks his sad story.

"We can help you to see the world," said the Ducks. "Bite* down hard on this stick with your mouth, and we will fly you high up in the sky so that you can see the world. No matter what* happens,* do not speak. Or you'll regret* it very badly."*

The Tortoise was very pleased.* He bit down on the stick as hard as he could, and the Ducks took hold of*

tortoise 거북 shell back 등 punishment lazy 게으른 refuse 거절하다, 거부하다 move about 돌아다니다 swiftly 빠르게 bite no matter what ~ happen regret 후회하다 badly pleased take hold of ~

우리말 번역

문장 구성과 어구의 쓰임을 효율적으로 학습할 수 있도록 직역을 기본으로 하여 번역하였다. 가능하면 번역에 의존하지 말고 영문과 어구만으로 이야기를 이해하도록 하며, 번역은 참고만 하도록 한다.

페이지 표시

영문을 읽다가 해결되지 않는 부분이 있을 때 그에 대응하는 번역 부분을 손쉽게 찾을 수 있도록 해당 영문 페이지의 번호를 표시해 놓았다.

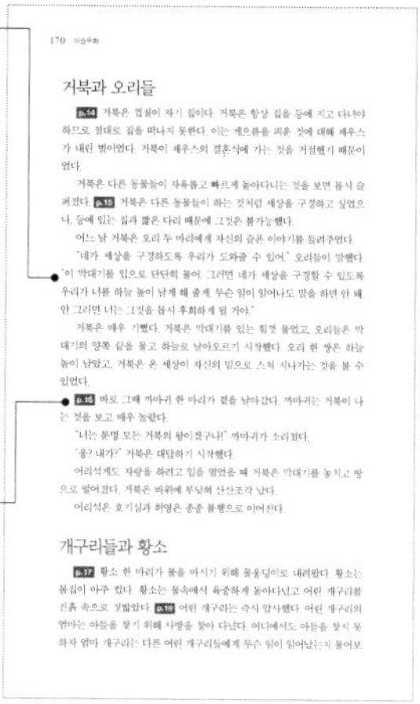

170 이솝우화

거북과 오리들

p.14 거북은 껍질이 자기 집이다. 거북은 항상 집을 등에 지고 다녀야 하므로 절대로 집을 떠나지 못한다. 이는 제우스를 피운 것에 대해 제우스가 내린 벌이었다. 거북이 제우스의 결혼식에 가는 것을 거절했기 때문이었다.

거북은 다른 동물들이 자유롭고 빠르게 돌아다니는 것을 보면 몹시 슬퍼졌다. p.15 거북은 다른 동물들이 하는 것처럼 세상을 구경하고 싶었으나, 등에 있는 집과 짧은 다리 때문에 그것은 불가능했다.

어느 날 거북은 오리 두 마리에게 자신의 슬픈 이야기를 들려주었다.

"네가 세상을 구경하도록 우리가 도와줄 수 있어." 오리들이 말했다. "이 막대기를 입으로 단단히 물어. 그러면 네가 세상을 구경할 수 있도록 우리가 너를 하늘 높이 날게 해 줄게. 무슨 일이 일어나도 말을 하면 안 돼. 안 그러면 너는 그것을 몹시 후회하게 될 거야."

거북은 매우 기뻤다. 거북은 막대기를 있는 힘껏 물었고, 오리들은 막대기의 양쪽 끝을 물고 하늘로 날아오르기 시작했다. 오리 한 쌍은 하늘 높이 날았고, 거북은 온 세상이 자신의 밑으로 스쳐 지나가는 것을 볼 수 있었다.

p.16 바로 그때 까마귀 한 마리가 곁을 날아갔다. 까마귀는 거북이 나는 것을 보고 매우 놀랐다.

"너는 분명 모든 거북의 왕이겠구나!" 까마귀가 소리쳤다.

"응? 내가?" 거북은 대답하기 시작했다.

어리석게도 자랑을 하려고 입을 열었을 때 거북은 막대기를 놓치고 땅으로 떨어졌다. 거북은 바위에 부딪혀 산산조각 났다.

어리석은 호기심과 허영은 종종 불행으로 이어진다.

개구리들과 황소

p.17 황소 한 마리가 물을 마시기 위해 물웅덩이로 내려왔다. 황소는 몸집이 아주 컸다. 황소는 물속에서 육중하게 돌아다녔고 어린 개구리를 진흙 속으로 짓밟았다. p.18 어린 개구리는 즉시 압사했다. 어린 개구리의 엄마는 아들을 찾기 위해 사방을 찾아 다녔다. 어디에서도 아들을 찾지 못하자 엄마 개구리는 다른 어린 개구리들에게 무슨 일이 일어났는지 물어보

MP3 파일
www.nexusbook.com에서 다운로드

전문 원어민 성우들의 생생한 연기를 귀로 들으며, 바로 옆에서 누군가가 동화책을 읽어주는 것처럼 더욱 흥미롭고 효과적으로 학습할 수 있다.

저자 소개

어니스트 헤밍웨이(Ernest Miller Hemingway, 1899-1961)는 미국 일리노이 주 오크파크의 유복한 가정에서 태어나 어린 시절부터 문학적 감수성을 충분히 키워 나갔다.

제1차 세계대전이 발발했을 때 헤밍웨이는 의용병으로 참전했고 제대 이후 유럽으로 건너갔다. 이때 파리에 머물면서 많은 문인들과 친교를 쌓으며 문학 수업을 받았고, 마침내 1923년에 「3편의 단편과 10편의 시」를 처녀작으로 발표했다. 이어서 1924년에는 「우리들의 시대」를, 1926년에는 「봄의 분류」를 발표했다. 같은 해인 1926년에 발표한 「해는 또다시 떠오른다」는 그의 이름을 본격적으로 알리는 계기가 되었다. 그의 작품은 전후 남녀들의 가볍고 향락적인 풍속을 묘사하여 헤밍웨이는 이른바 '로스트 제너레이션(Lost Generation)'의 대표적인 작가로 지목되었다.

이후 1929년에 발표한 「무기여 잘 있거라」는 전쟁문학의 백미이며, 1940년에는 스페인 내전을 배경으로 한 장편 소설 「누구를 위하여 종은 울리나」를 발표하여 큰 반향을 불러일으켰다. 제2차 세계대전 후 1952년에는 「노인과 바다」를 발표했고, 1953년에는 퓰리처상을, 1954년에는 노벨문학상을 수상했다.

1953년 아프리카 여행 중 비행기 사고를 당한 헤밍웨이는 요양 생활을 하며 우울증에 시달리고 집필 활동도 거의 중단했다. 결국 그는 1961년 7월, 자살로 추정되는 갑작스러운 엽총 사고로 사망했다.

작품 소개

제1차 세계대전 때 미국인 헨리는 이탈리아군에 자원하여 복무하던 중 친구인 리날디 중위를 통해 영국인 간호보조원 캐서린 바클리를 알게 되고 둘은 사랑에 빠진다. 헨리가 부상을 입어 병원에 입원하게 되면서 두 사람은 급속도로 가까워지고, 캐서린은 헨리의 아이를 갖는다. 하지만 부상에서 회복된 헨리는 캐서린과 이별을 하고 전선으로 복귀한다. 이탈리아군이 독일군과 오스트리아군의 공세에 밀리면서 헨리는 부대원들을 이끌고 후퇴하게 되는데, 대대에서 이탈했다가 탈영병으로 몰려 총살당할 지경에 이른다. 가까스로 도망친 헨리는 캐서린을 찾아가 스위스로 탈출한다. 그곳에서 둘은 꿈같은 시간을 보내지만, 캐서린은 허무하게도 아기를 낳다가 죽는다.

이 작품은 전쟁을 배경으로 한 남녀 간의 사랑 행각을 그리면서 인간들의 삶이 전쟁에 의해 얼마나 비참하게 무너질 수 있는지를 극적으로 그려내고 있다. 전쟁 속에서도 사랑은 싹트고, 어려운 환경 속에서 서로에게 절실한 사랑으로 발전하지만, 인간들이 초래한 전쟁이라는 커다란 역사의 흐름에 휘둘리는 인간의 나약한 운명은 우리에게 시사하는 바가 크다.

저자의 참전 경험을 바탕으로 한 이 작품에서는 허무한 사랑의 결말을 통해 반전 의식을 고취했다는 점에서 「누구를 위하여 종은 울리나」와 함께 헤밍웨이의 가장 유명한 전쟁 문학 작품으로 꼽히고 있다.

Contents

Chapter 1

미국인 헨리는 이탈리아군에 중위로 복무 중이다.
제1차 세계대전의 와중에 그의 부대는
이탈리아의 어느 마을에 주둔하게 된다.

In the late summer of that year, we were living in a house in a village that looked across the river and the plain* to the mountains. When troops* went by the house and down the road, the dust* they raised* powdered* the leaves of the trees.

The plain was covered with crops.*

There were many orchards* of fruit trees, and beyond the plain the mountains were brown and bare.* Battles* took place* in the mountains, and at night we could see the flashes* from the artillery.*

Sometimes in the dark we heard the troops marching* under the window. There was much traffic at night. There were many mules* on the roads with boxes of ammunition* on each side of their pack saddles.* There were also gray motor trucks that carried men, and other trucks with loads* covered with canvas.* There were big guns too that passed during the day, drawn by tractors.*

To the north, we could see a valley and a forest of chestnut trees, and behind

---

plain 평지, 벌판 **troops** 대규모 병력 **dust** 먼지 **raise** 일으키다 **powder** 뿌리다, 분을 바르다 **crop** 농작물, 수확물 **orchard** 과수원 **bare** 헐벗은, 노출된 **battle** 전투, 싸움 **take place** 일어나다 **flash** 번쩍임, 섬광 **artillery** 대포 **march** 진군하다, 행군하다 **mule** 노새 **ammunition** 탄약 **pack saddle** 짐 싣는 안장 **load** 적재 하물, 짐 **canvas** 범포, 캔버스 천 **tractor** 트랙터, 견인차

it was another mountain on this side of the river. There was fighting on that mountain too. There were mists* over the river and clouds on the mountain. The trucks splashed* mud* on the road, and the troops were muddy* and wet in their capes.*

Small gray motorcars passed very fast. There was usually an officer* on the seat with the driver and more officers in the back seat. If the car went especially fast, it was probably* the King. He lived in Udine and came out nearly every day to see how things were going. Things usually went very badly.

At the end of the autumn came the permanent* rain, and with the rain came the cholera.* But in the end* it was contained,* and only seven thousand soldiers died from it.

Chapter 2

최전선의 고리지아라는 마을에서 헨리 중위의 부대는
식사 때마다 농담을 주고받으며
비참한 전쟁 분위기를 잠시라도 잊어 보려고 한다.

The following year there were many victories.* The mountain beyond the valley was captured,* and there were

---

mist 안개 **splash** 튀기다 **mud** 진흙, 진창 **muddy** 진창의, 진흙의 **cape** 망토(어깨에 걸치는 옷) **officer** 장교, 무관 **probably** 아마도, 십중팔구 **permanent** 영구적인, 불변의 **cholera** 콜레라 **in the end** 결국 **contain** 방지하다, 저지하다 **victory** 승리, 승전보 **capture** 점령하다, 붙잡다

victories beyond the plain on the plateau* to the south. We crossed the river in August and lived in a house in Gorizia. Now the fighting was in the next mountains beyond, no more than a mile away.

The town was very pretty, and our house was very comfortable.* The river ran behind us and the town had been captured very easily, but the mountains beyond it could not be taken. I was very glad the Austrians seemed to want to come back to the town some time, for they did not bombard* it to destroy* it.

There were hospitals and cafés. The fall we spent in the town was very different from the last fall when we had been in the country. The war had changed too.

The forest of oak* trees on the mountain beyond the town had been green in the summer. By the time we had come into the town, there were only the stumps* and the broken trunks,* and the ground had been torn up.* One day, at the end of the fall, I saw a cloud coming over the mountain. It came very fast, and then everything was gray and the sky was covered. The cloud came on down the mountain, and suddenly we were in it and it was snow.

One day, while we were drinking coffee in the café, my friend saw the priest* going by in the street. He was walking carefully in the slush.* He saw us and smiled. My friend motioned for him to* come in. The priest shook his head and went on. That night in the mess* after the spaghetti course, the captain* started picking on*

---

plateau 고원 **comfortable** 기분 좋은, 편안한 **bombard** 포격하다, 폭격하다 **destroy** 파괴하다 **oak** 떡갈나무, 참나무 **stump** 그루터기 **trunk** (나무의) 몸통 **tear up** 갈기갈기 찢다 **priest** 신부, 목사 **slush** 녹기 시작한 눈, 눈이 녹아 질벅한 길 **motion for A to do** A에게 ~하라는 몸짓을 하다 **mess** 군대 식당 **captain** 대위 **pick on** ~을 괴롭히다, 못살게 굴다

the priest.

The priest was young and blushed* easily. He wore a uniform like the rest of us, but with a cross in dark red velvet above the left breast pocket of his gray tunic.* The captain spoke in simple Italian phrases so that I could understand perfectly.

"I see priest today with girls," the captain said, looking at the priest and then at me. The priest smiled and blushed and shook his head.

"Not true?" asked the captain. "Today I see priest with girls."

"No," said the priest. The other officers were amused.*

"Priest not with girls," went on the captain. "Priest never with girls. Priest always with boys and men." Everyone at the table laughed. The priest accepted* it as a joke.

"The Pope* wants the Austrians to win this war," the major* said. "He loves Franz Joseph, because that's where the money comes from. That's the kind of thing that makes me an atheist.*"

"Did you ever read the *Black Pig*?" asked the lieutenant,* turning to me. "I will get you a copy.* That book shook my faith.*"

"It is a vile* book," said the priest.

"It is very good," said the lieutenant to me. "It tells you about priests. You will like it."

I smiled at the priest and he smiled back.

"Don't you read it," he said.

"I will get a copy for you," said the lieutenant.

"All thinking men are atheists," the

blush 얼굴을 붉히다 **tunic** 군복 상의 **amused** 즐거워하는 **accept** 받아들이다, 수용하다 **Pope** 로마 교황 **major** 소령 **atheist** 무신론자 **lieutenant** 중위 **copy** (책의) 한 부 **faith** 신앙, 신앙심 **vile** 타락한, 부도덕한

major said.

At that moment, someone came in, and as the door opened I could see the snow falling.

"There will be no more offensive* now that it is snowing," I said.

"Certainly not," said the major. "You should go on leave.* You should visit Rome, Naples, Sicily...."

"He should go to Amalfi," said the lieutenant. "I will write you cards to my family in Amalfi. They will love you like a son."

"He should go to Palermo."

"He ought to go to Capri."

"You should go to Abruzzi and visit my family at Capracotta," said the priest.

"Abruzzi? There's more snow there than here. Besides, he doesn't want to see peasants.* Let him go to centers of culture and civilization.*"

"You must go on leave immediately,*" said the major.

"I would love to go with you and show you things," said the lieutenant.

"When you come back, bring a phonograph.*"

"Bring back good opera disks."

"Bring Caruso."

"No. Caruso bellows.*"

"Don't you wish you could bellow like him?"

"He bellows. He bellows!"

"You should go to Abruzzi," the priest said. "There is good hunting, and you would like the people. You could stay with my family. My father is a famous hunter."

"Come on," said the captain. "Let's go for a drink before it closes."

---

offensive 공격, 공세 **go on leave** 휴가를 가다 **peasant** 농부, 소작농
civilization 문명 **immediately** 즉시, 즉각 **phonograph** 축음기
bellow 고함지르다

"Good night," I said to the priest.

"Good night," he said.

Chapter 3

이탈리아 주요 도시를 돌아다니며 휴가를 마치고 돌아온 헨리 중위에게
친구인 리날디 중위는 영국군 병원에서 근무하는
캐서린 바클리에게 호감이 있다고 말한다.

When I came back to the front,* we were still in that town. There were many more guns around, and the spring had come. There were some new hospitals. Now you could meet British men and

front 최전선, 제1선

sometimes women on the street.

A few more houses had been hit by shellfire.* I walked down the warm alleyway* of trees and found we still lived in the same house. The door was open, and there was a soldier sitting on a bench outside in the sun. It was all as I had left it except that now it was spring. I went upstairs.

The room I shared with lieutenant Rinaldi looked out onto the courtyard.* The window was open, my bed was made up with blankets, and my things hung on the wall. My Austrian sniper*'s rifle* hung over the two beds. Lieutenant Rinaldi lay asleep on his bed. He woke when he heard me come in, and sat up.

"Ciao*!" he said. "How was it?"

"Magnificent.*"

We shook hands, and then he put his arm around my neck and kissed me.

"Where did you go and what did you do?"

"I went everywhere. Milan, Florence, Rome, Naples, Villa San Giovanni, Messina, Taormina...."

"Did you meet a beautiful girl?"

"Yes. In Milano."

"Good. Here now we have beautiful girls. New girls, never been to the front before."

"Wonderful."

"We will go this afternoon and see. And in the town we have new, beautiful English girls. I am now in love with Miss Barkley. I want to marry Miss Barkley."

"I have to get washed and report back in. Does nobody work now?"

"The war starts again next week.

---

shellfire 포화, 포격 **alleyway** 골목, 좁은 길 **courtyard** 안마당, 안뜰 **sniper** 저격병 **rifle** 라이플총, 소총 **ciao** 안녕(이탈리아 어 인사말) **magnificent** 훌륭한, 멋진

Perhaps it starts again. They say it will. Do you think I could marry Miss Barkley... after the war of course?"

"Absolutely,* if you love her," I said and poured* the basin* full of water.

"Tonight you will tell me everything," said Rinaldi. "Now I must sleep more to be fresh and beautiful for Miss Barkley."

I washed in the cold water in the basin. While I rubbed* myself with a towel, I looked at Rinaldi lying with his eyes closed on the bed. He was handsome, was my age, and he came from Amalfi. He loved being a surgeon* and we were close friends. He opened his eyes.

"You have money?"

"Yes."

"Loan* me fifty lire."

I dried my hands and gave him the money.

"I must make on Miss Barkley the

impression* of a man of wealth,*" he said, smiling. "You are my close friend and financial* protector.*"

"Go to hell," I said.

That night in the mess I sat next to the priest. He was disappointed* and suddenly hurt* that I had not gone to Abruzzi. He had written to his father that I was coming and they had made preparations.* I felt as bad as he did and could not understand why I had not gone. It was what I had wanted to do, and I tried to explain how one thing had led to another, preventing me from* going. Finally he saw it and understood that I had really wanted to go and it was almost all right.

By the time we stopped talking, I was

---

absolutely 정말 그래, 그렇고말고 **pour** 따르다, 붓다 **basin** 대야 **rub** 문지르다 **surgeon** 외과의 **loan** 대부하다, 빌려 주다 **impression** 인상, 감명 **wealth** 부 **financial** 재정(상)의, 재무의 **protector** 보호자, 옹호자 **disappointed** 실망한, 기대가 어긋난 **hurt** 다치게 하다, 아프게 하다 **make preparations** 준비를 갖추다 **prevent A from B** A가 B하는 것을 방해하다

very much drunk on wine. Then the captain shouted, "Priest not happy. Priest not happy without girls."

"I am happy," said the priest.

"Priest not happy. Priest wants Austrians to win the war," the captain went on. The others listened. The priest shook his head.

"No," he said.

"Priest wants us never to attack.*"

"No. If there is a war, we must attack."

"Must attack. Must attack!"

The priest nodded.*

"Leave him alone," the major said. "He's all right."

"He can't do anything about it, anyway," said the captain.

We all got up and left the mess.

Chapter 4

헨리 중위는 캐서린 바클리에게 호감을 품고 있는 리날디를 따라
그녀가 근무하는 영국군 병원을 방문한다.
그런데 헨리와 캐서린이 서로에게 호감을 느끼게 된다.

The battery* in the next garden woke me in the morning. I looked out the window. It fired twice more and the air came each time like a blow and shook the window. As I looked out at the garden, I

attack 공격하다 **nod** 끄덕이다 **battery** 포병 중대, 포대

heard a motor truck starting on the road. I dressed and went out to the garage.*

Ten cars were lined up side by side.* They were top-heavy,* blunt-nosed* ambulances, gray and built like vans.* A few mechanics* were working on one out in the yard.

"Do they ever shell* that battery?" I asked one of the mechanics.

"No, Signor* Lieutenant. It is protected* by that little hill."

"How's everything?"

"Not bad."

"Has there been any trouble getting parts?" I asked the sergeant* mechanic as we looked at the cars together.

"No, Signor Lieutenant."

"Where is the gasoline park* now?"

"The same place."

"Good," I said and went back to the house and drank some coffee at the mess table. Outside the window I saw a lovely spring morning. That day I visited the posts* in the mountains and was back in town by the end of the afternoon.

I was very dirty, so I went up to my room to wash. Rinaldi was sitting on the bed with a copy of Hugo's English grammar.

"Splendid,*" he said. "You will come with me to see Miss Barkley."

"All right."

I washed, brushed my hair and we started.

"Wait a minute," Rinaldi said. "Maybe we should have a drink first." He opened his trunk and took out a bottle of grappa.*

He poured two glasses. It was very

garage 차고 **side by side** 나란히 **top-heavy** 상부가 무거운 **blunt-nosed** 앞머리가 무딘 **van** 유개 운반차 **mechanic** 수리공, 공병 **shell** 포격하다 **Signor** 님, 씨(Mr.) **protect** 보호하다, 막다 **sergeant** 병장, 하사관 **gasoline park** 주유소 **post** 주둔 부대, 주둔지 **splendid** 멋진, 훌륭한 **grappa** 그랍파(술)

strong.

“Another?”

“All right,” I said. We drank the second glasses. Rinaldi put away the bottle and we went down the stairs. It was hot walking through the town, but the sun was starting to settle* and it was very pleasant. The British hospital was a big villa* built by Germans before the war. Miss Barkley was waiting for us in the garden. Another nurse was with her. We walked toward them. We saluted.*

“How do you do?” said Miss Barkley. “You're not an Italian, are you?”

“No.”

Rinaldi was talking with the other nurse. They were laughing.

“What a strange thing...to be in the Italian army.*”

“It's not really the army. It's only the ambulance corps.*”

"It's still very strange. Why did you do it?"

"I don't know," I said. "There isn't always an explanation for everything. What is that stick?"

Miss Barkley was quite tall. She was a blonde* and had tawny* skin and gray eyes. I thought she was very beautiful. She was carrying a thin stick, bound* in leather.*

"It belonged to a young man who was killed last year."

"I'm awfully* sorry."

"He was going to marry me, and he was killed in the Somme."

"Had you been engaged* long?"

"Eight years. We grew up together."

"And why weren't you married?"

settle 가라앉다 **villa** 별장, 시골의 큰 저택 **salute** 경례하다, 인사하다 **army** 육군, 군대 **ambulance corps** 야전 의무대 **blonde** 금발의; 금발의 사람 **tawny** 황갈색의 **bind** 묶다, 둘러 감다 **leather** 가죽 **awfully** 대단히, 몹시 **engage** 약혼시키다

"I don't know," she said. "I was a fool not to. Have you ever loved anyone?"

"No," I said.

We sat down on a bench. I turned and looked at her.

"You have beautiful hair," I said.

"Do you like it?"

"Very much."

"I was going to cut it all off when he died."

"Don't."

We looked at Rinaldi talking with the other nurse.

"What is her name?"

"Helen Ferguson. Your friend is a doctor, isn't he?"

"Yes, a very good one."

After a while, we said goodnight and left.

"Miss Barkley prefers you to me," said Rinaldi as we walked back. "That is very clear. But Miss Ferguson is very nice."

"Very nice," I said. I had not even noticed* her. "You like her?"

"No," said Rinaldi.

---

notice 주의하다, 주목하다

Chapter 5

그날 오후에 다시 캐서린을 만나러 간 헨리 중위는
캐서린의 미모에 반해 우발적으로 그녀에게 키스를 한다.

The next afternoon, I went to see Miss Barkley again. I came across* the head nurse, who said Miss Barkley was on duty.*

"There's a war on, you know," she said.

"I know."

"You're the American in the Italian

army?" she asked.

"Yes, ma'am."

"You can come and see her after seven o'clock if you wish. But don't bring a lot of Italians."

"Not even for the beautiful language?"

"No. Not even for the beautiful uniforms."

"Good evening," I said.

In the evening, I returned to call on* Miss Barkley. Miss Barkley was sitting on a bench in the garden, and she was with Miss Ferguson. They seemed glad to see me, and after a few minutes Miss Ferguson excused herself* and went away.

"I'll leave you two," she said as she got up.

"Don't go, Helen," said Miss Barkley.

"I really should. I need to write some

---

come across ~을 (뜻밖에) 만나다, 발견하다 **on duty** 근무 중인 **call on** ~을 방문하다 **excuse oneself** 양해를 구하고 자리를 뜨다

letters."

"Good night," I said.

"Good night, Mr. Henry."

We watched as she walked away.

"She's nice," I said.

"Yes, she's very nice. She's a nurse."

"Aren't you a nurse?"

"Oh, no. I'm something called a Voluntary Aid Detachment.*"

"What's the difference?"

"It takes a long time to become a nurse. A V. A. D. is a shortcut.*"

"I see."

"The Italians don't want women so near the front. So we don't go out."

"I can come here, though."

"Oh, yes."

"Let's drop* the war."

"It's very hard not to talk about it."

"Let's drop it anyway."

"All right."

I looked at her in the dark. I thought she was very beautiful and I took her hand. I leaned* forward to kiss her and there was a sharp stinging* flash. She had slapped* my face. Tears came in my eyes from the reflex.*

"I'm so sorry," she said. I thought I had a certain advantage.*

"I deserved* it."

"I'm so sorry," she said. "I didn't mean to hurt you."

She looked at me. I was angry and yet certain, seeing it all ahead like the moves* in a chess game.

"At least we are not talking about the war now," I said.

She laughed.

Voluntary Aid Detachment 구급간호봉사대 **shortcut** 지름길, 손쉬운 방법 **drop** 중단하다, 그만두다 **lean** 기대다 **stinging** 찌르는 듯이 아픈, 얼얼한 **slap** 찰싹 때리다 **reflex** 반사 작용, 반사 행동 **advantage** 유리한 점, 강점 **deserve** ~할 만하다 **move** 말의 움직임, 수

"You are sweet," she said. "I'd be glad to kiss you if you don't mind."

I looked in her eyes and kissed her hard and held her tight. I held her close against me and could feel her heart beating. The next moment she was crying on my shoulder.

"Will you be good to me?" she said.

I thought this was rather strange. Nevertheless, I stroked* her hair and patted* her shoulder.

"You need to be good to me," she said, looking up at me, "because we're going to have a strange life."

After she gathered herself,* I walked with her to the door of the villa and then walked home. Back at my room in the villa, Rinaldi was lying on his bed.

"You make progress* with Miss Barkley?"

"We are friends."

Chapter 6

캐서린은 이상할 정도로 사랑에 집착하고
헨리 중위는 이를 이상하게 여기면서도 그녀의 요구에 부응하는 척한다.

The next time I went to see Miss Barkley, she was not in the garden. I waited in the office of the hospital until she came down. I stood up when I saw Catherine Barkley coming down the hall.

---

stroke 쓰다듬다, 어루만지다 **pat** 톡톡 가볍게 치다, 토닥거리다 **gather oneself** 정신을 차리다, 마음을 추스르다 **make progress** 진행하다, 전진하다

She looked lovely.

"Good evening, Mr. Henry," she said.

"How are you?" I said. "Shall we sit here or go out into the garden?"

"Let's go out. It's much cooler."

I walked behind her out into the garden.

"Where have you been?" she asked.

"I've been out on post."

"Why didn't you send me a note?"

"I was only away for two days. But I'm back now."

She looked up at me.

"And you do love me?"

"Yes."

"You did say you love me, didn't you?"

"Yes," I lied. "I love you." I had never said it before.

"I love you and it's been awful. You won't go away again?"

"I will, but I'll always come back."

I turned her, so I could see her face

when I kissed her and I saw that her eyes were shut. I kissed her shut* eyes. I thought she was probably a little crazy. It was all right if she was. I did not care what I was getting into. This was better than going back to a villa full of men every night.

We sat on the flat* stone bench, and I held her hand.

"This is a silly game we play, isn't it?" she said.

"What game?"

"Don't pretend* you don't know what I'm talking about."

"I'm not pretending."

"You're nice," she said. "And you play the game as well as you know how. But it's a silly game."

"Do you always know what others

---

shut 감다, 닫다 **flat** 평평한 **pretend** ~인 체하다

think?"

"Not always, but I do with you. You don't have to pretend you love me."

"But I do."

"Please don't lie when we don't have to. But you are very nice. Will you come and see me again?"

"Of course."

She stood up and put out her hand.

"Good night."

I tried to kiss her.

"No," she said. "I'm very tired."

"Kiss me," I said.

"I'm very tired, darling."

"Kiss me."

We kissed, but she broke away* suddenly.

"No. Good night, please."

I went home. Rinaldi came as I was undressing.*

"Ah, ha!" he said. "It does not go so well?

Thank God I did not become involved with* the British lady."

---

break away 달아나다 **undress** 옷을 벗다 **involved with** ~와 관련된

Chapter 7

다음날 헨리 중위는 술을 마시고 캐서린을 만나러 가지만
그녀를 만나지 못하자 이상한 외로움과 공허감을 느낀다.

The next day, when I came back from our first mountain post, it was five o'clock. I went out where we washed the cars and took a shower. Then I wrote up my report in my room, sitting in my trousers and an undershirt* in front of the open window. In two days the offensive was to start and I would go to Plava.

They talked too much in the mess that evening. I decided to eat quickly and go and see Catherine Barkley. I drank wine because that night we were not all brothers unless I drank a little. I talked with the priest about Archbishop* of Ireland.

After many more cups of wine and jokes, I remembered Catherine Barkley.

"I have to go," I said. Everyone was tipsy* and happy.

Rinaldi walked out with me.

"You should not go up there drunk."

"I'm not drunk. Really."

"You should chew* some coffee."

"Nonsense."

"I'll get some, baby." He came back with a handful of roasted* coffee beans. "Chew those, baby, and good luck. I'll walk with

---

undershirt 속옷 상의 **Archbishop** 대주교 **tipsy** 얼근하게 취한 **chew** 씹다 **roasted** 구운, 볶은

you."

We walked together through the town and I chewed the coffee. At the gate of the driveway* that led up to the British villa, Rinaldi said goodnight.

I started down the driveway. I looked back and saw Rinaldi watching me. I waved* to him.

I sat in the reception hall* of the villa and waited for Catherine Barkley to come down. Someone came down the hallway.* It was not Catherine. It was Miss Ferguson.

"Hello," she said. "Catherine says she's sorry but she can't see you this evening."

"I hope she's not ill."

"She's not very well."

"Will you tell her that I am worried about her?"

"Yes, I will."

"Do you think I should come back to see

her tomorrow?"

"Yes, I do."

"Thank you very much," I said. "Good night."

I left the villa and suddenly I felt lonely* and empty.*

---

driveway 진입로 **wave** (손을 흔들어) 인사하다 **reception hall** 응접실
hallway 복도 **lonely** 외로운, 적적한 **empty** 공허한, 무의미한

Chapter 8

다음날 전선으로 향하던 헨리 중위는 병원 앞을 지나게 되고
캐서린은 헨리에게 성 안토니오 상을 건네며 행운을 빌어 준다.

The next afternoon, we heard there was to be an attack up the river that night. When the time came, we got into four cars and started on our way. I was riding in the first car and as we passed the entry* to the British hospital, I asked the driver to stop. I ran up the driveway and inside the reception hall I asked for Miss Barkley.

"I stopped to see if you were better," I said.

"I'm well," she said. "I think the heat got me yesterday."

"I have to go."

"I'll step out with you for a minute."

"Are you sure you're all right?" I asked outside.

"Yes, darling. Are you coming back tonight?"

"No."

"When will you be back?"

"Tomorrow."

She unclasped* something from her neck and put it in my hand.

"It's Saint* Anthony," she said.

"Are you a Catholic?"

"No. But they say a Saint Anthony's very

---

entry 입구 **unclasp** ~의 걸쇠를 벗기다 **saint** 성인, 성자

useful."

"I'll take care of him for you. Goodbye."

"Be careful. No, don't kiss me here."

"All right."

I climbed up into the seat of the ambulance and we started. The Saint Anthony was in a small white metal* capsule.* I opened the capsule and put him on my hand. I put him back in the capsule and put the gold chain around my neck. Then I forgot about him. After I was wounded,* I never saw him again. Someone probably got it at one of the dressing stations.*

We drove fast when we were over the bridge and soon we saw the dust of the other cars ahead down the road. Soon we were in the foothills* on the near side of the river and as the road mounted,* there were the high mountains off to the north with snow still on the tops.

The road was empty and we climbed through the hills and then went down into a river-valley. I could see the river, the water clear, fast and shallow.* Then, as the road mounted along the ridge,* I saw another range* of mountains. They were higher snow-capped* mountains that looked chalky* white and furrowed.*

It was nearly dark when we came down and entered the main road that ran beside the river.

---

metal 금속의 **capsule** 캡슐 **wound** 부상하게 하다 **dressing station** 응급 치료소 **foothill** 구릉지, 작은 언덕 **mount** 오르다, 올라가다 **shallow** 얕은 **ridge** 산등성이, 산마루 **range** 산맥 **snow-capped** 꼭대기에 눈이 덮인 **chalky** 백토질의 **furrow** 고랑을 만들다

Chapter 9

부대원들의 음식물을 공수하고 함께 먹던 중 적군의 포격이 시작된다.
포격 중에 부대원 한 명을 잃고 헨리 중위는 다리에 부상을 입는다.

The road was crowded* and there were screens* of cornstalk* and straw* matting* on both sides. We drove slowly in this matting-covered tunnel and came out onto a cleared space where the railway station had been. The road here was below the level of the riverbank.

Along the side of the sunken* road, there were holes dug* in the bank with infantry* in them. As we drove, I saw the Austrian observation* balloons* above the hills on the other side against the sunset. We parked the cars past a brickyard.* Some deep holes had been equipped* as dressing stations.

Here at the brickyard, we were safe from rifle or machine gun* fire by the riverbank. There was a smashed* bridge across the river. They were going to put over another bridge when the bombardment* started so that some troops could cross the river.

The major was a little man with a mustache.* He had been in the war in Libya. He said that if everything went well

---

crowd 가득 메우다 **screen** 차폐물, 장벽 **cornstalk** 옥수숫대 **straw** 짚, 밀짚 **matting** 거적, 매트 재료 **sunken** 움푹 들어간, 침하한 **dig** 파다, 파헤치다 **infantry** 보병, 보병대 **observation** 관찰, 정탐 **balloon** 기구 **brickyard** 벽돌 공장 **equip** 장비를 갖추어 주다, 장비하다 **machine gun** 기관총 **smashed** 격파된 **bombardment** 포격, 폭격 **mustache** 콧수염

he would see that I was decorated.[*] He asked me to have a drink with him and two other officers. We drank rum[*] and had a friendly conversation. It was getting dark.

I asked what time the attack was to start and they said as soon as it was dark. I went to the drivers. They were sitting in a dugout[*] talking, and when I came in they stopped. I gave them each a pack of cigarettes.[*] Manera lit his lighter and passed it around, and I told them what I had heard.

"What about food, lieutenant?" asked Manera. "We won't have a chance to eat after this thing starts."

"I'll go and find out," I said.

I went back to the major's dugout and he said the field kitchen would be ready soon and the drivers could come and get their stew.[*] I went back to the drivers and told them they would eat soon. We sat on the ground with our backs against the wall and smoked.

"Who goes to the attack?" asked Gavuzzi.

"Snipers."

"All the snipers?"

"I think so."

"There aren't enough troops here for a proper* attack."

"It is probably to draw attention away from where the real attack will be."

"Do the snipers know?"

"I don't think so."

"Of course they don't," said Manera. "They wouldn't attack if they knew."

"Yes, they would," Passini said. "Bersaglieri* are idiots."

"They are brave," I said.

---

decorated 훈장을 받은 **rum** 럼주 **dugout** 방공호, 참호 **cigarette** 궐련, 담배 **stew** 스튜(요리) **proper** 적절한 **bersagliere** 저격대

"They are brave because they have to be," said Manera. "If you do not attack, the police* shoot you. You have to follow orders, even if you're likely to die."

"I heard last week that a sergeant shot two officers who would not get out," said Gavuzzi.

"One of them was from my town," Passini said.

"We will shut up now," Manera said.

"I am hungry, lieutenant," Gavuzzi said.

"I will go and see," I said. Gordini got up and went outside with me.

"Is there anything I can do to help in any way?" He was the quietest one of the four drivers.

"Come with me if you want," I said. "We'll see."

I found the major on the telephone, sitting on a box inside a tent. One of the medical* captains offered* me a glass of cognac.* Gordini stood behind me. The major got off the telephone.

"It starts now," he said.

I looked outside. The Austrian searchlights* were moving on the mountains behind us. Then, suddenly, from all the guns behind us, the bombardment started.

"About the stew, major," I said.

"It's not here."

A big shell* fell and burst outside in the brickyard.

"What is there to eat?" I asked.

"We have a little pasta," the major said.

"I'll take what you have."

The major spoke to an orderly,* who went out the back and came back with a metal basin of cold macaroni* and a large

---

the police 헌병대 **medical** 의사의 **offer** 제공하다 **cognac** 코냑 **searchlight** 탐조등 **shell** 포탄, 유탄 **orderly** 당번병, 간호병 **macaroni** 마카로니

block of cheese. I gave them to Gordini.

"You'd better wait until the shelling is over," the major said.

"They need to eat," I said.

"As you wish."

Outside, we ran across the brickyard to the dugout where the three drivers were sitting against the wall, smoking.

"Here, you patriots,*" I said.

Gordini handed me the basin of macaroni.

"You eat first, lieutenant."

"No," I said. "Put it on the floor and we'll all eat."

"We have no forks."

"What the hell," I said in English.

I cut the cheese into four pieces and laid them on the macaroni. I put my hand into the macaroni and lifted. A mass loosened.*

"Lift it high, lieutenant."

I lifted higher and the strands* cleared.

I lowered* it into my mouth, sucked* and snapped* in the ends. I chewed, then took a bite of cheese, chewed, and then drank a little wine. Something landed outside that shook the ground.

"Skoda guns," said Gordini.

We went on eating. There was a noise like a railway engine starting and then an explosion* that shook the ground again.

"This isn't a deep dugout," Passini said.

"That sounded like a big trench mortar,*" I said.

"Yes, sir."

I ate the end of my piece of cheese and took a sip* of wine. Then there was a flash, as when a blast furnace* door is swung open, and a roar.*

When I could open my eyes again, I

---

patriot 애국자 **loosen** 풀다, 느슨해지다 **strand** (새끼, 철사 등을 꼬아 놓은) 한 가닥 **lower** 낮추다, 내리다 **suck** 빨다 **snap** 홱 잡다, 잡아채다 **explosion** 폭발, 파열 **trench mortar** 박격포 **sip** 한 모금 **blast furnace** 용광로, 고로 **roar** 포효

saw the ground was torn up and in front of my head there was a splintered* beam* of wood. I heard somebody crying. I tried to move, but I could not move. I heard the machine guns and rifles firing across the river. Then I heard the rockets and the bombs,* and then I heard close to me someone saying, "Mamma mia*! Oh, mamma mia!"

I turned around and touched him, and he screamed. It was Passini. His legs were toward me, and I saw that they were both smashed above the knee. One leg was completely gone and the other was held by tendons.* He bit his arm and screamed in pain.*

I tried to get closer to Passini, but I could not move. I tried again and my legs moved a little. I could move backward with my arms and elbows.* Passini was quiet now, and by the time I got to him he was already dead. There were three others to locate.* I realized* that my legs felt warm and wet and my shoes were wet and warm inside. I knew that I was hit. I put my hand on my knee. My knee wasn't there. My hand went in and my knee was down on my shin.* Somedody took hold of* me under the arms and somebody else lifted my legs.

"There are three others," I said.

"It's me, Manera. We went to get a stretcher* but there wasn't any. How are you, lieutenant?"

"Where are Gordini and Gavuzzi?"

"Gordini's at the post getting bandaged.* Gavuzzi's holding your legs. Hold on to my neck, lieutenant. Are you badly hit?"

splintered 쪼개진, 부서진 **beam** 들보, 도리 **bomb** 폭탄 **Mamma mia!** 어머니! **tendon** 건(腱), 힘줄 **pain** 아픔, 고통 **elbow** 팔꿈치 **locate** 위치 등을 알아내다 **realize** 실감하다, 깨닫다 **shin** 정강이 **take hold of** ~을 잡다 **stretcher** 들것 **bandage** ~에 붕대를 감다

"In the leg. How is Gordini?"

"He's all right. It was a big trench mortar shell."

"Passini's dead."

"Yes. He's dead."

Outside the post a great many of us lay on the ground in the dark. Some were wounded, many more were dead. As soon as I got to the dressing station, Manera brought a medical sergeant out and he put bandages on both my legs. Gordini could not drive, Manera said. His shoulder was smashed and his head was hurt. Then the British came with three ambulances, and they had two men on each ambulance. One of their drivers came over to me, brought by Gordini who looked very white and sick.

"Are you hit badly?" asked the British driver. He was a tall man and wore steel-rimmed* glasses.

"In the legs."

"It's not serious, I hope. Do you want a cigarette?"

"Thanks."

"They tell me you've lost two drivers."

"Yes. One was killed, and the other is the fellow that brought you."

"Do you want us to take the cars?"

"Yes."

"We'll take them to the villa. Two hundred and six, aren't you?"

"Yes."

"It's a charming* place. I've seen you around. They say you're an American."

"Yes."

"I'm English."

"I know."

"This chap* of yours was very anxious* for me to see you." He patted Gordini on

---

steel-rimmed 철제 테를 두른 **charming** 매력적인 **chap** 놈, 녀석
anxious 열망하는, 몹시 ~하고 싶어 하는

the shoulder. "I must do something about getting you out of here. I'll take you back with us."

He walked across to the dressing station.

"He will take care of you, lieutenant," Gordini said.

"How are you, Franco?"

"I am all right." He sat down next to me. In a moment the Englishman came back, followed by two soldiers carrying a stretcher.

"Here is the American lieutenant," he said in perfect Italian.

"I'd rather wait," I said. "There are much worse wounded than me."

"Don't be a bloody* hero," he said. Then in Italian: "Lift him very carefully. His legs are very painful.*" They picked me up and took me into the dressing room. Inside, they were operating* on all the tables. The little major looked at us angrily.

"I'll take the American lieutenant," said one of the captains. They lifted me onto a table. They took off my trousers and the medical captain commenced* dictating* to the sergeant-adjutant* while he worked, "Multiple* superficial* wounds of the left and right thigh* and left and right knee and right foot. Serious wounds to the right knee and foot. Lacerations* of the scalp* with possible fracture* of the skull.*"

The adjutant, looking up from the paper, asked "What inflicted* the wounds?"

"What hit you?" asked the medical captain.

"A trench mortar shell," I said.

"Here are the fragments* of an enemy trench-mortar shell," continued the

---

bloody 피투성이의 **painful** 아픈, 고통을 주는 **operate** 수술을 하다 **commence** 개시하다, 시작하다 **dictate** 구술하다, 명령하다 **sergeant-adjutant** 부관 상사 **multiple** 복합적인, 다수의 **superficial** 외면의, 외견상의 **thigh** 넓적다리, 허벅다리 **laceration** 찢어진 상처, 열상 **scalp** 두피 **fracture** 골절, 좌상 **skull** 두개골, 해골 **inflict** (괴로움, 부상 등을) 가하다, 안기다 **fragment** 부서진 조각, 파편

medical captain. "The pain hasn't started yet. Bring him a glass of brandy. And I think you have a fracture. I'll wrap you up.* Don't bounce* your head around." He bandaged, his hands moving very fast and the bandage coming taut.* "All right, good luck."

They lifted me and we went outside. By the time they loaded me onto the English ambulance, the pain that the captain had spoken about had started. There was another stretcher by the side with a man on it. I could only see his nose, waxy-looking,* out of the bandages. He breathed* very heavily. More stretchers were lifted and slid into the slings* above. The tall English driver came around and looked in.

"I'll drive very carefully," he said. "I hope you'll be comfortable." I felt the engine start, felt him climb up into the front seat, felt the brake come off and the clutch go in, and we started.

After some time, I felt something dripping* onto my arm. At first it dropped slowly, and then it turned into a stream. I shouted to the driver. He stopped the car and looked in through the hole behind his seat.

"What's wrong?"

"The man on the stretcher above me has a hemorrhage.*"

The ambulance stopped. Suddenly the stream from the stretcher above lessened* and started to drip again.

"How is he?" I asked as the Englishman opened the back door and looked at the man on the stretcher above.

"He's dead," he said.

---

wrap up 싸다 **bounce** 흔들다 **taut** 팽팽한 **waxy-looking** 창백해 보이는 **breathe** 숨 쉬다, 호흡하다 **sling** 들것걸이 **drip** 뚝뚝 떨어지다 **hemorrhage** 출혈 **lessen** 적어지다, 줄다

At the next post, they took the stretcher out and put another in and we went on.

Chapter 10

야전병원에 입원 중인 헨리 중위에게 리날디가 문병을 오고
캐서린 바클리를 만날 수 있게 조치해 주겠다고 말한다.

In the ward* at the field hospital, I was told a visitor was coming to see me in the afternoon. I was telling the orderly where to scratch* on the soles* of my feet against the itching* when one of the doctors

---

ward 병동, 병실 **scratch** 긁다 **sole** 발바닥 **itching** 가려운

brought in Rinaldi. He came in very fast and kissed me. He was wearing gloves.

"How are you? I bring you this...." It was a bottle of cognac. The orderly brought a chair and Rinaldi sat down. "And the good news is you will be decorated. They want to get you the silver medal but perhaps they can get only the bronze.*"

"Why?"

"Because you are badly wounded. If you can prove* you did any heroic* act, you can get the silver. Did you do anything heroic?"

"No," I said. "I was eating cheese."

"Try to remember. You must have done something heroic either before or after."

"No."

"Gordini said you carried several people on your back, but the medical captain at the first post declares* it is impossible."

"I couldn't carry anybody. I couldn't even move."

"It doesn't matter,*" said Rinaldi, taking off his gloves. "I think we can get you the silver. Didn't you refuse to be medically* aided* before the others?"

"Not very clearly."

"It doesn't matter. Look how badly you are wounded. And you are brave, always asking to go to the first line. Besides, the mission* was successful."

"Did they cross the river?"

"Yes. And they took nearly a thousand prisoners. It's in the bulletin.* I'll bring it to you."

"Have you seen Miss Barkley?" I asked.

"I will go and bring her."

"No, don't," I said. "Tell me about

---

bronze 청동, 브론즈 **prove** 입증하다 **heroic** 영웅적인 **declare** 단언하다, 선언하다 **matter** 중요하다 **medically** 의학적으로 **aid** 돕다 **mission** 임무, 의무 **bulletin** 공보, 회보

Gorizia and the girls?"

"There are no new girls. I don't go anymore."

"At all?"

"I just stop by to see if there is anything new. The girls all ask for you."

Rinaldi poured himself a glass of the cognac.

"I don't think it will hurt you, baby," he said. "Drink it."

I drank the cognac and felt the warmth go down my throat. Rinaldi poured another glass.

"To your brave wounds," he said. "To the silver medal. Oh, the priest is coming to see you. He makes big preparations."

Rinaldi stood up and put on his gloves.

"Be sensible* while I'm gone," he said.

"I will send Miss Barkley. Goodbye, baby. The cognac is next to the bed. Get well soon."

Chapter 11

헨리 중위에게 신부님이 문병을 온다.
신부님은 전쟁 후 고향에서 평화롭게 지낼 생각을 하고
헨리에게 진정한 사랑과 욕정의 차이를 상기시킨다.

It was dusk* when the priest came to see me. He stood awkwardly*—small, brown-faced, and embarrassed.*

"How are you?" he asked. He put some packages down on the floor.

---

sensible 분별 있는 **dusk** 땅거미, 황혼 **awkwardly** 어색하게, 서투르게
embarrassed 어리둥절한, 당혹한

"All right, Father."

He sat down and looked out of the window embarrassedly.* I noticed his face looked tired.

"I can only stay a minute," he said.

"How was the mess?"

He smiled.

"I am still a great joke," he said. "Thank God they are all okay."

I was not used to seeing him look so tired.

"I missed you in the mess."

"I wish I were there. I always enjoyed our conversations."

"I brought you some things," he said, picking up the packages. "A mosquito net,* a bottle of vermouth,* and some English papers."

"Thank you very much. Where did you get the papers?"

"I sent for them to Mestre. I will bring

more."

"Thank you for coming, Father." I poured out two glasses of vermouth and handed one to the priest. "What's wrong, Father? You look very tired."

"I don't know. I just feel very low."

"It's the war."

"Yes, I hate the war. But it will be over one day."

"What will you do when it's over?"

"If possible, I will return to Abruzzi."

His brown face suddenly turned very happy.

"You love Abruzzi?"

"Yes, very much."

"You should go there, then."

"I would be happy if I could live there and love God and serve Him."

I remained silent.

---

embarrassedly 곤란한 듯이, 멋쩍은 듯이 **mosquito net** 모기장
vermouth 베르무트(술)

"You do not love God?" he asked.

"No. But I fear him. I don't love much."

"What you tell me about the nights with the women—that is not love. That is just passion* and lust.* When you love something, you wish to do things for it. You wish to sacrifice* for it. You wish to serve it."

"Then I do not love."

"You will one day. Then you will truly be happy."

"I've always been happy."

"It is different. You cannot know about it unless you have it."

"If I ever get it, I will tell you."

"I stay too long and talk too much. I will take your greetings to the mess."

"Thank you for the presents."

"Goodbye," he patted my hand.

Chapter 12

헨리 중위는 후방에 있는 밀라노의 병원으로 후송되기로 결정 난다.
48시간의 끔찍한 여행 후 헨리는 미군 병원에 도착한다.

One morning, the major in charge of* the ward asked me if I felt that I could travel the next day. I said I could. I was told they would ship* me out early in the morning. He said I should take the trip

passion 열정 **lust** 육욕, 욕정 **sacrifice** 희생하다 **in charge of** ~을 맡고 있는, 담당의 **ship** 실어 나르다, 전속시키다

now before it got too hot.

The doctors were anxious to ship me to Milan where there were better X-ray facilities* and where, after the operation,* I could take mechanotherapy.* I wanted to go to Milan as well. They wanted to get us all out and back as far as possible from the front because all the beds were needed for the offensive.

I was told that I would go to an American hospital in Milan that had just been installed.* Some American ambulance units were to be sent down, and this hospital would look after them and any other Americans serving in the Italian army. There were many Americans in the Red Cross. The United States had declared war on Germany, but not on Austria.

The Italians were sure America would declare war on Austria too, and they were very excited about it. They asked me if I thought President Wilson would declare war on Austria, and I said it would happen very soon. I did not know what we had against Austria, but it seemed logical* that we should declare war on her if we did on Germany.

The night before I left, Rinaldi came to see me with the major. We shared a few glasses of the vermouth the priest had brought me. Somehow the conversation drifted* toward my life, and I explained to them that I live on money from my grandfather. Rinaldi also told me that Catherine Barkley had made plans to meet me in the hospital in Milan, and that it seemed she had managed to* get posted* there. After an hour and many more

---

facility 설비, 시설 **operation** 수술 **mechanotherapy** 기계(적) 요법, 기계로 하는 마사지 **install** 설치하다 **logical** 논리적인 **drift** 표류하다, 떠돌다 **manage to** 용케 ~을 해내다 **post** 파견하다, 전근시키다

glasses of vermouth, they got up to go.

"Goodbye, baby," said Rinaldi, kissing me. The major patted my shoulder. They staggered* out. I found I was quite drunk and went to sleep.

We left for Milan the next morning and arrived forty-eight hours later. It was a horrible* trip. We were sidetracked* for a long time this side of Mestre, and children came and peeped* in. I sent a little boy to go and get me a bottle of cognac, but he came back and said he could only get grappa. I told him to get it, and when he came back I gave him the change.*

The man next to me and I got drunk and slept until we were past Vicenza, where I woke up and was sick all over the floor. It did not matter because the man on that side had already been very sick on the floor several times.

Chapter 13

헨리 중위는 밀라노의 미군 병원에 도착하여 어렵게 병실에 입원하지만
의사도 부재중이고 캐서린도 아직 도착하지 않았음을 알게 된다.

We arrived in Milan early in the morning, and they unloaded* us in the freight yard.* An ambulance took me to the American hospital. When they unloaded my stretcher, I saw a

---

stagger 비틀거리다 **horrible** 무서운, 끔찍한 **sidetrack** 대피선에 넣다
peep 엿보다 **change** 잔돈 **unload** 짐을 내리다 **freight yard** 화물 조차장

marketplace and an open wine shop. People were watering the street, and it smelled of the early morning.

Inside the hospital, the stretcher could not fit* into the elevator, and they discussed whether it was better to lift me off the stretcher and go up in the elevator or carry the stretcher up the stairs. I listened to them as they discussed it. They chose the elevator and the Italian doorkeeper* lifted me from the stretcher.

"Be gentle," I said.

In the elevator my legs were bent* and the pain was very bad.

"Straighten* out my legs," I said.

"We can't, Signor lieutenant. There isn't enough space.*" The doorkeeper had his arm around me, and I had my arm around his neck. His face was sweating* and he grunted.*

"Heavy?" I asked.

"It's nothing."

The elevator doors opened, and we were on a balcony. The others had already arrived with my stretcher. There were several doors with brass* knobs.* One of the stretcher-bearers pushed a button that rang a bell. We heard it ring inside the doors. No one came.

"Where are they?" asked the stretcher-bearers.

"I don't know," said the doorkeeper. "They sleep downstairs."

"Go and get somebody."

The doorkeeper rang the bell, waited for a second, then he opened the door and went in. He came back with an elderly woman wearing glasses. Her hair was loose, and she wore a nurse's dress.

---

fit 맞다, 적합하다 **doorkeeper** 문지기, 수위 **bend** 구부리다 **straighten** 똑바르게 하다, 곧게 하다 **space** 공간 **sweat** 땀 흘리다, 땀나다 **grunt** 툴툴거리다, 불평하다 **brass** 놋쇠, 황동 **knob** 손잡이

"I don't understand," she said. "I don't speak Italian."

"I speak English," I said. "They want to know where they should put me."

"No rooms are ready. We weren't expecting any patients." She tucked* her hair and looked at me.

"Just show them any room where they can put me."

"I'm not sure," she said. "We weren't expecting any patients. I can't put you in just any room."

"Any room will do," I said. "Find an empty room," I said to the doorkeeper in Italian.

"Follow me," he said. They carried me down a long hallway and into a room. It smelled of new furniture. There was a bed and a large wardrobe* with a mirror. They put me down on the bed.

"I can't put on sheets," the woman said.

"They're locked up."

I ignored* her.

"Go into my pocket and take out my money," I said to the doorkeeper. The doorkeeper took out the money. The two stretcher-bearers stood next to the bed, holding their caps. "Give them five lire each and take five lire for yourself. My papers are in the other pocket. Please give them to the nurse."

The stretcher-bearers said thank you.

"Goodbye," I said. "And thanks." They saluted again and left.

"Those papers explain my case and the treatment* already given," I said to the nurse.

The woman looked at the papers through her glasses.

"I can't read Italian," she said. "I can't

---

tuck 집어넣다, 끼워 넣다 **wardrobe** 양복장, 옷장 **ignore** 무시하다, 모르는 체하다 **treatment** 치료

do anything without the doctor's orders." She began to cry and put the papers in her apron pocket. "Are you an American?" she asked, still crying.

"Yes. Please put the papers on the table by the bed."

The doorkeeper was still standing by the bed. He had a friendly face and was very kind.

"You can go," I said to him. "You can go too," I said to the nurse. "What is your name?"

"Mrs. Walker."

"You can go, Mrs. Walker. I think I will get some sleep now."

When I woke, sunlight was coming in through the shutters. I was thirsty, so I reached for the bell and pushed the button. The door opened and a nurse came in. She was young and pretty.

"Good morning," I said.

"Good morning," she said as she came over to the bed. "We couldn't get the doctor. He's at Lake Como. No one knew you were coming. Where are you hurt?"

"The legs and feet and my head are hurt."

"What's your name?"

"Frederic Henry."

"I'll get you cleaned up. But we can't do anything to the dressings* until the doctor is here."

"Is Miss Barkley here?"

"No. There's no one by that name here."

"Who was the woman that cried when I came in?"

The nurse laughed. "That's Mrs. Walker. She was on night duty, and she was asleep when you came."

While we were talking, she undressed

---

dressing (상처 따위의) 처치; 거즈, 탈지면

me. When I was undressed, except for* the bandages, she washed me. There was a bandage on my head, and she washed all around the edge.*

"Where were you wounded?"

"On the Isonze, north of Plava."

"Are you in a lot of pain?"

"No. Not anymore."

She went out of the room and came back with Mrs. Walker. Together, they made the bed with me still in it. That was new to me and I found it admirable.*

"Who is in charge here?"

"Miss Van Campen."

"And how many nurses are there?"

"Just us two."

"That's it?"

"More are coming."

"When will they be here?"

"I don't know. You ask a lot of questions for a sick boy."

"I'm not sick," I said. "I'm wounded."

After making the bed, Mrs. Walker went out and came back with a pajama jacket. They put that on me and I felt very clean.

"You're very nice to me," I said. The young nurse, who told me her name was Miss Gage, giggled.*

"Could I have some water?" I asked.

"Of course. Then you can have breakfast."

"I'm not hungry. Can you open the shutters please?"

The shutters were opened and I looked out onto a balcony. Beyond it were the tiled* roofs of houses and chimneys. I looked out over the tiled roofs and saw white clouds and the blue sky.

"When will the other nurses be coming?"

---

except for ~을 제외하고 **edge** 가장자리 **admirable** 감탄할 만한 **giggle** 낄낄 웃다 **tiled** 기와를 올린

"Why? Don't we take good care of you?"

"You're very nice."

"Do you want to use the bedpan*?"

"I'll try."

They helped me and held me up but it was of no use. I got back down on the bed and looked out the open doors onto the balcony.

"When will the doctor be here?"

"When he comes. We've tried to telephone him at Lake Como."

"There are no other doctors?"

"He's the doctor of our hospital."

Miss Gage brought a pitcher* of water and a glass. I drank some water and went back to sleep. Later, I ate some lunch and in the afternoon Miss Van Campen, the superintendent,* came up to see me. We did not like each other. She was small and suspicious* and too good for her position.* She asked many questions and seemed to think it was somewhat* disgraceful* that I was in the Italian army.

"Can I have some wine with my meals?" I asked her.

"Only if the doctor allows it."

"I can't have any until he comes?"

"Absolutely not."

"Are you planning on having him come in anytime soon?"

"We've telephoned for him."

She went out and Miss Gage came in.

"Why were you rude to Miss Van Campen?" she asked.

"I didn't mean to be. But she was snobbish.*"

"She thought you were domineering* and rude."

---

bedpan (환자용) 요강, 변기 **pitcher** 물 주전자 **superintendent** 수간호사, 관리자 **suspicious** 의심하는, 의혹을 품은 **position** 근무처, 직위 **somewhat** 얼마간, 약간 **disgraceful** 수치스러운, 불명예스러운 **snobbish** 속물의, 신사인 체하는 **domineering** 가부장적인, 횡포한

"I wasn't. And what's the idea of a hospital without a doctor?"

"He'll be here. We've telephoned for him to Lake Como."

"What's he doing there? Swimming?"

"No. He has a clinic* there."

"Why don't they just get another doctor?"

"Hush. Hush. Be a good boy. He'll be here."

I sent for the doorkeeper and when he came I told him in Italian to get me a bottle of Cinzano, a flask* of Chianti and the evening papers. He went away and brought them wrapped in newspaper. He unwrapped* them and drew the corks and put the wine and Cinzano under the bed. Later on, while I was drinking some vermouth, Miss Gage brought up a glass with some eggnog* in it. I hid the bottle of Cinzano to the other side of the bed when she came in.

"Miss Van Campen put some sherry* in this for you," she said. "You shouldn't be rude to her. She's not young, and this hospital is a big responsibility for* her."

"Tell her, I said thank you."

"I'm going to bring your supper now."

"It's all right," I said. "I'm not hungry."

She brought the tray* and put it on the bed table. I thanked her and ate a little of the supper. Soon afterward, I feel asleep and woke in the middle of the night. I stayed awake until I heard roosters* crowing* as it began to be light. I was tired and once it was really light I fell asleep again.

---

clinic 진료소 **flask** (위스키 등의 납작한) 휴대용 병 **unwrap** 풀다, 포장을 끄르다 **eggnog** 에그노그 **sherry** 셰리, 백포도주 **be responsibility for** ~에 대해 책임이 있다 **tray** 쟁반 **rooster** 수탉 **crow** (수탉이) 울다

Chapter 14

헨리 중위는 밀라노에 온 캐서린 바클리를 만난다.
헨리는 캐서린을 반기고 두 사람은 격렬한 사랑을 나눈다.

The room was full of sunlight when I woke. I thought I was back at the front and stretched out in bed. My legs were painful, and I looked down at them still in the dirty bandages. I realized where I was. I reached up for the bell and pushed the button. I heard it buzz* down the hall and then someone coming. It was Miss Gage. In the bright sunlight, she looked a little older and less pretty.

"Good morning," she said. "Did you sleep well?"

"Yes. Thanks very much," I said.

"I came in to see you and you were asleep with this in your arms." She reached under the bed and brought up the vermouth bottle. It was nearly empty. "Why didn't you ask me for a glass?"

"I thought you wouldn't let me drink."

"I would have had some with you."

"You're a nice girl."

"It isn't good for you to drink alone," she said. "Anyway, your friend Miss Barkley's come."

"Really?"

"Yes. I don't like her."

---

buzz 윙윙거리다

"You'll come to like her. She's very nice."

Miss Gage shook her head.

"Can you move just a little to this side?" she said. "I'll clean you up for breakfast." She washed me with a cloth and soap and warm water.

"Can you get a barber* for me before breakfast?"

"I'll send the doorkeeper for him." She went out and came back. "He'll be here shortly,*" she said and dipped* the cloth in the basin of water.

A few minutes later, the barber came with the doorkeeper. He was about fifty years old and had an upturned* mustache. Miss Gage was finished with me and went out and the barber lathered* and shaved* my face. He did not talk.

"What's the matter? Don't you know any news?" I asked.

"What news?"

"Anything. What's happening in town?"

"It is time of war," he said. "The enemy has ears everywhere."

I looked up at him.

"Please hold still," he said and went on shaving. "I won't tell you anything."

"What's the matter with you?" I asked.

"I am an Italian. I will not talk with the enemy."

I decided to let it go. If he was crazy, the sooner I could get out from under the razor* the better.

I paid him when it was over and tipped him half a lira. He refused to take the coins.

"No," he said. "I am not a soldier, but I am still an Italian."

"Get the hell out of here."

He went out, leaving the five copper*

---

barber 이발사 **shortly** 곧, 이윽고 **dip** 담그다 **upturned** 끝이 위로 향한
lather ~에 비누 거품을 칠하다 **shave** 면도하다 **razor** 면도칼 **copper** 구리

coins on the table beside the bed. I rang the bell and Miss Gage came in.

"Can you ask the doorkeeper to come, please?"

"All right."

The doorkeeper came in. He was trying very hard not to laugh.

"Is that barber crazy?" I asked.

"No. He made a mistake. He can't hear very well and he thought I said you were an Austrian officer."

"Oh," I said.

"Ha, ha, ha," the doorkeeper laughed. "It was funny. He said one move from you and he would have...." He drew his forefinger* across his throat.

"Ha, ha," he tried to stop laughing. "You should have seen his face when I told him you were not an Austrian!"

"Very funny," I said bitterly.* "How funny it would have been if he'd had cut my throat. Get out of here."

He went out, and I heard him laughing down the hall. Then I heard someone coming down the hallway. I looked toward the door. It was Catherine Barkley.

She came over to the bed.

"Hello, darling," she said. She looked young and very beautiful. I thought I had never seen anyone so beautiful.

"Hello," I said. When I saw her, I fell in love with her. Everything turned over inside me. She looked toward the door to check there was no one, and then she sat on the side of the bed and leaned over and kissed me. I pulled her down and kissed her and felt her heart beating.

"You're sweet," I said. "Did you have a difficult journey?"

"It wasn't very hard. It may be hard for

---

forefinger 집게손가락 **bitterly** 통렬하게, 쓰라리게

me to stay, though."

"You have to stay," I said. "Oh, you're beautiful." I was crazy about her. I could not believe she was really there and held her tight.

"You shouldn't," she said. "You're not well enough."

"Yes, I am. Come here."

"No. You're not strong enough."

"Yes, I am."

"Do you love me?"

"I love you. I'm crazy about you."

"Feel our hearts beating."

"I don't care about our hearts. I want you now. I'm crazy about you."

"You really love me?"

"Don't keep asking me that. Come on. Please, Catherine."

"All right. But only for a minute."

"Good," I said. "Close the door."

"You can't. You shouldn't."

"Don't talk. Just close the door."

As soon as she had closed the door and come back, I pulled her down onto the bed.

Afterward, Catherine opened the door and sat in a chair by the bed. The wildness* was gone, and I felt better than I had ever felt.

"Now do you believe I love you?" she asked.

"Oh, you're lovely," I said. "Stay. They can't send you away."

"We'll have to be more careful. That was crazy. We can't do that."

"At night we can."

"I have to go now, darling."

"Come back soon."

"I'll come when I can."

"Goodbye."

---

wildness 난폭함, 격렬함

"Goodbye, darling."

She left. God knows I had not wanted to fall in love. But God knows I had fallen in love with Catherine Barkley and I lay on the bed in the room of the hospital in Milan and felt wonderful. Finally, Miss Gage came in.

"The doctor's coming," she said. "He called from Lake Como. He'll be here this afternoon."

Chapter 15

헨리 중위의 다리 상태를 살펴보기 위한 검사가 진행된다.
발렌티니 박사가 헨리 중위의 다리 수술을 집도하기로 한다.

The doctor was a thin, quiet little man who seemed to hate the war. He took out a number of small steel splinters* from my thighs. After some time, he said it would be better to have an X-ray.

---

splinter 파편, 조각

The X-ray was taken at the Ospedale Maggiore, and the doctor who did it was efficient* and cheerful. Catherine Barkley had come with me, and we returned to the little hospital in the ambulance. The plates* came about an hour later. Catherine Barkley showed them to me. She took them out of the envelopes* and held them up to the light and we looked at them together.

"That's your right leg," she said, pointing.

"Put them away," I said, "and come here."

"No, I have to go," she said.

Soon after she left, three doctors came into the room. I had noticed that doctors who fail in the practice* of medicine* have a tendency to* seek one another's company. A doctor who cannot take out your appendix* properly* will refer you to* a doctor who will be unable to remove* your tonsils.* These three were such doctors.

"This is the young man," said the house doctor.*

"How do you do?" said the tall, thin doctor with the beard. The third doctor, who picked up the X-ray plates, said nothing.

"Remove the dressings?" asked the bearded doctor.

"Yes. Remove the dressings, please, nurse," the house doctor said to Miss Gage. Miss Gage removed the dressings, and I saw that my legs looked a lot better than they did at the field hospital.

"They look clean," said the house doctor.

---

efficient 유능한, 능률적인 **plate** 금속판 **envelope** 봉투 **practice** 실무, 실습 **medicine** 의학, 의료 **have a tendency to** ~의 경향이 있다 **appendix** 충수, 맹장 **properly** 적당히, 알맞게 **refer A to B** A에게 B를 참조하게 하다 **remove** 제거하다, 없애다 **tonsil** 편도선 **house doctor** (병원에서 숙식하는) 입주 의사

The second and third doctor looked over the house doctor's shoulder.

"Try moving the knee," said the bearded doctor.

"I can't," I said.

Two of them grabbed my right leg very gently and bent it.

"That's painful," I said.

"May I see the plates again, please, doctor?" asked the bearded doctor. The third doctor handed him one of the plates. "Can you pass me the left leg?"

"That is the left leg, doctor," said the house doctor.

"Oh, that's right. I was looking from a different angle.*"

They examined* the plates for some time.

"I think it's clear," said the bearded doctor. "It is going to take some time. Probably six months, at least."

"Yes. The synovial fluid* needs to reform,*" said the house doctor.

"Yes. We cannot open a knee like that."

"I agree, doctor."

"I have to wait six months?" I asked. "For what?"

"Six months before the knee can be opened safely."

"I don't believe it," I said.

The bearded doctor patted me on the shoulder.

"I can only say that to be on the safe side, you should wait at least six months before operating on such a knee," he said. "You are welcome, of course, to seek a second opinion.*"

"Thank you," I said.

"You are most welcome," he said. "Hope you get well soon."

---

angle 각도, 각 **examine** 검사하다, 조사하다 **synovial fluid** 관절 낭액
reform 다시 만들다 **opinion** 견해, 의견

All three shook my hand and went out of the room.

"Miss Gage," I called. She came in. "I cannot stay in bed for six months. Can you get another doctor to come and see me?"

"I will ask Dr. Valentini."

"Who is he?"

"He is a surgeon of the Ospedale Maggiore."

Two hours later, Dr. Valentini came. He was a major, and his face was tanned* and the ends of his moustache pointed straight up. He smiled and laughed all the time.

"How did this happen?" he asked. "Let me see the plates. Yes. Yes. That's it. You look very healthy. I'll make you better than new."

"That's all I wanted to hear."

Dr. Valentini patted me on the shoulder.

"Leave the dressings off."

"Would you like a drink, Dr. Valentini?"

"A drink? Of course. I will have more than one."

I poured him a glass of Cinzano.

"Thank you, thank you. I will bring you some cognac next time."

"When do you think my knee can be operated on?"

"Tomorrow morning. Your stomach must be empty. I will see the old lady downstairs and leave instructions. See you tomorrow. I'll bring you some cognac." He waved from the doorway, his brown face smiling.

---

tanned 햇볕에 그을린

Chapter 16

수술을 앞둔 헨리 중위를 캐서린은 정성껏 간호한다.
헨리도 이제 캐서린을 진심으로 사랑하며 그녀에게 의지한다.

Catherine stayed with me that night. I worried in the night about someone coming up, but she said they were all asleep. When I woke in the morning, she was gone. A few minutes later, she came in looking fresh and lovely and sat on the bed.

"I wish we could go for a walk," Catherine said. "Let's get you ready for your friend Dr. Valentini."

"Can you be on night duty tonight?"

"Yes. But you won't want me tonight."

"Yes, I will."

"You've never been operated on. You'll be in a lot of pain."

"I'll be all right."

"You'll feel sick, and I won't be anything to you."

"Then come here now."

"No," she said. "I have to do the chart,* darling, and fix you up.*" She kissed me. "The chart's ready. Your temperature*'s normal.* Your temperature's always normal. You have such a lovely temperature."

"Maybe all our children will have lovely

---

chart 차트, 병력 **fix up** 준비하다 **temperature** 온도, 체온 **normal** 정상의

temperatures."

"Our children will probably have horrible temperatures."

"What do you have to do to get me ready for Dr. Valentini?"

"I have to give you an enema.* It'll be quite unpleasant."

"I wish you didn't have to do it."

"I don't want anyone else to touch you. It's silly of me, but I get furious* when the nurses touch you. And there are too many nurses here now. If we don't get more patients, they'll send us away."

"Then I'd go with you."

"Don't be silly, darling. You can't move yet. But get well quickly, and then we will go somewhere. Hopefully* the war will be over soon."

"Dr. Valentini will fix me."

Soon I was clean inside and outside and waiting for the doctor.

"What do you want me to do now that you're all ready?" asked Catherine.

"Come to the bed."

"All right."

"Oh, darling, darling," I said.

"Now you see," she said, "I do anything you want."

"You're so lovely."

"I'm all for you now. I'm no longer myself. I only want what you want."

---

enema 관장 **furious** 화내어 날뛰는, 격노한 **hopefully** 바라건대

Chapter 17

헨리 중위의 무릎 수술은 성공적으로 끝나고
캐서린은 그와 함께 시간을 보내기 위해 계속 밤 근무를 선다.
캐서린의 친구 헬렌 퍼거슨은 이를 염려하여 헨리에게 충고한다.

When I woke from after the operation, I felt sick. I looked around and saw Miss Gage and she said, "How do you feel?"

"All right," I said.

"He did a good job on your knee."

"How long did it take?"

"Two hours."

There were three other patients in the hospital now. One was a thin boy in the Red Cross from Georgia with malaria.* There was another thin boy from New York, with malaria and jaundice,* and a handsome boy who had tried to unscrew* the fuse-cap* from a combination* shrapnel* and high explosive shell* as a souvenir.*

All the nurses were greatly fond of Catherine Barkley, because she would do night duty indefinitely.* She had little work taking care of the malaria people, and the boy who had unscrewed the fuse-cap was a friend of ours, so he never rang at night.

I loved her very much and she loved me. I slept in the daytime, and we both

---

malaria 말라리아, 학질 **jaundice** 황달 **unscrew** ~의 나사를 빼다 **fuse-cap** 신관 뚜껑 **combination** 결합 **shrapnel** 유산탄 **high explosive shell** 고성능 포탄 **souvenir** 기념품 **indefinitely** 막연히, 무기한으로

wrote notes during the day when we were awake, which Ferguson delivered.* I never learned anything about Ferguson except that she had a brother in the Fifty-Second Division* and a brother in Mesopotamia. I also learned that she was very good to Catherine Barkley.

"Will you come to our wedding, Fergy?" I asked her once.

"You'll never get married."

"Why not?"

"You two will fight before you'll marry."

"We don't fight."

"You'll die, then. Fight or die. That's what people do. They don't marry. But maybe you two will be all right. But don't get her in trouble. You get her in trouble and I'll kill you."

"I won't."

"Don't get her pregnant.* I don't want her with a war baby."

"You're a good girl, Fergy."

"And you ought to ask Catherine not to do night duty for a while. She's getting very tired. Also, Miss Van Campen is getting suspicious about you sleeping all morning."

"I want her to stay off night duty."

"No, you don't."

"I do."

"I don't believe you. But if you make her take the nights off for a while, I will have great respect* for you." With that, she took my note and went out.

Later that day, I rang the bell and in a little while Miss Gage came in.

"What is it?" she asked.

"I just wanted to talk to you. Don't you think Miss Barkley should go off night duty for a while? She looks very tired. Why

---

deliver 전하다 **division** (육군의) 사단 **pregnant** 임신한 **respect** 존경, 존중

does she have to stay on so long?"

Miss Gage looked at me in a funny way.

"I'm your friend," she said. "You don't have to talk to me like that."

"What do you mean?"

"Don't be silly. Will that be all?"

"Do you want a glass of vermouth?"

"All right. Just one."

She poured out a glass.

"You take the glass," I said. "I'll drink out of the bottle."

"Cheers," said Miss Gage.

"What did Van Campen say about me sleeping in*?"

"She's just annoyed. She calls you 'the privileged* patient'."

"She can go to hell."

"She isn't a mean* person," Miss Gage said. "She's just old and cranky.* And she never liked you."

"I know."

"Well, I like you. And I'm your friend. Don't forget that. You don't know it yet, but you will some day."

Catherine Barkley took three nights off night duty that week. When she came back, it was as though we met again after each of us had been away on a long journey.

---

sleep in 늦잠 자다 **privileged** 특권이 있는 **mean** 비열한 **cranky** 짜증을 잘 내는

Chapter 18

헨리 중위의 몸은 많이 회복되고
이제는 병원 밖에서도 캐서린과 즐거운 시간을 가진다.
헨리는 캐서린과 결혼식을 올리기를 바라지만
그녀는 결혼한 것이나 다름없다며 이를 꺼린다.

We had a lovely time in Milan while I recovered* from my surgery.* When I was well enough to go out, we rode in a carriage* in the park. I remember the carriage, the horse going slowly, and Catherine sitting beside me. When I was well enough to get around on crutches,* we went to dinner at Biffi's or the Gran Italia and sat at the tables outside on the floor of the galleria.*

After dinner, we would walk through the galleria, past the other restaurants and the shops with their steel shutters down. We usually stopped at a little place where they sold sandwiches; ham and lettuce* sandwiches and anchovy* sandwiches made of very tiny brown glazed* rolls. We bought them so we could eat in the night when we were hungry. Then we would get into an open carriage outside the galleria in front of the cathedral* and go back to the hospital.

At the hospital, the doorkeeper usually came out to help with the crutches. I would pay the driver, and then we would

---

recover 건강을 회복하다 **surgery** 외과, (외과) 수술 **carriage** 사륜마차 **crutch** 목발 **galleria** 갤러리아(유리 지붕으로 된 넓은 통로나 상점가) **lettuce** 양상추 **anchovy** 멸치 **glazed** (설탕물, 달걀 등으로) 광택을 낸 **cathedral** 대성당

go upstairs in the elevator.

Catherine always got off at the lower floor where the nurses lived, and I went on up and went down the hall on crutches to my room. Sometimes I undressed and got into bed, and sometimes I sat out on the balcony and watched the swallows* over the roofs and waited for Catherine.

When all the patients were asleep and Catherine was sure they would not call, she came in. I loved to take the pins out of her hair and let it surround us both. It made me feel as though we were inside a tent or behind a waterfall.* She had beautiful hair and a lovely face. We would be lying together, and I would touch her cheeks and her forehead* with the tips of my fingers and say, "Smooth as piano keys."

We said to each other that we were married on the first day she had come to

Milan. I wanted to be legally* married, but Catherine said that if we were they would send her away. I wanted us to be married because I worried about having a child, but we just pretended to ourselves we were married and did not worry much.

"I want us to be married for your sake,*" I said.

"I'm you. We are the same person. We are not separate.*"

"I thought girls always wanted to be married."

"Darling, I am married. I'm married to you. Besides, I've already had one experience of waiting to be married."

"I don't want to talk about it."

"You know I don't love anyone but you. You shouldn't care that someone else loved me."

---

swallow 제비 **waterfall** 폭포 **forehead** 이마 **legally** 법률적으로, 법률상
for one's sake ~을 위해서 **separate** 따로따로의

"I do."

"You shouldn't be jealous of* someone who's dead."

"I said I don't want to talk about it."

"I know you've been with all sorts of girls, and it doesn't matter to me."

"Couldn't we get married privately*?"

"There's no way to be married except by church or state.* It would mean everything to me if I had any religion, but I don't have a religion.*"

"But you gave me the Saint Anthony."

"That was for luck. It was a gift from someone else."

"I'll need luck, because I'll have to go back to the front pretty soon."

"Let's not think about that until you go. I'm happy, darling, and we are having a lovely time. I haven't been happy for a long time. When I first met you, I was nearly crazy. Now we're happy and we love each other. Let's just be happy. Is there anything I do you don't like? What would you like me to do? Would you like me to take down my hair?"

"Come to bed."

"Let me go and see the patients first."

---

be jealous of ~을 질투하다 **privately** 남몰래, 은밀히 **state** 국가 **religion** 종교

Chapter 19

헨리 중위의 건강은 거의 회복되고
혼자 바깥나들이도 할 수 있게 된다.
비가 내리는 창밖을 보며
캐서린은 불길한 꿈 이야기를 들려주고 불안해한다.

The whole summer went that way. I do not remember much about the days, except that they were hot and that there were many stories of victory in the papers. I was very healthy and my legs healed* quickly.

Soon I was on crutches, and then

walking with a cane.* Then I started receiving physical therapy* at the Ospedale. I went over there in the afternoons and afterward stopped at the café and had a drink and read the papers. I did not roam* around the town; all I wanted was to see Catherine. I was simply killing time when I was not with her.

I usually slept in the mornings, and in the afternoons, sometimes, I went to the races,* which made me late for physical therapy. Sometimes I went to the Anglo-American* Club and sat in a deep leather-cushioned chair in front of the window and read the magazines. They would not let me and Catherine go out together when I was off crutches, because it was unseemly* for a nurse to be seen with

heal 치료하다, 낫다 **cane** 지팡이 **physical therapy** 물리 치료 **roam** 배회하다, 돌아다니다 **race** 경마 **Anglo-American** 영국계 미국인의, 영미의 **unseemly** 보기 흉한, 꼴사나운

a patient who did not look as though he needed attendance.* However, we sometimes went out to dinner if Ferguson went along.

It was a hot summer, and I knew many people in Milan, but I was always anxious to get back home to the hospital as soon as the afternoon was over. At the front, we were advancing* on the Carso, had taken Kuk across from Plava and were taking the Bainsizza plateau. We were not doing so well on the western front. It looked as though the war would go on for a very long time.

One afternoon, I left the club and went down the steps carefully and walked up the Via Manzoni. Outside the Gran Hotel, I met old Meyers and his wife coming back from the races. She was a big-busted woman in black satin.* He was short and old, with a white mustache. He walked flat-footed* with a cane.

"How do you do?" said Mrs. Meyers. I shook her hand.

"Hello," said Mr. Meyers.

"How were the races?" I asked.

"Wonderful. I had three winners," said Mrs. Meyers.

"And you?" I asked Mr. Meyers.

"All right. I had a winner. You should come out with us."

When he talked, you had the impression that he was not looking at you or that he mistook you for* someone else.

"I will," I said.

"I'm coming up to the hospital to see you," Mrs. Meyers said. "I have some things for my boys. You're all my dear boys."

---

attendance 간병, 간호 **advance** 나아가다, 전진하다 **satin** 공단, 새틴 **flat-footed** 평발인; 어색한, 서투른 **mistake A for B** A를 B로 잘못 알다, 오해하다

"They'll be glad to see you," I said. "I have to get back."

"You give my love to all those dear boys."

"Will do. Goodbye," I said.

I went on down the street. At the Cova, I bought a box of chocolates for Catherine, and while the girl wrapped it up I walked over to the bar.* I had a martini alone, paid for it, picked up the box of chocolates at the outside counter* and walked back toward the hospital.

Outside the little bar up the street from the Scala, I met some people I knew—a vice-consul,* two men who studied singing, and Ettore Moretti, an Italian from San Francisco who was in the Italian army. I had a drink with them. One of the singers was named Ralph Simmons who sang under the name of Enrico DelCredo. I never knew how well he could sing, but he always said he was on the verge of* something very big happening. He was fat and looked worn around the nose and mouth as though he had hay fever.* He had come back from singing in Piacenza. He had sung Tosca and according to him, it had been wonderful.

"When will you sing here?" I asked.

"I'll be at the Scala in the fall."

"They'll probably throw the benches at you," Ettore said. "Did you hear how they threw the benches at him in Modena?"

"That's a damned* lie."

"I was there," Ettore said. "I threw six benches myself."

"You're just a wop* from San Francisco."

"They throw benches at him everywhere

bar 술집 **counter** 계산대, 카운터 **vice-consul** 부영사 **on the verge of** ~하기 직전에, ~에 직면하여 **hay fever** 건초열 **damned** 얼토당토않은, 천벌 받을 **wop** 이탈리아 녀석

he goes," said Ettore, "because he can't pronounce* Italian."

"He's a nut,*" said Edgar Saunders, a tenor who sang under the name of Edouardo Giovanni. "All he knows how to say is throw benches."

"That's all people know how to do when you two sing," Ettore said. "Then when you go back to America, you'll lie about your "triumphs" at the Scala. They wouldn't even let you get by* the first note* at the Scala."

"I'll sing Tosca at the Scala in October," Simmons said.

"We'll have to go, won't we, Mac?" Ettore said to the vice-consul. "They'll need someone to protect them."

"Maybe the American army will protect them," the vice-consul said.

"I hear you're going to get the silver medal," Ettore said to me. "What kind of citation* are you going to get?"

"I'm not even sure if I'm going to get it."

"You will. Oh, boy, the girls at the Cova will think you're fine, then. They'll all think you killed two hundred Austrians by yourself."

"How many do you have, Ettore?" asked the vice-consul.

"He's got everything," Simmons said. "He's their poster boy.*"

"I've got two bronze and three silver medals," said Ettore.

"He's been badly wounded many, many times," added* Simmons.

"How long have you been an officer, Ettore?" I asked.

"Two years. I'm going to be a captain soon. How long have you been a

---

pronounce 발음하다 **nut** 괴짜, 멍텅구리 **get by** 그럭저럭 살아 나가다 **note** 곡조 **citation** 표창장, 감사장 **poster boy** 이미지 캐릭터, 심벌 **add** 덧붙이다

lieutenant?"

"Just under three years."

"You can't be a captain because you don't know the Italian language well enough," Ettore said. "You can talk, but you can't read and write well enough. Why don't you join the American army?"

"Maybe I will."

"I wish I could. Oh, boy, how much does a captain get in the American army, Mac?"

"Around two hundred and fifty dollars, I think."

"Jesus Christ! What I could do with two hundred and fifty dollars! You'd better join the American army quick, Fred. See if you can get me in too."

"All right."

"Let's go, Sim," said Saunders standing up.

"All right."

"I have to go too," I said. It was a quarter

to six. "Ciao, Ettore. Keep out of trouble."

"When are you going back to the front?"

"Pretty soon."

"Well, I'll see you around."

I walked on down a back street that led to a shortcut to the hospital. Ettore was twenty-three years old. He had been brought up by his uncle in San Francisco and was visiting his father and mother in Torino when war was declared. He was a real hero, but he bored every person he met. Catherine could not stand him.

"We have heroes too, you know," she said. "But they do not talk so much."

"I think he's all right."

"I'd think he's all right if he wasn't so conceited* and didn't bore me, and bore me, and bore me."

"He bores me too."

---

conceited 자부심이 강한, 우쭐한

We were talking out on the balcony. Outside, it began to rain and we heard it drumming* on the roof.

"Who else did you see today?" Catherine asked.

"Mr. Meyers and his wife."

"They're a strange couple."

"They say he was in prison before he got back home. They let him out because he's old and he'll die soon."

"And he lived happily forever after in Milan. She's bringing some things here."

"It's raining hard."

"You'll always love me, won't you?"

"Yes."

"And the rain doesn't make any difference?"

"No."

"I'm afraid of the rain."

"Why?" The steady* rain was making me sleepy.

"I don't know, but I've always been afraid of the rain."

"Why?"

"I'm not sure."

"Tell me."

"I don't want to."

"Tell me."

"No."

"Tell me."

"All right. I'm afraid of the rain because sometimes I see me dead in it. And sometimes I see you dead in it."

She began to cry. I held her and she stopped crying. But outside the rain did not stop.

---

drum (북 등을) 둥둥 치다 **steady** 규칙적인, 끊임없는

Chapter 20

헨리 중위와 캐서린은 친구들과 함께 경마장으로 가서
마권도 사고 여러 사람들과 어울리며 즐거운 시간을 보낸다.

One day, we went to the races with Helen Ferguson and Crowell Rodgers, the boy from the hospital who had been wounded in the eyes by the explosion of the shell nose-cap.

The four of us drove out to San Siro in an open carriage. It was a lovely day, and we drove out through the park and out of town where the road was dusty.* There were villas with iron fences and big overgrown* gardens. There were many carriages going into the race track. We left the carriage, bought programs, and walked to the paddock.*

The grandstands* were old and made of wood, and the betting booths* were under the stands.* We met with Mr. and Mrs. Meyers. There was a crowd of soldiers along the fence in the infield,* and the paddock was filled with* people. We saw some people we knew and got chairs for Ferguson and Catherine and watched the horses.

There was one horse, a purplish* black, Crowell swore* was dyed* that color. We

---

dusty 먼지투성이의, 먼지가 많은 **overgrown** 무성하게 우거진 **paddock** 경주마 대기소 **grandstand** 특별관람석 **betting booth** 마권 매표소 **stand** 대기소 **infield** 내야 **be filled with** ~로 가득 채워지다 **purplish** 자줏빛을 띤 **swear** 맹세하다, 단언하다 **dye** 물들이다, 염색하다

watched him and he looked suspicious. We looked him up in the program, and he was listed* as a black gelding* named Japalac. The race was for horses that had never won a race worth more than one thousand lire. Catherine was sure his color had been changed. We all agreed we should bet on him and pooled* one hundred lire. The program showed he would pay thirty-five to one. Crowell went over and bought the tickets.

Japalac won the race.

"Isn't it wonderful?" Catherine said. "We'll have over three thousand lire."

"I hope the purple dye doesn't run before they pay off," Crowell said.

"I wonder if Mr. Meyers backed* him," said Catherine.

"Did you have the winner?" I called to Mr. Meyers. He nodded.

"I didn't," Mrs. Meyers said. "Who did

you children bet on?"

"Japalac."

"Really? He's thirty-five to one!"

"He won't pay much," Mr. Meyers said.

"He's marked thirty-five to one in the program," I said.

"He won't pay much. They put a lot of money on him in the last minute. It was Kempton and his boys. You'll see. He won't even pay two to one."

"Then we won't get three thousand lire," Catherine said. "I don't like this crooked* racing!"

"Let's go down and get a drink and see what they're paying," Crowell said. We went down and found that Mr. Meyers was right. They were paying less than two to one.

We went to the bar under the

---

list 명부에 올리다 **geld** (말을) 거세하다 **pool** 공동 출자하다 **back** (경마에서) 돈을 걸다 **crooked** 부정직한, 사기의

grandstand and ran into* a couple of polite* Italians we knew and McAdams, the vice-consul. They came up with us when we joined the girls. The Italians were full of manners and McAdams talked to Catherine while we went down to bet again. We ran into Mr. Meyers and bet a hundred lire on the same horse as him. I was feeling very good and we picked up* a couple more Italians, who each had a drink with us, and went back to the girls. These Italians were also very polite and matched manners with the two we had met before. Soon no one could sit down.

Our horse won but did not pay anything. Mr. Meyers was angry.

"You have to put up* two hundred lire to make twenty!" he said. "It's just not worth it."

I got up to go down to the paddock.

"I'll go down with you," said Catherine,

standing up. The Italians all rose. We went downstairs and out to the paddock.

"Do you like this?" Catherine asked.

"Yes. I'm having a good time."

"I can't stand being with so many people."

"Then let's stay out here and watch the race from the fence."

"That will be nice. Let's bet on a horse we've never heard of and that Mr. Meyers won't be betting on."

"All right."

We bet on a horse named Light For Me that finished fourth in a field of five. We leaned on the fence and watched the horses go by.

"Don't you prefer it when we're alone?"

"Yes," I said.

"I felt very lonely when we were with

run into ~와 우연히 마주치다 **polite** 공손한, 예의 바른 **pick up** (우연히 만난 사람과) 친해지다 **put up** 돈을 걸다

the others. But don't let me spoil* your fun, darling. We'll go back whenever you want."

"No. We'll stay here and have a drink."

Once Catherine was feeling better, we went back. We were glad to see the others again, and we had a good time.

Chapter 21

헨리 중위의 부대 복귀 일자가 정해진다.
캐서린은 헨리에게 임신 사실을 알린다.

In September, the weather became much cooler. Things were going very bad at the Italian front. The Italian army could not take San Gabriele. The fighting on the Bainsizza plateau was over, and by the

---

spoil 망치다

middle of the month the fighting for San Gabriele was nearly over too. Ettore had been sent back to the front. There was no more racing. Crowell had been sent back to America.

One afternoon, I stopped at a barber shop and got a shave and went back to the hospital. My leg was much better. I walked along the side street, practicing not limping.* An old man was making silhouettes* under an arcade.*

"Would you like one, lieutenant?" he asked.

"All right," I said.

"Take your cap off."

"I want to keep it on."

"It will not be as nice," the old man said. "But it will be more military.*"

He cut away at the black paper, then pasted* the profiles* on a white card and then handed them to me.

"How much?" I asked.

"Nothing." He waved his hand.

"Please." I took out some coppers.

"No. I made them for you. Give them to your girl."

"Many thanks."

I went back to the hospital and found some letters waiting for me. Papers with my orders had come. I was to have three more weeks of "convalescent leave*" before returning to the front.

I told Catherine about my papers later that day.

"We should go away during the three weeks," she said.

"Where?"

"Anywhere. Somewhere no one knows us."

---

limp 절뚝거리다 **silhouette** 반명 영상, 실루엣 **arcade** 아케이드, 상가
military 군의, 군대의 **paste** 풀칠하다, 풀로 붙이다 **profile** 옆얼굴, 반면상
convalescent leave (군대) 요양 휴가

She seemed upset.

"What's the matter?" I asked.

"Nothing."

"I know something's wrong. Tell me, darling."

"I don't want to worry you."

"You won't."

"Are you sure? I'm not worried, but I'm afraid it might worry you."

"Just tell me."

"I'm three months pregnant, darling. You're not worried, are you? Please don't worry."

"All right."

"Are you sure?"

"Of course. I'm not worried. In fact, I feel cheerful."

"Now just pick out a place for us to go. Anywhere would be lovely in October. We'll have a beautiful time, darling, and I'll write you every day while you're at the front."

I poured out a glass of cognac and drank it.

"Do you want a drink?" I asked.

"No. It always makes you happy, but it only makes me dizzy."

I poured another glass.

"I'd better go take a look at the patients," Catherine said. "I'll come back later."

"I'll read the papers," I said.

Chapter 22

헨리 중위는 황달에 걸리고
수간호사는 헨리가 복귀를 피하려고 일부러 벌인 짓이라고 생각한다.
헨리의 휴가는 취소되고 전선으로 복귀할 날은 가까워진다.

The next day was cold and rainy. It rained very hard when I was coming back from the Ospedale Maggiore. I changed into dry clothes and drank some brandy, but the brandy did not taste good. I became sick during the night.

"He's got jaundice," the house surgeon

said. "Look at the whites of his eyes."

Miss Gage looked, and the whites of my eyes were yellow. I was sick for two weeks, and for that reason Catherine and I could not spend a convalescent leave together.

One day while I was in bed with jaundice, Miss Van Campen came in the room, looked under the bed and saw the empty bottles there. I had sent a load of them down by the doorkeeper and I thought she must have seen them going out and come up to find some more.

"These are all brandy bottles, aren't they?" Miss Van Campen asked.

"Probably."

"And I was pitying you for having jaundice. Pity is a waste on you."

"Thanks."

"I suppose* you can't be blamed* for

---

suppose 추측하다, 생각하다 **blame** 나무라다, 비난하다

not wanting to return to the front. But I hope you had tried something more intelligent* than giving yourself jaundice with alcoholism.*"

"With what?"

"With alcoholism. You heard me. Once you feel better, you'll have to go back to the front. Self-inflicted* jaundice doesn't entitle you to* a convalescent leave."

"Have you ever had jaundice, Miss Van Campen?"

"I haven't had it myself, but I have seen a great deal of it."

"Did it seem like any of the patients enjoyed it?"

"It is still better than going back to the front."

"Miss Van Campen," I said, "have you ever seen a man who tried to disable* himself by injuring himself*?"

She ignored my question. She had to

ignore it or leave the room. She did not want to leave because she had disliked me for a long time and this was her chance to torment* me.

"I have seen many men escape the front through self-inflicted wounds."

"That wasn't my question. I have also seen self-inflicted wounds. I asked you if you had ever seen a man who had tried to disable himself by injuring himself."

She left the room, and then soon afterward Miss Gage came in.

"What happened? Miss Van Campen was furious."

"She thinks I've drunk myself into jaundice to avoid* going back to the front."

"Huh," said Miss Gage. "I'll swear

---

intelligent 지적인, 이성적인 **alcoholism** 알코올 중독 **self-inflicted** 스스로 초래한, 자초한 **entitle A to B** A에게 B할 자격을 주다 **disable** 불구로 만들다 **injure oneself** 자해하다 **torment** 괴롭히다, 고문하다 **avoid** 피하다, 회피하다

you've never had a drink. Everybody will swear you've never taken a drink."

"She saw the bottles."

"I've told you a thousand times to clear out those bottles. Where are they?"

"Below the bed."

"Do you have a suitcase*?"

"No. Use that rucksack.*"

Miss Gage packed the bottles and started for the door.

"I'll ask the doorkeeper to take them out," she said.

"Hold on," Miss Van Campen said. She was standing at the door "I'll take them, thank you." The doorkeeper was with her. "Take them, please," she said. "I want to show them to the doctor when I make my report."

She went down the hall, followed by the doorkeeper carrying the sack.

I was afraid that I would be court-martialed,* but I only lost my leave.

---

suitcase 여행 가방 **rucksack** 배낭, 룩색 **court-martial** 군사 법원에 회부하다

Chapter 23

헨리 중위가 전선으로 복귀하기로 예정된 날 밤,
헨리와 캐서린은 시내에서 마지막 데이트를 즐긴다.

I met up with Catherine on the night I was to return to the front. We walked through the streets together and I stopped in front of a gun shop.

"Let's go in for a minute," I said. "I lost my pistol.* I need to buy a new one."

I bought a used pistol and two extra*

clips* and a box of cartridges.*

I paid for the cartridges and the pistol, filled the magazine* and put it in place, put the pistol in my empty holster,* filled the extra clips with cartridges and put them in the leather slots* on the holster.

We left the shop and crossed the street and started to walk up the other side.

"I feel better," Catherine said. "I felt terrible before."

"We always feel good when we're together."

"We will always be together."

"Yes, except that I'm getting on a train at midnight."

"Are you tired?" Catherine asked.

"No. You?"

"I'm enjoying the walk. It's fun, walking with you."

---

pistol 권총 **extra** 여분의, 추가의 **clip** 탄창, 장전된 총알 한 세트 **cartridge** 탄약통 **magazine** 탄창 **holster** 권총집 **slot** 홈, 가늘고 긴 구멍

"But let's not walk for too long. Let's go in somewhere," I said.

"Let's get a room. I want to be alone with you."

It began to rain, so we took a carriage ride to the station. It was a long ride.

"What about dinner?" Catherine asked.

"We'll get room service."

At the hotel, I asked Catherine to wait in the carriage while I went in and spoke to the receptionist.* There were plenty of rooms. I went back out to the carriage, paid the driver, and Catherine and I walked in together.

The receptionist bowed* us toward the elevator. He went up in the elevator with us and showed us to the room.

"Will you have the dinner menu sent up, please?" I said.

"Of course," the receptionist said. He bowed and went out.

I went to the window and pulled a cord* that shut the thick plush* curtains. Catherine was sitting on the bed, looking at the chandelier.* She took her hat off and her hair shone under the light. She seemed unhappy.

"Come here please," Catherine said, smiling.

I went over and kissed her on the head.

"You're always my good girl."

"I'm always yours," she said.

We felt better after we ate. After coffee, the room felt like our own home. My room at the hospital had been our home and now this room was our home.

"It's a lovely room," Catherine said.

I poured out a glass of wine.

"I love wine," I said. "It makes you forget all the bad things in life."

---

receptionist 접수원 **bow** 머리를 숙여 절하다 **cord** 끈, 줄 **plush** 플러시(천) **chandelier** 샹들리에

"It's nice," said Catherine. "But it made my father very sick."

"Tell me about your father."

"He's very sick. You won't ever have to see him. Don't you have a father?"

"I have a stepfather.*"

"Will he like me?"

"You won't ever have to see him."

My head was suddenly very clear and cold and I wanted to talk facts.

"Where will you have our baby?"

"I'm not sure yet. But it'll be the best place I can find. Don't worry about me, darling. Just look out for yourself."

"How often will you write me?"

"I will write daily.*"

"I'm afraid we have to go. I might miss the train."

"All right, darling."

"I hate to leave our new, fine house."

"Don't worry. I'll have a beautiful home

for you when you get back."

---

stepfather 계부 **daily** 매일, 날마다

Chapter 24

헨리 중위는 캐서린과 아쉬운 작별을 하고 기차에 오른다.
객차 안의 적대적인 분위기에 헨리는 사람을 시켜 맡아 두었던 자리를 양보하고
기차 복도에서 잠을 자며 부대로 복귀한다.

I paid the bill* and asked the waiter to get us a carriage. We watched him cross the street in the rain.

"How do you feel, Cat?" I asked.

"Sleepy."

The carriage came and the waiter stepped out, opened his umbrella, and came toward the hotel. We met him at the door and walked out under his umbrella down the wet walk to the carriage at the curb.*

He stood with the umbrella until we were in the carriage and I had tipped* him.

We drove down the street and turned left, then came around* to the front of the station. A porter* came out from under the shelter* of the station.

"No," I said. "Thanks, but I don't need you." I had already had my baggage* put on the train by the doorkeeper from the hospital, and arranged* for him to pay a soldier to save a seat for me.

"Let's just say goodbye here," I said, turning to Catherine.

"You don't want me to come in?"

"No. Goodbye, Cat."

---

bill 계산서 **curb** (인도와 차도 사이의) 연석 **tip** 팁을 주다 **come around** 도달하다 **porter** 짐꾼 **shelter** 대기소 **baggage** 수하물 **arrange** 준비하다, 마련하다

"Will you tell him to take me to the hospital?"

I told the driver the address of the hospital.

"Goodbye," I said. "Take good care of yourself and our baby."

"Goodbye, darling."

"Goodbye," I said. I stepped out into the rain and the carriage took off. Then I went through the station and down the platform to the train.

The doorkeeper was on the platform waiting for me. I followed him into the train, and went along the aisle* and in through a door into a compartment.* My rucksack and duffel bags* were above his head on the baggage rack.* There were many men standing in the corridor,* and the men in the compartment all looked at us when we came in.

There were not enough places in the

train and everyone was hostile.* A soldier, who had been paid by the doorkeeper to save me the seat, stood up to give me his seat. Someone tapped me on the shoulder. I turned around. It was a very tall, thin captain with a red scar* along his jaw.* He had looked through the glass from the corridor and then come in.

"What?" I asked. I turned to face him. Everyone in the compartment was watching us.

"You can't do that," he said. "You can't have someone save you a place."

"Well, I did."

"You don't have the right* to do that. I was here for two hours before you came."

"What do you want?"

"The seat."

---

aisle 통로, 복도 **compartment** 칸막이한 객실 **duffel bag** 더플 백 **baggage rack** (버스, 기차 등의 짐 올려 두는) 선반 **corridor** 복도 **hostile** 적의 있는, 적대하는 **scar** 상처, 흉터 **jaw** 턱 **right** 권리

I could feel the whole compartment against me. I did not blame them. The captain was right.

"Sit down, Signor Captain," I said. The soldier who had saved me a seat moved out of the way and the tall captain sat down. "Get my things," I said to the soldier. We went out into the corridor. The train was full and there was no chance I would find a seat. I gave the doorkeeper and the solider ten lire each. I said goodbye to them and we shook hands and they left. They both felt terrible.

Inside the train, we were all standing in the corridor when the train left the station. Later, I slept on the floor of the corridor. I slept all night, waking only briefly* at Brescia and Verona when more men got on the train. Men slept on the floor all down the corridor, and the train was always crowded.

Chapter 25

부대로 복귀한 헨리 중위는 동료들과 재회하고 리날디와도 다시 만난다.
헨리는 부대원들이 전쟁에 모두 지쳐 있다는 느낌을 받는다.

I rode from Udine to Gorizia on a camion.* I got off the camion in the big square* in front of the Town Major*'s house, the driver handed down my rucksack and I put it on and swung on the

---

briefly 잠깐, 잠시 **camion** 군용 트럭 **square** 광장 **Town Major** 시장

two duffel bags and walked to our villa.

At the villa, I found the major sitting at a table in the bare room with maps and typed sheets of paper on the wall.

"Hello," he said. "Are you feeling better?" He looked older than before.

"Yes, thanks," I said. "How are things here?"

"It was a bad summer," the major said. "Did you get the decorations?"

"Yes," I put my bags down. "What do you want me to do?"

"The cars are not here. There are six up north at Caporetto. You know Caporetto?"

"Yes," I said. I remembered it as a little white town with a bell tower in a valley.

"That's where they're working from. The fighting is over, but many are sick."

"Where are all the other cars?"

"There are two up in the mountains

and four on the Bainsizza. You can go and take over* the four cars on the Bainsizza if you want. Gino has been up there for a long time. You haven't been up there, have you?"

"No."

"It was bad. We lost three cars."

"I heard."

"That's right. Rinaldi wrote you."

"Where is he?"

"He is here at the hospital. Go get cleaned up and see your friend Rinaldi."

I went to my room, unpacked my bags and lay on the bed. I was tired and my feet hurt. It was getting dark outside. I thought about Catherine and waited for Rinaldi. I had decided I was going to try not to think about Catherine except at night before I went to sleep. But I was tired and there was

---

take over ~을 맡다, 인수하다

nothing to do, so I lay and thought about her. Then Rinaldi came in. He looked a little thinner, but more or less* the same.

"Hey, baby," he said. I sat up. He came over and put his arm around me. "Let me see your knee."

"I'll have to take off my pants."

"Then take them off, baby. I want to see what kind of a job the doctors in Milan did."

I got up, took off the pants and pulled off the knee brace.* Rinaldi sat on the floor and bent the knee back and forth.* He ran his fingers along the scar, put his thumbs* together over the kneecap* and moved the knee gently with his fingers.

"You can't move it more than that?"

"No."

"Then it's a crime* to send you back. They should rest you more."

"It's a lot better than it was."

"You need more physical therapy."

"I'm fine."

"Baby, this is something I know more about than you." He got up and sat down on the bed. "The knee will be okay." He was done with the knee. "Tell me about everything."

"There's nothing to tell," I said. "I didn't do much."

"You sound like a married man," he said. "What's wrong with you?"

"Nothing," I said. "What's wrong with you?"

"This war is killing me," he said. "It is very depressing.*"

"I bet you had a great time while I was gone. Tell me."

"All summer and all fall I was operating.

---

more or less 얼마간, 더도 말고 덜도 말고 **knee brace** 무릎 보호대 **back and forth** 앞뒤로 **thumb** 엄지손가락 **kneecap** 슬개골, 무릎뼈 **crime** 죄, 범죄 **depressing** 침울하게 만드는, 울적한

I work all the time. They give me all the hard work. I am becoming a good surgeon, baby. And it was okay, because when I was operating, I did not have to think. I hate thinking, because of the war, you know? But now, baby, it's all over. I don't operate anymore and I feel like hell.* The war is terrible, baby. But now you are here to cheer me up. Did you bring the phonograph records?"

"Yes."

They were in a cardboard* box in my rucksack. I was tired and had not bothered to get them out.

"Do you feel good yourself, baby?" Rinaldi asked.

"I feel horrible."

"This war is horrible," Rinaldi said. "Come on. Let's get drunk and be cheerful. Then we'll feel fine."

"I can't drink. I've had jaundice."

"Oh, baby, you came back from Milan and with a seriously damaged liver.*"

"Oh, hell, we'll have a drink. I don't want to get drunk. I'll have one drink."

Rinaldi glided* across the room to the washstand* and brought back two glasses and a bottle of cognac.

"It's the finest Austrian cognac," he said. "They brought it back from San Gabriele."

We drank. Rinaldi laughed.

"I will get you drunk and take out your liver and put in a strong Italian liver and make you a man again."

I held out the glass for more cognac. It was getting dark outside now. Holding the glass of cognac, I went and opened the window. The rain had stopped.

"Don't throw the cognac out the window," said Rinaldi. "Just give it to me if

hell 지옥 **cardboard** 마분지 **liver** 간 **glide** 미끄러지다 **washstand** 세면대

you can't drink it."

"Go to hell," I said. I was happy to see Rinaldi again. He had teased* me for two years, and I had always liked it. We understood each other perfectly.

"Are you in love?" he asked. I was standing against the wall by the window.

"Yes."

"With Miss Barkley?"

"Yes. She is pregnant with my baby."

"She is good to you?"

"Yes."

"I want to know everything. I mean, does she...?"

"Rinaldi," I said, "please shut up. If you want to be my friend, don't say more."

"I don't want to be your friend, baby. I am your friend."

"Then shut up."

"All right. I see how it is."

I went over to the bed and sat down

next to Rinaldi. He understood me.

"To your girl," Rinaldi said, smiling. He held out the glass.

"All right."

"I'll never say anything dirty about her. Come on, baby, let's go down and eat something."

I washed, combed* my hair and we went down. Rinaldi was a little tipsy. The meal was not quite ready, so Rinaldi went back upstairs to get the bottle of cognac. I sat at the table, and he came back with the bottle and poured us each a glass of cognac.

I drank half my glass. In the hall, I heard the orderly calling. "Soup! Soup is ready!"

The major came in and sat down.

"Is this everyone?" he asked. The orderly put the soup bowl down and he ladled*

---

tease 괴롭히다, 곯리다 **comb** 빗질하다, 빗으로 빗다 **ladle** 국자로 뜨다

out a plate* full.

"This is it unless the priest comes," Rinaldi said. "If he knew baby was here, he would be here."

"He'll be here," said the major. "I left word that you were here."

"I miss the noise of the mess," I said.

"It's too quiet," the major said.

"I will be noisy," said Rinaldi.

We were finishing the spaghetti when the priest came. He was the same as ever, small and brown and compact.* I got up and we shook hands.

"Sit down," said the major. "You're late."

"Good evening, priest," Rinaldi said, using the English word. They had learned that from the captain, who spoke a little English and liked to tease the priest.

"Good evening, Rinaldi," the priest said.

"How are you?" the priest asked me.

"Fine," I said. "How have you been?"

"Drink some wine, priest," interrupted* Rinaldi.

"All right," said the priest politely. Rinaldi filled his glass.

It was clear Rinaldi wanted to tease the priest, maybe because of the captain's absence.* The priest turned to me and smiled. I could see that the teasing did not bother him now.

"Where are all the good old priest-teasers? Where is Cavalcanti? Where is Brundi? Where is Cesare? Do I have to tease this priest alone without support*?"

"He is a good priest," the major said.

"He is a good priest," said Rinaldi, "But a priest nonetheless.* I want to make the mess like the old days. I want to make baby happy. To hell with you, priest!"

---

plate 접시 **compact** (체격이) 탄탄한, 다부진 **interrupt** (말 등을) 도중에서 방해하다 **absence** 부재 **support** 지원, 원조 **nonetheless** 그럼에도 불구하고

The major looked at Rinaldi and noticed that he was drunk.

"To hell with you," said Rinaldi. "And to hell with the whole goddamned* war."

"He's been under a lot of stress and he's tired," the major said to me.

"You should take a leave," the priest said.

The major shook his head secretly at him. Rinaldi stared at the priest.

"You think I should take a leave?"

The major shook his head again at the priest. Rinaldi was still staring at the priest.

"Not if you don't want to."

"To hell with you," said Rinaldi. "They always try to get rid of* me. Every night they try to get rid of me. I fight them back. So what if I'm sick? Yes, I have it, but everybody has it. The whole army's got it. First, it's a little pimple.* Then you notice a rash* between the shoulders. Then you notice nothing at all. But don't worry, good old priest. You'll never get it. Baby will get it, but you won't."

The orderly brought in the dessert. Rinaldi was quiet. He seemed all right. We chatted* and after the coffee we all went out into the hall.

"You wanted to talk to the priest. I have to go into town," Rinaldi said. "Good night, priest."

"Good night, Rinaldi," the priest said.

"I'll see you, baby," Rinaldi said.

"Yes," I said. "Come back early." He went out the door without answering.

"He's very tired and overworked,*" the major said.

---

goddamned 망할, 빌어먹을 **get rid of** ~을 제거하다 **pimple** 여드름, 뾰루지 **rash** 발진, 뾰루지 **chat** 담소하다, 수다 떨다 **overworked** 과로한

Chapter 26

헨리 중위는 오랜만에 만난 신부님과 그동안의 일을 이야기한다.
신부님은 전쟁이 그리 오래가지 않을 것 같다는 의견을 밝힌다.

The major went into his office, and I invited the priest up to my room. I lay down on Rinaldi's bed and the priest sat on mine. The room was dark.

"How are you really?" asked the priest.

"I'm good. I'm just tired tonight."

"I'm tired too. I'm tired of the war. But I

think it will be over soon. I can feel it."

"What do you mean?"

"Everyone's become gentle, like the major."

"I feel the same way," I said.

"The summer was terrible," said the priest. He was surer of himself now than when I had gone away. "You won't believe how it has been. And I feel it cannot go on much longer."

"What will happen, then?"

"Both sides will stop fighting."

"I hope so," I said.

"You don't believe it will happen?"

"I don't think both sides will stop fighting at once."

"You are probably right. It is too much to expect. But I see the changes in men, so I do not think it can go on."

"Who won the battles this summer?"

"No one."

"The Austrians won," I said. "They managed to defend San Gabriele. They won, so they won't stop fighting. No one stops when they are winning."

"You tread on* my hopes."

"I'm just being honest."

"Then you think it will never stop? Nothing will change?"

"I don't know. I just think the Austrians will not stop when they are winning. We only become Christian when we are losing."

The priest said nothing.

"We are all gentler now because we are losing," I continued.

"I still want to believe and pray that something will happen. Anyway, I am very sorry to have stayed so long. You must be very tired. But I like talking with you."

"It was very nice to talk again."

We stood up and shook hands in the

dark.

"I'm going to the front early tomorrow."

"I'll see you when you come back."

---

tread on ~을 발로 밟다

Chapter 27

독일군과 오스트리아군의 공세에 바인시짜 고원의 전선은 무너진다.
헨리 중위는 부대원을 이끌고 우디네로 철수하라는 명령을 받는다.

I woke when Rinaldi came in but we did not talk and I went back to sleep again. In the morning, I was dressed and gone before Rinaldi was up.

I had not seen the Bainsizza before, and it was strange to go up the slope* where the Austrians had been, beyond the place on the river where I had been wounded. The houses were badly smashed but things were very well organized* and there were signboards* everywhere. We found Gino and he gave us some coffee and later I went with him and met various* people and was shown all the posts.

Gino told me there were Croatians* in the lines opposite* us now and some Magyars.* Our forces* were still in the attacking positions. There was no wire* to speak of and no place to fall back* to in case of* an Austrian attack. There were fine defensive* positions along the low mountains that came up out of the plateau, but nothing had been done about organizing them for defense.*

---

slope 비탈, 비탈면 **organize** 조직하다, 편성하다 **signboard** 간판, 현판 **various** 가지각색의, 여러 가지의 **Croatian** 크로아티아 인 **opposite** 반대편의, 맞은편의 **Magyar** 마자르 인 **forces** 군대, 부대 **wire** 전선, 케이블 **fall back** 후퇴하다, 물러나다 **in case of** ~의 경우에는 **defensive** 방어적인 **defense** 방어, 수비

I told Gino that I did not believe in war in the mountains.

"You should always have possible mobility,*" I said. "A mountain is not very mobile.* Also, people always overshoot* downhill.* If the flank* were taken, the best men would be left on the highest mountains. You end up* taking and defending mountains. But when something really starts, everyone has to get down off the mountains."

Gino and I ended up talking for a long time. At some point, he told me that food had become scarce.*

"I myself have never had enough to eat," said Gino. "But I eat a lot, and I have not starved.* The regiments* in the foremost* line get pretty good food but those in support don't get so much. Something is going wrong somewhere. There should be plenty of* food for all the soldiers."

"Some of the food must be going somewhere it shouldn't."

"Yes, they give the battalions* in the front line as much as they can, but the ones in back are not getting much. It is very bad for soldiers to be short of food. Have you ever noticed the difference food makes in the way you think?"

"Yes," I said. "It can't win a war but it can make you lose one."

"Let's not talk about losing. There is already enough talk about losing. What was done this summer cannot have been done in vain.*"

I said nothing. I was always embarrassed by the words "sacred,*" "glorious,*" and "sacrifice" and the expression "in vain."

---

mobility 기동력, 기동성 **mobile** 기동력 있는, 기동성의 **overshoot** (목표 지점보다) 더 가다 **downhill** 내리막길 **flank** 측면 **end up** ~으로 끝나다 **scarce** 부족한, 모자라는 **starved** 굶주린, 허기진 **regiment** 연대 **foremost** 맨 앞의 **plenty of** 많은 **battalion** 대대 **in vain** 헛되이 **sacred** 신성한, 성스러운 **glorious** 영광스러운

I had heard them being used often in the war, but I had seen nothing sacred. Things that were glorious had no glory* and the sacrifices were useless.* There were many words that I could not stand* to hear and finally only the names of places had dignity.* Gino was a patriot, so he used such words at times.* But he was a nice boy, and I understood his being a patriot. He was born that way. He left with Peduzzi, who had brought me to the Bainsizza, in the car to go back to Gorizia.

It stormed* all day that day. The winds became stronger in the night and at three o'clock in the morning, with the rain coming down harder, there was a bombardment and the Croatians came over across the mountain meadows* and into the front line. They fought in the dark in the rain and a counterattack* from the second line drove them back. There was much shelling, and I saw many rockets flying back and forth in the rain. Machine gun and rifle fire did not cease* for what seemed like eternity.* They did not come again and it became quieter. Between the gusts* of wind and rain, I could hear the sounds of a great bombardment to the north.

Many were wounded that night. The wounded came into the post, some carried on stretchers, some walking and some brought on the backs of men that came across the field. They were all wet to the skin* and scared. We filled two ambulances with stretcher cases and as I shut the door of the second car and fastened* it, I felt the rain on my face turn

---

glory 영광, 영예 **useless** 쓸모없는, 무용한 **stand** 참다, 견디다 **dignity** 존엄, 위엄 **at times** 때때로 **storm** 폭풍이 불다 **meadow** 초원 **counterattack** 역습, 반격 **cease** 중지하다, 그만두다 **eternity** 영원, 영구 **gust** 세찬 바람, 돌풍 **wet to the skin** 흠뻑 젖어 **fasten** 죄다, 잠그다

to snow. The flakes were coming down heavy and fast with the rain.

At dawn,* it was still storming but the snow had stopped. There was another attack just after daylight but it was unsuccessful. We expected an attack all day but it did not come until the sun was beginning to fall. It was getting dark when I heard guns firing from the field behind the village and the shells.

Later, we heard that the attack to the south had been unsuccessful. They did not attack that night but we were told that they had broken through to the north. In the night, we were told to prepare to retreat.* Later, the captain of the post came and told us that we had new orders, that the line of the Bainsizza should be held no matter what happened. He said that the Austrians had broken through the twenty-seventh army corps* up toward Caporetto.

"If those bastards* let them through we are doomed,*" he said.

"It's the Germans that are attacking," one of the medical officers said. The word "Germans" was something to be frightened of. We did not want to have anything to do with the Germans.

"There are fifteen divisions of Germans," the medical officer continued. "They have broken through, and soon we will be cut off.*"

"So am I to stay or to leave?" I asked.

"The latest orders are that we stay here. You clear* the wounded from here to the clearing station.*"

"Sometimes we clear from the clearing station to the field hospitals as well," I said. "Tell me...I have never taken part in* a

---

dawn 새벽, 동틀 녘 **retreat** 후퇴하다, 퇴각하다 **corps** 군단 **bastard** 개자식, 새끼 **doomed** 운이 다한, 불운한 **cut off** 차단하다, 끊다 **clear** 깨끗하게 하다, 치우다 **clearing station** 치료 후송소 **take part in** ~에 참가하다

retreat…if there is a retreat, how will we evacuate* all the wounded?"

"We take as many as we can and leave the rest."

"What do I take in the cars?"

"Medical equipment.*"

"All right," I said.

The retreat started the following night. We heard that Germans and Austrians had broken through in the north and were coming down the mountain valleys toward Cividale and Udine. The retreat was organized, wet and sullen.* In the night, going slowly along the crowded roads, we drove past troops marching under the rain, guns, horses pulling wagons,* mules,* motor trucks, all moving away from the front. It was just like an advance.*

We arrived at Gorizia in the middle of the next day. The rain had stopped, and the town was nearly empty. They were loading the girls into a truck. There were seven girls in total and they were wearing their hats and coats and carried small suitcases. Two of them were crying, and another smiled at us and put out her tongue and fluttered* it up and down.

I jumped out as we came into the drive to the villa.

"Take the car out and have the mechanics take a look at it," I said to the driver. "Change the oil and check the differential.* Fill her up and then get some sleep."

"Yes, lieutenant."

The villa was empty, and Rinaldi and the major had left me a note on the window. I was instructed* to fill the cars

---

evacuate 비우다, 철수시키다 **equipment** 장비, 설비 **sullen** 뚱한, 침울한 **wagon** 짐마차, 사륜마차 **mule** 노새 **advance** 전진, 진군 **flutter** 펄럭이다, 나부끼다 **differential** 차동 장치 **instruct** 지시하다, 명령하다

with the material* piled* in the hall and to proceed* to Pordenone. The mechanics had gone already. I went out to the garage. The other two cars came in while I was there and the drivers got down. It began to rain again.

"I'm so sleepy. I fell asleep three times coming here from Plava," Piani said. "What do you want us to do, lieutenant?"

"We'll change the oil, grease* them, fill them up, then take them around in front and load up the things they've left."

"We'll we leave straight away?"

"No, we'll sleep for three hours."

"I'm glad to hear that," Bonello said. "I couldn't stay awake driving."

"How's your car, Aymo?" I asked.

"It's all right."

"I'll help you with the oil."

"That's all right, lieutenant," Aymo said. "I can do it myself. You go and pack your things."

"My things are already packed," I said. "I'll go and take out the things that they left for us. Bring the cars around as soon as they're ready."

They brought the cars around to the front of the villa and we loaded them with the hospital equipment which was piled in the hallway.

"Make a fire in the kitchen and dry your clothes," I said.

"I don't care about dry clothes," Piani said. "I want some sleep."

"I'm going to sleep on the major's bed," Bonello said.

"I don't care where I sleep," Piani said.

"There are two beds in the major's room," I said. "You two sleep in there. I'll wake you."

---

material 재료, 물질 **pile** 쌓아 올리다 **proceed** 나아가다, 가다 **grease** 기름을 바르다, 기름을 치다

"The Austrians will wake us if you oversleep,* lieutenant," Bonello said.

"I won't," I said. "Where's Aymo?"

"He went in the kitchen."

"Get to sleep," I said.

I went to the kitchen. Aymo had a fire in the stove and a kettle of water on.

"I thought I'd cook some pasta," he said. "Everyone will be hungry when they wake up."

"Aren't you tired, Bartolomeo? You should get some sleep," I said. "We can eat cheese and monkey meat.*"

"This is better," he said. "Something hot will be good for those two fools. You get some sleep, lieutenant."

"Do you want a drink, Bartolomeo?"

"When we leave, lieutenant. It wouldn't do me any good now."

"If you're up in three hours and I haven't called you, wake me, will you?"

"I don't have a watch, lieutenant."

"There's a clock on the wall in the major's room."

"All right."

I fell asleep as soon as I lay down and got up in three hours. We ate in the kitchen before we started. Aymo had a basin of spaghetti with onions and tinned* meat in it. We sat around the table and drank two of the bottles of wine that had been left in the cellar* of the villa. It was still dark and raining outside.

"I have a bottle of wine for each of us to take in the cars," Aymo said.

"Did you sleep at all*?" I asked.

"I slept a little. I don't need much sleep."

"Tomorrow we'll sleep in the king's bed," Bonello said. The wine was making him feel very good.

---

oversleep 너무 자다, 늦잠 자다 **monkey meat** 통조림 소고기 **tinned** 통조림으로 된 **cellar** 지하실, 지하층 **at all** 조금이라도

We loaded the cars with our things and left for Udine.

Chapter 28

퇴각하는 병사들과 차량들이 몰리면서 도로는 정체되고,
헨리 중위의 부대원들은 낙오한 두 명의 공병 병장과
민간인 소녀 두 명을 차에 태워 준다.

Soon after we drove out of town, the road became heavily congested* with the retreating troops. A couple of hours later, we were not moving at all. I got out and walked ahead, going between the trucks

---

congested 혼잡한, 정체된

and carts and under the wet necks of the horses. The whole column* of vehicles* did not move as far as I could see.

On the other side beyond the stalled* vehicles, however, I could see the troops moving. I went back to our cars. I thought this block* might extend* as far as Udine. Piani was asleep over the wheel.* I climbed up beside him and went to sleep as well.

After a few hours, I heard the truck ahead of us grinding* into gear.* I woke Piani and we started, moving a few yards, then stopping, then going, then stopping. We continued like this for several hours until the column stalled again in the night and did not start. I got down and went to the other cars to see Aymo and Bonello. Bonello had two engineering sergeants on the seat of his car with him. They stiffened* when I opened the door.

"They were left to do something on a

bridge," Bonello said. "They can't find their unit,* so I gave them a ride."

"We apologize* for not having asked your permission,* lieutenant."

"You have my permission," I said.

"The lieutenant is an American," Bonello said. "He'll give anyone a ride."

One of the sergeants smiled, and the other asked Bonello if I was an Italian from North or South America.

"He's not Italian. He's American."

The sergeants did not seem to believe it. I left them and went back to Aymo. He had two girls on the seat with him and was sitting back in the corner smoking.

"Well, well," I said. Aymo laughed.

"Talk to them, lieutenant," said Aymo. "I can't understand them. Hey!" He

---

column 종대 **vehicle** 탈것, 차 **stalled** 꼼짝 못하는, 정체된 **block** (길 등을) 막는 것 **extend** 연장하다, 늘이다 **wheel** (자동차의) 핸들 **grind** 삐걱거리다, 삐걱거리게 만들다 **gear** 기어 **stiffen** 뻣뻣하게 굳다, 경직되다 **unit** 부대 **apologize** 사과하다, 사죄하다 **permission** 허락, 허가

squeezed* one of the girls' thighs in a friendly way. The girl drew her shawl* tight around her and pushed his hand away. "Hey!" he said. "Tell the lieutenant your name and what you're doing here."

The girl looked at me angrily. The other girl looked down on the floor. The girl who looked at me said something in a dialect* I could not understand. She looked about sixteen.

"Sister?" I asked and pointed at the other girl.

She nodded and smiled.

"All right," I said and patted her knee. I felt her stiffen when I touched her. Her sister never looked up. She seemed about a year younger. Aymo put his hand on the elder girl's thigh and she pushed it away again. He laughed.

"Good man," he pointed at himself. "Good man," he pointed at me. "Don't worry." The girl looked at him angrily. The two girls were like wild birds.

"Why does she ride with me if she doesn't like me?" Aymo asked. "They got right up in the car the second* I motioned to them." He turned to the elder girl. "Don't worry," he said. "We are not going to touch you." Her eyes looked at him very scared. She pulled the shawl tighter. "The car is all full," Aymo said. "We won't touch you." The girl's lips shook and then tears came down her plump* cheeks. She began to sob.*

"I think I scared her," Aymo said. "I didn't mean to." He took out two pieces of cheese from his knapsack.* "Here," he said, handing them to the girls. "Stop crying."

The elder girl shook her head and

---

squeeze 쥐어짜다, 죄다 **shawl** 숄 **dialect** 사투리, 방언 **the second** ~하자마자 **plump** 포동포동한 **sob** 흐느껴 울다 **knapsack** 배낭

continued to cry, but the younger girl took the cheese and began to eat. After a while, the younger girl gave her sister the second piece of cheese and they both ate.

"She'll be all right," Aymo said.

An idea suddenly came to him.

"Virgin[*]?" he asked the girl next to him. Both girls nodded vigorously.[*] The elder said something in her dialect.

"That's all right," Aymo said. "That's all right."

As I walked back to my car, I thought about how beautiful the girls were. A retreat was no place for two beautiful virgins. I fell asleep for a couple more hours in the car until Piani woke me. I had dreamt about Catherine.

"They've started again," he said, gently shaking me by the shoulder.

I looked at my watch. It was three o'clock in the morning. I reached back behind the seat for my bottle of wine.

"You talked in your sleep," Piani said.

Before daylight, we were stalled again and about an hour later we started to move again. Seeing the rate* of progress* in the daylight,* I knew we were going to have to get off that main road and go across country if we ever hoped to reach Udine.

When we came across a small road that led off to the north between two fields with a hedge* of trees on both sides, I thought that we had better take it and hurried back to the other cars to tell Bonello and Aymo.

"If it leads nowhere, we can come back," I said.

"What about them?" Bonello asked. The two engineering sergeants were beside him on the seat. They were unshaven* but still

---

virgin 처녀 **vigorously** 격렬하게 **rate** 속도 **progress** 전진, 진행
daylight 낮 **hedge** 산울타리 **unshaven** 면도하지 않은

military-looking* in the early morning.

"They'll help us push the cars if we get stuck* in the mud," I said. I went back to Aymo and told him we were going to try it across country.

"How's your leg, lieutenant?"

"Fine. How are you?"

"Fine. But very hungry, lieutenant," he said.

"There should be something up that road and we will stop and eat."

A little way down the side road, we came across a deserted* farmhouse.* I looked back down the road, and saw that the farmhouse was on a slight* elevation* above the plain, and we could see over the country. The two sergeants looked through the house and one of them came out with a clock in his hand.

"Put it back where it was," I said. He looked at me, went back in the house and returned without the clock.

"Where's your friend?" I asked.

"He's gone to the toilet.*" He went back in the ambulance. He seemed to be afraid we would leave him.

"What about breakfast, lieutenant?" Bonello asked.

"All right. Let's eat." Piani and Bonello went in the house.

"Come on," Aymo said to the girls. He held his hand to help them down. The elder sister shook her head. They were not going into any deserted house with soldiers.

We went into the farmhouse. It was large and dark, and Bonello and Piani were in the kitchen.

"There's not much to eat," Piani said.

---

military-looking 군인처럼 보이는 **get stuck** 갇히다, 옴짝달싹 못하다 **deserted** 인적이 끊긴 **farmhouse** 농가 **slight** 근소한, 약간의 **elevation** 높은 곳, 고지 **toilet** 변소, 화장실

"They've cleaned most of it out."

Bonello sliced* a big cheese on the heavy kitchen table.

"Where was the cheese?"

"In the cellar. Piani found some wine and apples too."

"That's a good breakfast," I said.

The two engineering sergeants came in.

"Have some cheese, sergeants," Bonello said.

"We should go," one of the sergeants said, eating his cheese and drinking his wine.

"We'll go soon. Don't worry," Bonello said.

"We need to eat first," I said.

"Yes. But time is precious,*" said the other sergeant.

"I think these bastards had eaten already," Piani said. The sergeants stared at him. They hated us.

"You know the road?" one of them asked me.

"No," I said. They looked anxiously at each other.

"We really should start," the first one said.

"We will," I said. I drank another cup of the red wine. It tasted very good with the cheese and apple.

"Bring the cheese," I said and went out. Bonello came out carrying the great jug of wine.

"That's too big," I said. "Fill up the canteens* with it."

Bonello filled the canteens and some of the wine ran out on the stone paving* of the courtyard. Then he picked up the jug and put it just inside the door.

"This way the Austrians can find it

---

slice 얇게 썰다, 잘라 내다 **precious** 귀중한 **canteen** 수통 **paving** 포석

without breaking the door down," he said.

"Let's go." I said. "Piani and I will lead."

The two engineering sergeants were already on the seat beside Bonello. The girls were eating cheese and apples and Aymo was smoking. We started off down the narrow side road.*

Chapter 29

차가 진흙탕에 빠지자 공병 병장들은 미련 없이 떠난다.
헨리 중위는 배신감을 느끼고 도망치는 그들 중 한 명을 사살한다.

The next day, at around midday, I figured* we were about ten kilometers from Udine. The rain had stopped by then, but Aymo's car became stuck in the mud. Our only option* was to dig out in

---

side road 샛길, 곁길 **figure** 여기다, 판단하다 **option** 선택, 선택권

front of the wheels and then push until the car was able to move forward again. We were all down on the road around the car. The two engineering sergeants examined the wheels. Then, without a word, they started off down the road. I went after them.

"Come back," I said. "Help us dig the car out."

"We are going," one said.

"I said to come back and help us," I said.

"We have to go," the other said. They were in a hurry to leave. They did not even look at me.

"Come back and help us dig the car out. That's an order," I said.

"We have to go on," said the first. "You can't give us orders. You're not our officer."

They turned and headed down the road.

"Stop," I said. They kept on moving

down the muddy road. "I order you to stop," I called. They moved a little faster. I took my pistol out of the holster, aimed* at the one who had talked the more, and fired. I missed and they started to run. I shot three more times and dropped one. The other ran away into the field. I fired at him. The pistol clicked* empty and I loaded another clip. Bonello came up.

"Let me go and finish the son of a bitch,*" he said. I handed him the pistol and he walked down to where the engineering sergeant lay face down across the road. Bonello leaned over, put the pistol against the man's head and pulled the trigger* twice. Then he took hold of the sergeant's legs and pulled him to the side of the road so he lay beside a hedge.

We spent the next hour trying to get the

---

aim 겨누다 **click** 딸깍 소리가 나다 **son of a bitch** 개자식 **trigger** 방아쇠

car out of the mud. It was no use.

"What shall we do, lieutenant?" Bonello asked.

"We leave the car," I said. "What shall we do with Aymo's virgins?"

"They can get in the back," Piani said. "We are not going far, anyway."

I opened the back door of the ambulance.

"Get in," I said. The girls climbed in and sat in the corner. They seemed to have taken no notice of* the shooting. I got up on the seat next to Piani and we started. We tried to cross the field to the road on the other side, but we couldn't. The ground was too soft and muddy for the cars. When they were finally and completely stalled, we left them in the field and started on foot for Udine.

When we came to the road which led back toward the main highway,* I pointed down it to the two virgins.

"Go down there," I said. "There'll be people there." I gave them each a ten-lira note. "Go there," I said, pointing. "Friends! Family!"

We watched them go down the road, their shawls close around them, looking back apprehensively* at us. The three drivers laughed.

"How much will you give me to go with them, lieutenant?" Bonello asked.

"They're better off in a group of people than alone if the Austrians catch them," I said.

We started on foot to Udine.

"You killed a man today, Bonello," said Aymo. "What will you say in confession*?"

"I'll say, 'Bless me, Father, for I have killed a sergeant.'"

---

take notice of ~을 알아차리다 **highway** 간선 도로 **apprehensively** 우려하여, 통찰하여 **confession** 고해, 자백

We all laughed.

"He's an anarchist,*" Piani said. "He doesn't go to church."

"You're an anarchist too," Bonello said.

"Are you really anarchists?" I asked.

"No, lieutenant. We're socialists.* We're from Imola. Have you ever been there?"

"No," I said.

"It's a beautiful place, lieutenant. You come there after the war and we'll show you a good time."

"How did you become socialists?"

"We've always been socialists."

"Come to Imola, lieutenant. We'll make you a socialist too."

As the road went uphill,* we stopped talking.

Chapter 30

헨리 중위는 이탈리아 헌병에게 붙잡혀 부대 이탈 죄로 처형당할 위기에 처한다.
강물에 뛰어든 헨리는 나무토막을 잡고 탈출을 감행한다.

Later, we came across a high river. Along the riverbank there was nothing but the wet and muddy ground. We went up to the bank and finally we saw a railway bridge.

---

anarchist 무정부주의자 **socialist** 사회주의자 **uphill** 올라가는, 오르막의

"That's a beautiful bridge," Aymo said. It was a long, plain* iron bridge across what was usually a dry riverbed.*

"We'd better hurry and cross it before they blow it up,*" I said.

"There's nobody left to blow it up," Piani said. "Everyone's gone."

"It's probably rigged* with explosives," Bonello said.

"I'll cross it first," I said. "It won't be rigged to blow up with one man. Come one at a time."

I started across the bridge. I watched the rails for any tripwires* or signs of explosives, but I saw nothing. Ahead, across the wet countryside and through the rain, I could see Udine in the distance. I looked back across the bridge. Just up the river there was another bridge.

As I watched, a motorcar crossed it. The sides of the bridge were so high that the body of the car, once on the bridge, was out of sight.* But I saw the heads of the driver and the passengers. They were all wearing German helmets. Then the car went over the bridge and out of sight behind the trees and the abandoned* vehicles on the road. I waved to Aymo who was crossing and to the others to hurry up. I climbed down and crouched* beside the railway embankment.* Aymo soon joined me.

"A German car crossed the upper bridge."

"Holy Mary."

The others came, and we all crouched in the mud behind the embankment.

"Do you think we're cut off then, lieutenant?" asked Aymo.

---

plain 소박한 **riverbed** 강바닥 **blow up** 폭파하다 **rig** 각 부품을 조립하여 장비하다 **tripwire** 덫으로 쳐 놓은 철사 **out of sight** 보이지 않게 되어 **abandoned** 버려진 **crouch** 몸을 쭈그리다, 웅크리다 **embankment** 둑, 제방

"I'm not sure."

"Let's have a drink," Piani said. "If we're cut off, we might as well have a drink." He unhooked* his canteen.

"Look! Look!" Aymo said, pointing toward the road. Along the top of the stone bridge, we saw German helmets moving. As they came off the bridge, we saw them. They were motorcycle* troops. Stick bombs hung down from their belts. Their helmets and their gray uniforms were wet and they rode comfortably, looking ahead and to both sides. There were more than two dozen of them. Soon they were gone out of sight up the road.

"Holy Mary," Aymo said.

"They were Germans, not Austrians," Piani said.

"Why isn't there somebody here to stop them?" I said. "Why don't they blow up the bridge? Why aren't there machine guns along this embankment?"

I was angry. I took a big sip of wine from Piani's canteen.

"Let's move," I said.

We walked along the railway track* for some time.

"Down! Down!" Aymo said. We dropped down beside the embankment. There was another group of motorcycle troops passing along the road. I looked over the edge* and saw them going past.

"They saw us, but they did not fire," Aymo said.

"They don't want us," I said. "They're going after something else."

We continued on our way. The railway moved south, away from the highway now and we could not see what passed along the road. A short bridge over a canal* was

---

unhook 갈고리를 벗기다 **motorcycle** 오토바이 **railway track** 철도 선로, 궤도 **edge** 가장자리, 모서리 **canal** 운하, 인공 수로

blown up, but we climbed across on what was left of it. We heard gunfire ahead of us.

We came to the railway beyond the canal. It went on straight toward the town across the fields.

Then a shot was fired at us from the side road.

We ran down into the embankment. The drivers were ahead of me. Two more shots came from the thick brush* and Aymo, as he was crossing the tracks, tripped* and fell face down. We pulled him down on the other side and turned him over. The three of us squatted around him in the rain. He was hit low in the back of the neck, and the bullet* had ranged* upward and come out under the right eye. He died almost instantly.* Piani laid Aymo's head down and wiped* his face with a piece of emergency* dressing.

"They weren't Germans," I said. "There

can't be any Germans over there."

"Italians!" Piani said. Bonello said nothing. He was sitting beside Aymo. Piani picked up Aymo's cap and put it over his face.

"We are in more danger from Italians than Germans," I said. "The rear guards* are afraid of everything, whereas* the Germans know exactly what they're after."

"What do we do now?" Piani asked.

"We'd better lay low till it gets dark. If we can get south, we'd be all right."

We went down the north side of the embankment. I looked back at Aymo, lying in the mud. He was quite small and his arms were by his side. He looked very dead, and I realized how much I had liked him. I had his papers in my pocket, and I

brush 덤불, 잡목림 **trip** 걸려 넘어지다 **bullet** 총탄, 탄환 **range** (총 등의) 조준을 맞추다 **instantly** 즉시, 즉석에서 **wipe** 씻다, 닦다 **emergency** 비상용의, 긴급한 **rear guard** 후위 **whereas** ~에 반하여, 그러나

decided I would write to his family. Ahead across the fields we saw a farmhouse. The house was empty. We looked around, but we could not find anything to eat.

"We should get some sleep in the barn,*" I said. "Do you think you could find anything to eat, Piani, and bring it up there?"

"I'll try," Piani said.

"I'll look as well," Bonello said.

"All right," I said. "I'll go and check out the barn."

The barn, like the house, was mostly empty, but there was enough hay* for us to sleep on, and we had a better view of the surrounding than from the farmhouse. Piani came a few minutes later with a long sausage, a jar of something and two bottles of wine under his arm.

"Where's Bonello?" I asked.

"He left, lieutenant," he said. "He

decided to become a prisoner of war.*"

I said nothing.

"He was afraid that we'd get killed."

I said nothing.

"We don't believe in the war anyway, lieutenant."

"Why didn't you go with him?" I asked.

"I didn't want to leave you."

"Where did he go?"

"I don't know, lieutenant. He just left."

"All right," I said. "Let's eat."

We sat in the hay and ate the sausage and drank the wine.

"You look out of this window, Piani," I said. "I'll go look out of that one."

I watched out of my window until it was dark. I went over to Piani and woke him up.

"Let's move when it is dark," I said, and

---

barn 헛간, 광 **hay** 건초, 꼴 **prisoner of war** 전쟁 포로

we started.

Nothing happened that night, and at around five in the morning, we found ourselves walking along the side of a road crowded with vehicles and troops. All of a sudden, I felt that the retreat would not have felt at all dangerous if Aymo had not died.

"Bonello was a fool," said Piani.

"You're right."

"What will you do about him, lieutenant?"

"I don't know."

"Can't you just report him as taken prisoner?"

"I don't know."

"You see, if the war continues, they would make trouble for his family."

"The war won't go on," a soldier said. "We're going home. The war is over."

"Everybody's going home," said another

soldier.

"Come on, lieutenant," Piani said. He wanted to overtake* them.

"Lieutenant? Who's a lieutenant? Down with the officers!"

Piani took me by the arm.

"I'd better call you by your name," he said. "They might try and cause trouble. They've shot some officers."

Before dawn, we reached the bank of the Tagliamento and followed down along the flooded* river to the bridge where all the traffic was crossing. We joined the massive* crowd of people crossing a bridge. Everyone was silent, and the tightly-packed* crowd moved very slowly. Piani was a little ahead in the jam.* We were almost across.

At the far end of the bridge, there were

---

overtake 따라잡다, 따라붙다 **flooded** 물에 잠긴, 침수된 **massive** 대규모의, 대량의 **tightly-packed** 빽빽한 **jam** 붐빔, 혼잡

officers and carabinieri* standing on both sides. As we came close to them, I saw one of them point to a man in the column. A carabiniere went in after him and came out holding him by the arm. He took him away from the road. As we came closer, I saw one or two of them look at me. Then one pointed at me and said something. I saw a carabiniere come for me, then felt him take me by the collar.*

"What's wrong with me?" I said and hit him in the face. Soon I was subdued* by half a dozen carabinieri.

"What is going on?" I asked.

"Take him back there with the others," the first officer said. "He speaks Italian with an accent."

"So do you, you fool," I said.

They took me down behind the line of officers below the road in a field by the riverbank. As we walked toward them, shots were fired. There were four officers standing together, with a man in front of them with a carabiniere on each side of him. Four other carabinieri stood near the questioning* officers, leaning on their rifles. I looked at the man the officers were questioning. He was the lieutenant-colonel* I had seen them take from the bridge.

"Your brigade*?"

He answered.

"Regiment?"

He answered.

"Why are you not with your regiment?"

He answered.

"Don't you know that an officer should be with his troops?"

He said yes.

---

carabiniere (이탈리아) 경찰관, 헌병 **collar** 칼라, 깃 **subdue** 진압하다, 압도하다 **questioning** 심문 **lieutenant-colonel** 중령 **brigade** (군대) 여단

"It is people like you that have let the barbarians* onto the sacred soil* of the fatherland.*"

"Have you never been in a retreat before?" the lieutenant-colonel asked.

"Italy should never have to retreat."

We stood there in the rain and listened.

"If you are going to shoot me, please shoot me now without further questioning," said the lieutenant-colonel. "The questioning is stupid." He made the sign of the cross. The officers spoke to each other. One wrote something on a piece of paper.

"Executed* for abandoning his troops," he said.

Two carabinieri took the lieutenant-colonel to the riverbank and shot him in the head. Some of the carabinieri were looking at the newcomers.* The others were looking at the dead lieutenant-colonel. I ducked* down, pushed between two men, and ran for the river. I jumped in with a splash.* The water was very cold, but I stayed under as long as I could. The second I came up, I took a breath and went down again. It was easy to stay submerged* with so much clothing and my boots.

When I came up the second time, I saw a piece of timber* ahead of me and reached for it and held on with one hand. I kept my head behind it and did not dare look over it. I had heard shots when I was running and when I first came up for air. Some minutes later I heard no more shots. The piece of timber swung in the current* and I held it with both hands now. I was moving very fast, and I held onto the timber and let it take me along.

---

barbarian 야만인 **soil** 땅 **fatherland** 조국 **execute** 사형에 처하다, 처형하다 **newcomer** 새로 온 사람 **duck** 머리를 홱 숙이다, 몸을 홱 굽히다 **with a splash** 텀벙(철벅)하는 소리를 내고 **submerge** 잠수하다, 물에 잠기다 **timber** 재목, 목재 **current** 조류, 물결

Chapter 31

헨리 중위는 가까스로 물에서 빠져나와 베네치아 평원을 횡단한다.
그리고 후방으로 가는 기차에 몰래 올라탄다.

After many torturing* minutes in the cold water, I finally managed to make it to a riverbank. After making sure that no one was around, I sat down by some bushes along the bank of the ditch* and took off my shoes and emptied* them of water. I took off my coat, took my wallet* with my papers and my money all wet in it out of the inside pocket and then wrung the coat out.* I took off my trousers and wrung them too, and then my shirt and underwear.* I rubbed myself* and then dressed again.

Before I put my coat back on, I cut the insignia* of a lieutenant off my sleeves and put them in the inside pocket with my money. I had a little over three thousand lire. They had taken my pistol, and I put the holster on under my coat. It was cold in the rain. I came up onto a road. Ahead, I saw some troops coming down the road. I limped along the side of the road and they paid no attention to* me. I continued down the road.

I crossed the Venetian plain that day.

---

torturing 고통스러운 **ditch** 수로, 도랑 **empty** 비우다 **wallet** 지갑 **wring out** 짜다, 쥐어짜다 **underwear** 속옷, 내의 **insignia** 계급장 **pay attention to** ~에 유의하다

It was mostly flat* countryside, and the closer I got to the sea, the fewer roads there were. When I came across a railroad, I waited for a train to pass by. After some hours, a train came along. It was so long that the engine moved it very slowly, and I was sure I could get aboard* it. I watched it go past carefully, then I saw a low open car coming, covered with canvas. I jumped and caught the rear* hand-rods* and pulled up.

I looked at how the canvas was fastened. It was laced* down at the edge with cord. I took out my knife, cut the cord and put my arm under. There were hard bulges* under the canvas that had tightened* in the rain. I looked up ahead. There was a guard on the freight car ahead, but he was looking forward. I ducked under the canvas. My forehead hit something violently,* and I felt blood on my face but I crawled* on in and lay flat. Then I turned around and fastened the canvas back down.

I realized I was under the canvas with guns. They smelled clean greasy.* I lay and listened to the rain on the canvas and the clicking of the car over the rails. A little light came through, and I lay and looked at the guns. The bump* on my forehead was swollen,* and I stopped the bleeding* by keeping still and letting it coagulate,* then picked away the dried blood except over the cut.

I had no handkerchief, so feeling with my fingers I washed away where the dried blood had been with rainwater that dripped from the canvas. Then I wiped it clean with the sleeve of my coat. I did

flat 평평한 **get aboard** 올라타다 **rear** 뒤, 배후 **hand-rod** 후방 손잡이 **lace** 끈으로 묶다 **bulge** 불룩한 것 **tighten** 죄다, 죄이다 **violently** 맹렬하게, 격렬히 **crawl** 기어가다, 포복하다 **greasy** 기름이 묻은 **bump** 혹, 융기 **swollen** 부푼 **bleeding** 출혈 **coagulate** 응고시키다, 굳히다

not want to look suspicious. I knew the guns must be going to Mestre and that I would have to get out before they got there because they would be taking care of these guns. They had no guns to lose. I was very hungry.

Chapter 32

기차 안에 숨은 헨리 중위는 추위와 배고픔에 시달린다.
그에게 생각나는 것은 맛있는 식사와 캐서린뿐이다.

I was wet, cold and hungry. I rolled over and lay flat on my stomach with my head on my arms. My knee was stiff,* but it had not hindered* me in any way. Dr. Valentini had done a great job. I thought

stiff 뻣뻣한, 딱딱한 **hinder** 방해하다, 저지하다

of Catherine, but I knew I would get crazy if I continued to think about her when I was not sure yet I would see her. I tried not to think about her, or to think about her only a little.

I thought about the cars and the men I had lost. I had tried my best, but I had lost them all. And the carabinieri had tried to kill me. I began to feel no longer obligated* to the army. I was not angry, however. I was not against the Italian army. I wished them all the luck in the world. But it was not my show anymore, and I just wished that the bloody train would get to Mestre and I would eat and stop thinking.

Piani would tell them I had been shot. They went through the pockets of the people they shot and took the papers. They did not have my papers, so they might write me up* as drowned.* I wondered what they would hear in the States. I was so hungry. I wondered what had become of the priest. And Rinaldi. And the major. Well, I would never see them now. I would never see any of them ever again. That part of my life was over. I worried about Rinaldi. It was not a serious disease anyway if you took the medicine in time, they said. But Rinaldi would worry.

I did not want to think. I wanted to eat. I wanted to eat and drink and sleep with Catherine. Tonight, maybe. No. That was impossible. But tomorrow night, we'll share a good meal and sheets and never go away again except together. We'd have to move fairly* quickly. She would go with me. I knew she would go. When would we go? And where? That was something to think about. It was getting dark. I lay and thought of the places we could go. There were so many places.

---

obligate 의무를 지우다, 강요하다 **write ~ up** ~에 대해 공식 기록을 만들다
drowned 물에 빠져 죽은 **fairly** 꽤, 상당히

Chapter 33

밀라노에 도착한 헨리 중위는 캐서린이 스트레사로 갔다는 소식을 듣는다.
그는 친구인 시몬즈를 찾아가 도움을 청한다.

In Milan I was told, by the doorkeeper at the American hospital, that Catherine had gone to the town of Stresa with Helen Ferguson. I asked the doorkeeper to keep my visit a secret and got into a cab. I gave the driver the address of Simmons, one of the men I knew who was studying singing.

Simmons lived far from the town toward the Porta Magenta. He was still asleep when I went to see him.

"You get up awfully early, Henry," he said, sitting up in bed and lighting* a cigarette.

"I need help, Sim," I said. "Do you know how I can cross into Switzerland?"

"The Italians wouldn't let you out of Italy."

"I know. But what about the Swiss? What will they do?"

"Nothing. You can go anywhere in Switzerland. I think you just have to tell the authorities where you're going. Why? Are you running from the police?"

"Not yet."

"My dear Henry. What would you like me to do?"

---

light 불을 붙이다

"You're about my size. Can you go out and buy me some civilian* clothes? I have clothes, but they're all at Rome."

"Rome's a filthy* place. What were you doing there?"

"I was studying architecture.*"

"You don't need to buy clothes. I'll give you all the clothes you want. Go into that dressing room. Take all the clothes you want. Where are you headed?"

"I have to get to Stresa first."

"That's ideal.* You can just row a boat across from Stresa into Switzerland."

I looked out of the window.

"I'll go down and let my cab go," I said.

"Come back up and have breakfast with me."

I went down and paid off the cab.

Chapter 34

헨리 중위는 스트레사에 도착해서 캐서린과 재회한다.
그는 캐서린에게 스위스로의 탈출 의사를 밝힌다.

In civilian clothes, I felt like I was wearing a costume* for masquerade.* But once I was on the train to Stresa I did not care. I just wanted to see Catherine.

Catherine and Helen Ferguson were

civilian 일반 시민, 민간인 **filthy** 불결한 **architecture** 건축 **ideal** 이상적인
costume 복장, 옷차림 **masquerade** 가면무도회

having dinner when I came to their hotel. Ferguson was talking, but she stopped when I came in.

"My God," she said.

"Hello," I said.

"It's you!" Catherine said. She looked overjoyed.* I kissed her and I sat down at the table.

Ferguson did not seem too happy to see me.

"You're not happy to see me?" I asked Ferguson with a smile.

"No, I'm not. You had a love affair* all summer and got this girl pregnant and sneaked off.* And now I suppose you'll sneak off again."

I smiled at Catherine and she smiled at me.

"We'll sneak off together," she said.

"You two are the same," Ferguson said. "I'm ashamed of* you, Catherine Barkley.

You have no shame* and no honor and you're as sneaky* as he is."

"Don't, Fergy," Catherine said and patted her hand. "You know we like each other."

Catherine managed to calm Helen Ferguson down,* and the three of us had dinner together.

That night at the hotel, I finally felt I was home, and that I was not alone. I felt as part of one as I held Catherine and felt the beating of her heart. I told her that I was through with the army, and that I wanted to go away with her.

I remember when I woke up that morning. Catherine was asleep and the sunlight was coming in through the window. I walked over to the window.

---

overjoyed 매우 기뻐하는 **love affair** 연애 사건 **sneak off** 살짝 떠나다 **be ashamed of** ~을 부끄러워하다 **shame** 수치, 치욕 **sneaky** 교활한, 엉큼한 **calm down** 가라앉히다, 진정시키다

Down below were the gardens, bare now but beautifully regular,* the gravel* paths,* the trees, the stone wall by the lake and the lake in the sunlight with the mountains beyond. I stood at the window looking out and when I turned around I saw Catherine was awake and watching me.

"I feel like a criminal,*" I said. "I've deserted* the army."

"Darling, don't be silly. It's only the Italian army."

I laughed.

"You're a good girl," I said.

"And you be a good boy and find us a way into Switzerland quickly."

Chapter 35

헨리는 그레피 백작을 만나 당구를 치고 환담을 나눈다.
백작은 헨리에게 사랑은 종교적인 감정과 마찬가지라고 충고한다.

Catherine went to see Ferguson and I sat in the bar and read the papers.

"Count* Greffi was asking for you," Emilio, the bartender,* said.

"Who?"

---

regular 규칙적인, 정연한 **gravel** 자갈 **path** 작은 길, 오솔길 **criminal** 범인, 범죄자 **desert** 버리다, 탈영하다 **count** 백작 **bartender** 바텐더

"Count Greffi. You remember the old man who was here when you were here last time."

"Is he here?"

"Yes, he's here with his niece. I told him you were here. He wants to play billiards* with you."

"Where is he?"

"He's out on a walk."

"How's his billiard game?"

"Good. He beats most people. When I told him you were here, he was very happy. He has nobody else to play with."

Count Greffi was ninety-four years old. He was an old man with white hair and mustache and beautiful manners. He had been a diplomat* for both Austria and Italy and his birthday parties were the great social event of Milan.

I had some time to kill before dinner with Catherine and Helen Ferguson, so

I invited Emilio to come fishing with me. After that, I had a quick dinner with Catherine and Ferguson, and went to meet Count Greffi.

I found him in the billiard room. His face lightened up when he saw me, and he put out his hand.

"It is such a great pleasure that you are here," he said. "How kind of you to come and play with me."

"It was very nice of you to ask me."

"Are you well?"

"I'm very well. And you?"

"I'm always well. But I am getting old. I detect* signs of age now."

"I don't believe it."

We opened a bottle of champagne and played billiards. He wanted to talk about the war, but I did not give him detailed*

---

billiards 당구 **diplomat** 외교관 **detect** 간파하다, 인지하다 **detailed** 상세한

answers.

After a couple of games, we sat in the deep leather chairs, the champagne in the ice bucket* and our glasses on the table between us.

"What do you value most in life?" he asked me.

"Someone I love."

"It is the same with me. Because she is all I have. And to give birthday parties," he laughed. "You are wiser than I am. You do not give birthday parties."

We both drank the champagne.

"Shall we drink some more?" he asked.

"I should get back to my girl."

"Are sure you don't want more?"

"Yes."

He stood up.

"I hope you will be very healthy and very happy."

"Thank you. And I hope you will live

forever."

"Thank you. And remember, love is a religious feeling. Do not forget that."

---

ice bucket 얼음 통

Chapter 36

폭풍우가 치는 밤에 바텐더가 찾아와
헨리를 체포하러 이탈리아군이 올 것이라며 헨리의 탈출을 도와준다.

That night, I woke to the sounds of a storm. Then I heard someone knock on the door. I went to the door very softly so as not to disturb* Catherine, and opened it. It was Emilio. He had on his overcoat and carried his wet hat.

"What's the matter, Emilio? Are you in

trouble?"

"No. You are, lieutenant. They are coming here to arrest* you in the morning."

"Really?"

"Yes. What will you do now? If you have nothing to fear, an arrest is nothing. But it is always bad to be arrested during wartime.*"

"I don't want to be arrested."

"Then you have to go to Switzerland."

"How?"

"In my rowboat.*"

"But there is a storm outside," I said.

"The storm is nearly over. It is rough, but you will be all right. But you have to go right now. Pack your bags and dress your lady. I will take care of the rest."

Emilio took the bags and told us to meet

---

disturb 방해하다, 어지럽히다 **arrest** 체포하다 **wartime** 전시 **rowboat** (노 젓는) 보트

him at the quay* where his boat should be. We went there, with me holding an umbrella over Catherine. When we got there, the water was dark against the stone. Emilio stepped out from beside the row of trees.

"Your bags are in the boat," he said.

"I must pay you for the boat," I said.

"How much money do you have?"

"Not much."

"Then send me the money later. It's all right."

"How much?"

"However much you want."

"Tell me how much."

"Just send me five hundred francs."

"All right."

"Here are some sandwiches." He handed me a package. "And here's a bottle of brandy and a bottle of wine." I put them in my bag. "Do you know where to go?"

"Up the lake."

"And do you know how far?"

"Past Luino."

"Past Luino, Cannero, Cannobio, Tranzano. You won't be in Switzerland until you come to Brissago. You have to pass Monte Tamara. If you don't stop, you should be there by seven o'clock in the morning."

"Is it that far?"

"It's thirty-five kilometers."

I stepped in the boat and helped Catherine in.

"Did you leave the money for the hotel?" asked Emilio.

"Yes. In a white envelope in the room."

"All right. Good luck, lieutenant."

"Good luck. Thank you for everything."

Emilio bent down and shoved us off.*

---

quay 선창, 부두 **shove ~ off** ~을 밀어내다

Chapter 37

밤새 노를 저어 헨리와 캐서린은 스위스에 도착한다.
그들은 임시 비자를 받고 스위스에 머문다.

By the time we were in Switzerland, we were both completely exhausted.* We had eaten and drank everything Emilio had given us, but we were both famished.* We pulled into a lake, and I was sure that we were in Switzerland. I saw a road that came quite close to the lake, and I saw a soldier coming out of a café on the road. He wore a gray-green uniform and a helmet like the Germans. He noticed us.

"Wave to him," I said to Catherine. She waved and the soldier smiled and gave a wave of his hand. I eased up* rowing.* We were passing the waterfront* of a village.

"I think we're in Brissago," I said.

"Should we land then and have some breakfast?"

"All right."

We hid the boat in some bushes and left our bags in the boat. We stepped on land and we were in Switzerland together.

"What a beautiful country," she said.

"Isn't it lovely?"

"Let's go and have breakfast!"

We went inside the café the soldier had come out of and sat down at a clean

---

exhausted 기진맥진한 **famished** 굶주린, 몹시 배고픈 **ease up** (운행) 속도를 줄이다 **rowing** 노 젓기, 조정 **waterfront** 선창가, 부두

wooden table. We were very excited. Soon after we had had a nice breakfast of toast and eggs, we went back to our boat. A soldier was standing by our boat.

"Is this your boat?" he asked.

"Yes."

"Where did you come from?"

"Up the lake."

"I'll have to ask you to come with me."

"How about the bags?"

"Bring them with you."

We were taken to a customhouse,* where a lieutenant, very thin and military, questioned us.

"What nationality* are you?"

"American and British."

"Show me your passports.*"

We gave him our passports. He examined them for a long time.

"Why did you enter Switzerland this way in a boat?"

"I am a sportsman," I said. "Rowing is my favorite. I always row whenever I get a chance."

"Why did you come here?"

"For winter sports."

"This is no place for winter sports."

"I know. I want to go where they have winter sports."

"What were you doing in Italy?"

"I was studying architecture. But the war broke out* and I couldn't study anymore."

"I'm afraid I will have to send you into Locarno," he said. "You can get a carriage, and a soldier will accompany* you."

"All right," I said. "What about the boat?"

"It will be confiscated.* How much money do you have?"

---

customhouse 세관 **nationality** 국적 **passport** 여권 **break out** (전쟁이) 발발하다 **accompany** 동행하다, 함께 가다 **confiscate** 몰수하다, 징발하다

"Two thousand and five hundred lire."

He was quite impressed.* "And what about you, lady?"

Catherine had a little over a thousand lire. The lieutenant was pleased. His attitude toward us changed favorably.*

"If you are here for winter sports, Wengen is the place," he said. "My father has a hotel at Wengen. You should go there."

"That's great," I said. "Could you give me the name?"

"I will write the details on a card." He handed me the card very politely.

"The soldier will take you into Locarno. I am sure they will give you a visa* or a police permit* in Locarno."

He was right. In Locarno, we were given provisional* visas. It helped that we had passports and money to spend. The visas could be withdrawn* at any time, however, and we were to report to the police wherever we went.

After getting the visas, we found a nice hotel and checked in. We were exhausted, but we were both overjoyed at having made it safely to Switzerland.

impress ~에게 깊은 인상을 주다 **favorably** 호의적으로 **visa** 비자 **permit** 허가증 **provisional** 임시의, 일시적인 **withdraw** 철회하다, 취소하다

Chapter 38

헨리와 캐서린은 스위스의 산에 있는 민박집에서 지낸다.
오랜만에 평온하고 행복한 날들이 지속된다.

The snow did not come till very late that fall. We lived in a brown wooden house in the pine trees* on the side of the mountain, and at night there was frost* so that there was thin ice over the water in the two pitchers on the dresser* in the morning. Mrs. Guttingen came into the room early in the morning to shut the windows and started a fire in the tall stove.

The pine wood crackled* and sparked* and then the fire roared* in the stove. The second time Mrs. Guttingen came into the room, she brought big chunks* of wood for the fire and a pitcher of hot water. Once the room was warm, she brought in breakfast. Sitting up in bed having breakfast, we could see the lake and the mountains across the lake on the French side. There was snow on the tops of the mountains.

Outside, in front of the chalet,* a road went up the mountain. The wheel ruts* and ridges were hard with the frost, and the road climbed steadily through the forest and up the mountain to where there

---

pine tree 소나무 **frost** 서리, 서릿발 **dresser** 화장대 **crackle** 우지끈 소리를 내다 **spark** 불꽃이 튀다, 불똥이 튀다 **roar** 으르렁거리다 **chunk** 큰 덩어리 **chalet** 샬레, 스위스의 농가 **rut** 바퀴 자국, 홈

were meadows. Barns and cabins* in the meadows at the edge of the woods looked across the valley. There was a stream at the bottom of the valley that flowed down into the lake. When the wind blew across the valley, you could hear the stream in the rocks.

Sometimes we went off the road and trekked* up a path through the pine forest. The floor of the forest was soft; the frost did not harden* it as it did the road. We did not mind the hardness* of the road either because we had nails* in the soles and heels* of our boots. But it was not as lovely as walking in the woods.

In front of the house the mountain went down steeply* to the little plain along the lake. We sat on the porch* of the house in the sun and saw the winding* of the road down the mountainside. The vines* in the terraced* vineyards* on the side of the lower mountain were all dead now. There was an island with two trees on the lake, and the trees looked like the sails* of a boat.

The mountains were sharp and steep* on the other side of the lake. Down at the end of the lake was the plain of the Rhone Valley, which was flat between the two ranges of mountains. Up the valley where the mountains cut it off was the Dent du Midi. It was a high snowy mountain, but it was so far away that it did not make a shadow.

We only ate breakfast on the porch when it was very sunny. The rest of the time we ate upstairs in a small room with plain wooden walls and a big stove in the

---

cabin 오두막집 **trek** 길고 힘든 여행을 하다, 트레킹을 하다 **harden** 단단하게 만들다 **hardness** 단단함, 견고함 **nail** 못 **heel** 발뒤꿈치 **steeply** 가파르게 **porch** 현관 **winding** 꾸불꾸불한 **vine** 포도나무 **terraced** 테라스 식의(비슷한 생김새의 집들이 죽 늘어서 있는 집이나 거리) **vineyard** 포도밭 **sail** 돛 **steep** 가파른, 경사가 급한

corner. We bought books and magazines in the town. The small room with the stove was our living room. We had two comfortable chairs and a table for books and magazines, and we played cards on the dining table.

Mr. and Mrs. Guttingen lived downstairs, and we sometimes heard them talking in the evening and they were very happy together too. Mr. Guttingen had been a headwaiter* and his wife had worked as maid in the same hotel. They had saved their money together to buy this place. They had a son who was also studying to be a headwaiter at a hotel in Zurich. Downstairs, there was a shop where they sold wine and beer, and sometimes in the evening we would hear carts stop outside on the road and men come up the steps to go in the shop to drink wine.

One day, I suggested to Catherine that we should be married.

"No," Catherine said. "I'm too plain right now. Let's get married once I've had the baby and lost some weight.*"

Snow did not come until just three days before Christmas. We woke one morning and everything was white.

"I wish I could ski," said Catherine.

"I can't ski either," I said. "We'll learn together once you've had the baby."

"But you could learn it now."

"I want to wait until you can learn it with me."

"But aren't you bored because you haven't got anything to do?"

"No. I love being with you. I'm enjoying life in Switzerland. Aren't you?"

"I think I have a lovely life. But I was

---

headwaiter 급사장 **weight** 체중

afraid because I'm big now that maybe I bore you."

"Oh, I wish you knew how crazy I am about you."

"I do, but I thought you were restless* sometimes."

"Sometimes I am, because I wonder about the front and about people I know."

"What do you wonder about?"

"About Rinaldi and the priest and the others. But I don't think about them much because I don't want to think about the war."

"When I first met you, I was a crazy little girl. But I am never crazy now. I'm just very, very happy."

"Go to sleep, darling," I said.

"All right. Let's go to sleep at exactly the same time."

"All right."

We did not go to sleep at the same time.

I was awake for quite a long time, thinking about things and watching Catherine sleeping, before I fell asleep.

---

restless 불안한, 들뜬

Chapter 39

1월이 되고 겨울은 점점 춥고 깊어진다.
헨리와 캐서린은 태어날 아기와 결혼에 대해 생각한다.

By the middle of January I had a full beard and the winter had settled into* bright cold days and hard cold nights.

"I love your beard," Catherine said. "It looks so stiff and fierce, but it's very soft and nice to touch."

"Do you like me better with a beard?"

"I think so. After young Catherine's born, I'm going to be thin again. I'm going to cut my hair and then I'll be a fine new and different girl for you."

I did not say anything.

"You won't mind me cutting my hair, will you?"

"No. I think it would be fun."

"Oh, you're so lovely. And maybe I'd look sweet, darling, and be so thin and exciting to you that you'll fall in love with me all over again."

"Hell," I said, "I already love you enough. What do you want to do? Ruin* me?"

"Yes. I want to ruin you."

"Good," I said. "That's what I want."

---

settle into ~로 틀이 잡히다 **ruin** 파멸시키다, 망치다

Chapter 40

2월이 지나고 캐서린의 해산이 가까워지자
헨리와 캐서린은 병원이 있는 로잔으로 거처를 옮긴다.

We had a happy life. We lived through the months of January and February and the winter was very beautiful and we were very happy. Then, in March, when the baby was about a month away, we decided to move to Lausanne where the hospital was.

We took the train from Montreux to Lausanne. We found a nice, medium-sized hotel. It was raining gently as we drove through the streets and into the carriage entrance* of the hotel. Everything about the hotel seemed luxurious* after staying with the Guttingens. The windows of the room looked out onto a wet garden with a wall topped* by an iron fence.

Catherine turned on all the lights and began unpacking. I ordered a whiskey* and soda* and lay on the bed and read the papers I had bought at the station. It was March, 1918, and the German offensive had commenced* in France.

The town was wonderful, and we had the most splendid three weeks together. We never had a bad time during those

---

entrance 입구, 문간 **luxurious** 사치스러운, 호화로운 **top** 위에 놓다, 얹다
whiskey 위스키 **soda** 소다수, 탄산음료 **commence** 개시하다, 시작하다

three weeks. We knew the baby was very close now, and it made us both feel that we could not lose any time together.

Chapter 41

캐서린이 진통을 시작하고 분만실로 들어간다.
헨리는 초조하게 분만을 기다리지만 병원 분위기는 심상치 않다.

Catherine went into labor* at around three o'clock one morning.

"Are you all right, Cat?" I asked, panicking.*

"I've been having some pains, darling."

---

go into labor 산고를 치르다, 진통을 겪다 **panic** 공황 상태에 빠지다

I called the receptionist for a cab and we went down. The night was clear and the stars were shining brightly. Catherine was very excited.

"I'm so happy it's started," she said. "The waiting will be over soon."

"You've been a good, brave girl."

At the hospital, we were greeted by a nurse, who showed us to our room.

"This is your room," the woman said. "Please get undressed and get into the bed. Here is a nightgown for you to wear."

Before I had time to say anything, Catherine was taken into the delivery room.* I was given a gown, so I could follow her in.

"Hello, darling," Catherine said in a strained* voice. "I'm nervous."

"Are you Mr. Henry?" the doctor asked.

"Yes. How is everything, doctor?"

"Things are going very well," the doctor

said. "We came in here because it is easy to give gas* for the pains.*"

"I want it now," Catherine said. The doctor placed the rubber* mask over her face and turned a dial, and I watched Catherine breathing deeply.

"I want it again," Catherine said. She held the rubber tight to her face and breathed in rapidly. I heard her moan.* Then she pulled the mask away and smiled.

"The pains are getting worse," she said. "But don't you worry, darling. You go away. Go and have some breakfast."

I did as I was asked. When I returned, the doctor seemed relieved* to see me.

"Here is your husband," he said.

"Oh, darling, this doctor is wonderful,"

---

delivery room 분만실 **strained** 팽팽한, 긴장한 **gas** (마취용) 가스 **pains** 진통 **rubber** 고무 **moan** 신음하다, 끙끙대다 **relieved** 안심한, 안도한

Catherine said in a very strange voice.

"You're intoxicated,*" I said.

"I know," Catherine said. "Give me some more. Give me some more." She clutched hold of* the mask and breathed short and deep, making the respirator* click. The doctor motioned for me to come outside with him.

"She's in a lot of pain," said the doctor. "We have two options. Either a high forceps delivery,* which can be quite dangerous for both mother and child, or a Caesarean.*"

"What if she dies during a Caesarean?"

"A Caesarean is no more dangerous than an ordinary* delivery."

"Will you be doing it yourself?"

"Yes."

"Then go ahead, doctor."

Inside the delivery room, I could hear Catherine screaming in pain. The doctor went in, followed by nurses who were saying, "It's going to be a Caesarean. It's going to be a Caesarean."

About an hour later, the doctor came out, followed by a nurse. He held something in his two hands that looked like a freshly* skinned* rabbit. He hurried across the corridor with it and went through another door. I followed him and found them in the room doing things to a newborn* child. The doctor held him up by the heels and slapped him.

"Is he all right?"

"It's a magnificent boy. He'll weigh* at least five kilos."

I had no feelings for the baby. He did not seem related to* me in any way. I felt

---

intoxicated 취한 **clutch hold of** ~을 꽉 잡다, 붙들다 **respirator** 인공호흡 장치 **forceps delivery** 겸자 분만 **Caesarean** 제왕 절개의 **ordinary** 일반적인, 정상의 **freshly** 새로이, 새롭게 **skinned** 가죽을 벗긴 **newborn** 갓 태어난 **weigh** 무게가 ~ 나가다 **related to** ~와 관련이 있는

no feeling of fatherhood.*

"Aren't you proud of your son?" the nurse asked.

"He nearly killed his mother," I said, "so no!"

"Aren't you happy you have a boy?"

"We didn't want a boy," I said.

I rushed down the hall and went to the door of the delivery room. Catherine looked dead. Her face was gray. Down below, under the light, another doctor was sewing her up.* After a while the doctor came out.

"How is she?"

"You can go in and see her now."

I went into the room and Catherine put out her hand.

"Hello, darling," she said. Her voice was very weak.

"Hello."

"Was it a boy or a girl?"

"Sh…don't talk," the nurse said.

"A boy. He's strong and healthy."

The nurse looked at me strangely.

"Please go out now," the nurse said. "Madame Henry needs to rest."

"I'll be right outside. May I speak to you?" I said to the nurse. She followed me out into the hall. We walked a little way down the hall.

"What's wrong with the baby?" I asked.

"Didn't you know?"

"No."

"He wasn't alive."

"He was stillborn*?"

"He wasn't breathing. The umbilical cord* was caught around his neck or something."

"So he's dead?"

"Yes. I'm so sorry. He was such a

---

fatherhood 부성애 **sew up** 꿰매다 **stillborn** 사산된, 유산된 **umbilical cord** 탯줄

beautiful, big boy."

I sat down on the chair in the corridor that looked out of the window. I could see nothing but the dark sky and the rain falling across the light from the window. So that was it. Our baby was dead. That was why the doctor looked so tired. But why had they acted so positively* in the room with him? They must have supposed he would come around* and start breathing properly.

So now I sat out in the corridor and waited to hear how Catherine was. The nurse did not come out, so after a while, I went to the door and opened it very gently and looked in. I could not see at first because there was a bright light in the corridor and it was dark inside the room. Then I saw the nurse sitting by the bed and Catherine's head on a pillow. The nurse came quietly to the door.

"How is she doing?" I asked.

"She's all right," the nurse said. "You should go and get some dinner and then come back. She needs to rest."

I went down the hall and then down the stairs and out the door of the hospital. I walked down the dark street in the rain to the café. The café was brightly lit inside and there were many people at the tables.

I ate the ham and eggs and drank beer. The ham and eggs were in a round dish, with the ham underneath* and the eggs on top. It was very hot and at the first mouthful* I had to take a drink of beer to cool my mouth. I was very hungry, and I asked the waiter for another order. I drank four glasses of beer with the food. I could not think at all but read the paper of the man opposite me. It was about the

---

positively 긍정적으로, 적극적으로 **come around** 의식을 회복하다
underneath ~의 아래에 **mouthful** 한 입 가득

breakthrough* on the British front.

When he saw that I was reading the back of his paper, he folded* it over. I thought of asking the waiter for a paper, but I could not concentrate.* It was hot in the café and the air was smoky.* Most of the people at the tables knew one another. There were several card games going on. The waiters were busy taking drinks from the bar to the tables. I had two more glasses of beer before I got up and returned to the hospital.

At the hospital, I met the nurse coming down the hall.

"I've been calling you at the hotel," she said. My heart dropped inside me.

"What's wrong?"

"Your wife has had a hemorrhage."

"Can I go in and see her?"

"No, not yet, I'm afraid. The doctor is with her."

"Is it serious?"

"It is very serious." The nurse went into the room and closed the door. I sat outside in the corridor. I was completely empty inside. I did not think. I could not think. I just knew she was going to die, and I prayed that she would not. "Don't let her die. Oh, God, please don't take her from me. I'll do anything for you if you don't let her die. Please, please, please, dear God, don't let her die. Dear God, don't let her die. Please, please, please don't let her die. God please don't take her away. I'll do anything you say if you don't let her die. You already took our baby! Don't let her die. You can take the baby but don't let her die. Please, please, dear God, don't let her die."

The nurse opened the door and

---

breakthrough 돌파 (작전) **fold** 접다, 접어 포개다 **concentrate** 집중하다 **smoky** 연기 나는, 연기 자욱한

motioned with her finger for me to come in. I followed her into the delivery room. Catherine did not look up when I came in. I went over to the side of the bed. The doctor was standing by the bed on the opposite side. Catherine saw me and smiled. I bent down over the bed and began to cry.

"Poor darling," Catherine said very gently. She was all gray.

"You're all right, Cat," I said. "It's all going to be all right."

"I'm going to die," she said. She waited a little and said, "I hate it."

I held her hand.

"Don't touch me," she said. I let go of her hand. She smiled. "Poor darling. You can touch me all you want."

"You'll be fine, Cat. We'll get through* this. I know you'll be all right."

"I meant to write you a letter to have if

anything happened, but I didn't have time to write it."

"Do you want me to get a priest or anyone to come and see you?"

"Just you," she said. "I'm not afraid of dying. I just hate it."

"Please don't talk so much," the doctor said.

"All right," Catherine said.

"Do you want me to do anything, Cat? Can I get you anything?"

"No," she said, smiling. Then a little later, "You won't do our things with another girl, or say the same things you said to me to another girl, will you?"

"Never."

"I want you to meet girls, though."

"I don't want to."

"You are talking too much," the doctor

---

get through ~을 타개해 나가다, 극복하다

interrupted. "Mr. Henry must go now. He can come back again later. No one is going to die. You must not be silly."

"All right," Catherine said. It was very hard for her to talk.

"Please leave the room for now," the doctor said to me. "You cannot talk," he said to Catherine.

She winked at me, her face was even grayer than before.

"I'll be right outside," I said.

"Don't worry about me, darling," Catherine said. "I'm not afraid at all."

I waited outside in the corridor. I waited for a very long time. The nurse came to the door and came over to me.

"I'm afraid your wife is very ill, Mr. Henry," she said.

"Did she die?"

"No, but she is unconscious.*"

I was told she had one hemorrhage after

another. The doctors couldn't stop it. I went into the delivery room and stayed with Catherine until she died. She never regained consciousness,* and it did not take her very long to die.

Outside the delivery room, in the corridor, I spoke to the doctor.

"Is there anything you need me to do here tonight?"

"No, Mr. Henry. There is nothing for you to do. Would you like me to take you to your hotel?"

"No, thank you. I am going to stay here for a bit."

"I know there is nothing for me to say. I cannot tell you how sorry...."

"That's all right," I said. "There's nothing to say."

"Good night," he said. "Are you sure I

---

unconscious 의식을 잃은, 의식 불명의 **regain consciousness** 의식을 회복하다

cannot take you to your hotel?"

"No, thank you."

"The Caesarean was our only option," he said.

"It's all right," I said. "I do not want to talk about it."

"Please let me take you to your hotel."

"No, thank you."

He went down the corridor. I went to the door of the delivery room.

"You can't come in now," said one of the nurses.

"Yes, I can," I said.

"Mr. Henry, you can't come in yet."

"No. You get out," I said. "All of you, get out."

I got them out and shut the door and turned off the light, but it was all useless. It was like saying goodbye to a statue. After a while, I left the hospital and walked back to the hotel in the rain.

전문번역

제1장

p.12 그해 늦은 여름, 우리는 강과 산 쪽으로 난 벌판을 가로질러 보이는 어느 마을에 있는 집에서 살고 있었다. 부대가 그 집을 지나쳐 길 아래쪽으로 내려갈 때, 그들이 일으킨 먼지가 나무의 잎들을 뽀얗게 뒤덮었다.

벌판은 농작물로 뒤덮여 있었다. **p.13** 그곳에는 많은 과수원들이 있었고, 벌판 너머 산들은 헐벗어 갈색을 띠었다. 산에서는 전투가 벌어졌고, 밤에는 대포에서 나오는 섬광들을 볼 수 있었다.

때때로 어두울 때 우리는 부대들이 창문 아래쪽에서 행군하는 소리를 들었다. 밤에는 교통량이 많았다. 양 옆구리 쪽에 올려 놓은 짐 싣는 안장마다 탄약 상자들을 채운 많은 노새들이 도로 위에 있었다. 또한 사람들을 실어 나르는 회색의 군용 트럭과 캔버스 천을 씌워 놓은 짐을 실은 다른 트럭들도 있었다. 낮에 트랙터에 견인되어 지나가는 커다란 대포들도 있었다.

북쪽으로는 계곡과 밤나무 숲을 볼 수 있었고 그 뒤에 우리가 있는 강 쪽에는 또 다른 산이 있었다. **p.14** 그 산 위쪽에서도 또한 전투가 벌어지고 있었다. 강 위로는 안개가 끼어 있었고 산은 구름에 가려져 있었다. 트럭들은 도로에 진흙을 튀겼고, 부대원들은 망토가 진흙투성이에다 젖어 있었다.

작은 회색 자동차들이 아주 빠르게 지나갔다. 차 안에는 대개 장교 한 명이 운전사와 함께 앉아 있고 뒷좌석에는 보다 많은 장교들이 앉아 있었다. 만약 자동차가 유난히 빠르게 달리면, 그것은 십중팔구 왕이었다. 왕은 우디네에 살았고 전황이 어떻게 전개되는지 알아보려고 거의 날마다 시찰을 나왔다. 전황은 대체로 아주 나쁘게 전개되었다.

가을의 끝 무렵에는 끝도 없이 비가 내렸고 그 비와 함께 콜레라가 찾아왔다. 하지만 결국 콜레라는 저지되었고, 단지 7천 명의 병사들만 콜레라로 죽었다.

제2장

p.15 이듬해에는 많은 승전보가 있었다. 골짜기 너머의 산이 점령되었고, 남쪽으로 고원의 벌판 너머에서도 승전보가 있었다. **p.16** 8월에 우리는 강을 건너가 고리지아에 있는 어떤 집에서 살았다. 이제 전투는 채 1마

일도 떨어져 있지 않은 저 너머 인접한 산에서 벌어지고 있었다.

마을은 아주 아름다웠고, 우리의 집은 아주 편안했다. 강은 우리 뒤쪽으로 흘렀고 마을은 아주 쉽게 점령되었지만, 그 너머의 산은 점령되지 못했다. 나는 오스트리아 인들이 언젠가는 마을로 돌아오고 싶어 하는 것 같아서 아주 기뻤는데, 그들이 그 마을을 파괴하려고 포격하지 않았기 때문이었다.

마을에는 병원과 카페가 있었다. 우리가 그 마을에서 지낸 가을은 우리가 시골에 있었던 지난 가을과는 사뭇 달랐다. 전쟁도 변해 있었다.

마을 너머 산에 있는 떡갈나무 숲은 여름에 초록색이었다. 우리가 마을로 들어갔을 때, 그루터기와 부러진 나무 몸통들만 있었고, 땅은 파헤쳐져 있었다. **p.17** 가을이 끝나가던 어느 날, 나는 구름이 산을 넘어오는 것을 보았다. 구름은 아주 빨리 다가왔고, 그런 다음 모든 것은 회색이 되었고 하늘은 구름으로 가려졌다. 구름은 산 아래로 내려왔으며, 갑자기 우리는 그 안에 있었는데, 그것은 눈이었다.

어느 날 우리가 카페에서 커피를 마시고 있는 동안, 내 친구는 신부님이 거리를 지나가고 있는 것을 보았다. 신부님은 눈이 녹아 질벅한 길을 조심조심 걷고 있었다. 신부님은 우리를 보고 미소를 지었다. 내 친구는 신부님에게 들어오라는 몸짓을 했다. 신부님은 고개를 젓고 가던 길을 계속 갔다. 그날 밤 식당에서 스파게티 코스의 식사를 마친 후, 대위는 신부님을 괴롭히기 시작했다.

p.18 신부님은 젊었고 얼굴을 쉽게 붉혔다. 신부님은 나머지 우리들과 같은 군복을 입었지만, 신부님의 회색 군복 상의의 왼쪽 가슴 주머니 위에는 검붉은 색깔의 우단으로 만들어진 십자가가 있었다. 대위는 내가 알아들을 수 있도록 쉬운 이탈리아 말로 말했다.

"요즘 신부님이 아가씨들과 함께 있는 것이 눈에 띄던데요." 대위가 신부님을, 그런 다음 나를 쳐다보며 말했다. 신부님은 미소를 짓고 얼굴을 붉혔으며 고개를 저었다.

"사실이 아닌가요?" 대위가 물었다. "저는 요즘 신부님이 아가씨들과 함께 있는 것을 보는데요."

"아닙니다." 신부님이 말했다. 다른 장교들은 즐거워했다.

"신부님은 아가씨들과 있지 않았어." 대위가 계속해서 말을 했다. "신부님은 아가씨들과 있는 법이 절대 없으시지. 신부님은 늘 남자아이들과

사나이들과만 계시다니까." 식탁에 앉아 있던 모든 사람들이 웃었다. 신부님은 그것을 농담으로 받아들였다.

p.19 "로마 교황은 오스트리아 인들이 이번 전쟁을 이기기를 원해." 소령이 말했다. "교황은 프란츠 요제프를 좋아하는데 그곳에서 돈이 나오기 때문이지. 나를 무신론자로 만드는 일이 바로 그런 거라니까."

"「검은 돼지」를 읽어 본 적 있나?" 중위가 나에게 몸을 돌리며 물었다. "내가 자네에게 한 권 구해 주지. 그 책이 내 신앙심을 흔들어 놓았다네."

"그것은 부도덕한 책입니다." 신부님이 말했다.

"그 책은 아주 괜찮아." 중위가 나에게 말했다. "그 책은 신부님들에 관해 쓰고 있어. 자네는 그 책을 좋아할 거야."

나는 신부님에게 미소를 지었고 신부님도 답례로 미소를 지었다.

"읽지 마세요." 신부님이 말했다.

"신부님께도 한 권 구해 드릴게요." 중위가 말했다.

"모든 사상가들은 무신론자야." 소령이 말했다.

p.20 바로 그 순간 누군가가 들어왔고, 문이 열릴 때 나는 눈이 내리고 있는 것을 보았다.

"눈이 오고 있으니까 더 이상 공격은 없을 것입니다." 내가 말했다.

"분명히 없을 거야." 소령이 말했다. "자네는 휴가를 가야 해. 로마, 나폴리, 시칠리아 등등을 가 봐야 한다고."

"그는 아말피로 가야 합니다." 중위가 말했다. "내가 자네한테 아말피에 있는 내 가족에게 보내는 카드를 써 줄게. 우리 가족들이 자네를 아들처럼 아껴 줄 거야."

"그는 팔레르모로 가야 해."

"그는 카프리로 가야 해."

"중위님은 아브루찌로 가서 카프라코타에 있는 제 가족을 방문하셔야 합니다." 신부님이 말했다.

"아브루찌요? 그곳에는 이곳보다 더 눈이 많이 내려요. 게다가 이 친구는 농부들을 보고 싶어 하지 않아요. 문화와 문명의 중심지로 가게 해 줍시다."

p.21 "자네는 즉시 휴가를 떠나야 하네." 소령이 말했다.

"자네와 함께 가서 안내를 해 주고 싶군." 중위가 말했다.

"돌아올 때 축음기를 가져오게."

"멋진 오페라 판도 가지고 와."

"카루소를 가져와."

"안 돼. 카루소는 고함만 질러."

"자네는 카루소처럼 고함을 지를 수 있으면 좋겠지 않나?"

"카루소는 고함을 지른다니까, 노래를 부르는 게 아니라 고함을 질러!"

"중위님은 아브루찌로 가셔야 해요." 신부님이 말했다. "멋진 사냥도 하고, 중위님은 사람들도 마음에 드실 거예요. 제 가족과 함께 지내셔도 되고요. 제 부친은 유명한 사냥꾼이시거든요."

"자자." 대위가 말했다. "문 닫기 전에 우리는 한잔하러 가자."

p.22 "안녕히 주무세요." 내가 신부님에게 말했다.

"안녕히 주무세요." 신부님이 말했다.

제3장

p.23 내가 최전선으로 복귀했을 때, 우리 부대는 여전히 그 마을에 있었다. 주변에는 보다 많은 대포들이 있었고, 봄은 와 있었다. 몇몇 새 병원들이 들어서 있었다. 이제는 거리에서 영국인 남자들과 때로는 여자들도 만날 수 있었다.

p.24 조금 더 많은 집들이 포탄을 맞았다. 나는 가로수가 늘어선 따뜻한 골목길로 걸어 내려갔고 우리 부대가 여전히 같은 집에 살고 있다는 것을 알았다. 문이 열려 있었고, 바깥의 양달에는 벤치에 앉아 있는 병사 한 명이 있었다. 지금이 봄이라는 것만 제외하면 모든 것이 내가 떠날 때와 마찬가지였다. 나는 위층으로 올라갔다.

내가 리날디 중위와 함께 사용하는 방은 앞마당으로 툭 튀어나와 있었다. 창문은 열려 있었고, 내 침대는 담요로 만들어져 있었으며, 내 물건들은 벽에 걸려 있었다. 나의 오스트리아제 저격수용 라이플총은 두 개의 침대 위에 걸려 있었다. 리날디 중위는 자기 침대에서 잠들어 있었다. 내가 들어오는 소리를 듣고 중위는 잠에서 깨서 일어나 앉았다.

"차우!" 중위가 말했다. "어땠나?"

"훌륭했지."

우리는 악수를 했고, 그런 다음 중위는 자신의 팔을 내 목에 감고 나에게 입을 맞추었다.

p.25 "어디로 가서 무엇을 했나?"

"여기저기 다 갔지. 밀라노, 피렌체, 로마, 나폴리, 빌라 산 지오반니, 메시나, 타오르미나……."

"예쁜 아가씨는 만났나?"

"그럼. 밀라노에서."

"잘 했네. 여기에도 이제 예쁜 여자들은 많아. 전에 한 번도 전선에 나와 본 적이 없는 새로운 여자들이지."

"굉장하군."

"오늘 오후에 가서 보게 될 거야. 그리고 마을에는 새로 온 예쁜 영국 여자들이 있지. 지금 나는 바클리 양을 사모하고 있다네. 나는 바클리 양과 결혼하고 싶어."

"나는 씻고 나서 보고하러 돌아가야 하네. 이제 아무도 전쟁은 안 하는 거야?"

"전쟁은 다음 주에 다시 시작되네. p.26 아마 다시 시작되겠지. 사람들이 그럴 거라고 말한다네. 자네는 내가 바클리 양과 결혼할 수 있을 것이라고 생각하나? 물론 전쟁 후에?"

"당연하지. 자네가 그녀를 사랑한다면." 내가 말하고 대야에 물을 가득 부었다.

"오늘 밤에 자네는 나에게 다 털어놓게 될 거야." 리날디가 말했다. "이제 바클리 양을 위해 기운 넘치고 멋있어지려면 나는 좀 더 자야 해."

나는 대야에 담겨 있는 찬물로 씻었다. 수건으로 문질러 닦는 동안 나는 침대 위에 눈을 감고 누워 있는 리날디를 쳐다보았다. 리날디는 잘생겼고, 내 나이 또래였으며, 아말피 출신이었다. 리날디는 외과 의사가 된 것을 아주 마음에 들어했고 우리는 절친한 친구였다. 리날디가 눈을 떴다.

"자네 돈 있나?"

"응."

"50리라만 빌려줘."

나는 손의 물기를 닦고 리날디에게 돈을 주었다.

"나는 바클리 양에게 돈이 많은 남자라는 인상을 주어야 하거든." 리날디가 미소를 지으며 말했다. p.27 "자네는 나의 절친한 친구이며 재정 보호인이잖아."

"지옥에나 가게." 내가 말했다.

그날 밤 식당에서 나는 신부님 옆에 앉았다. 신부님은 내가 아브루찌에 가지 않았다는 것에 실망하고 갑자기 상처를 받았다. 신부님은 자기 아버지에게 내가 갈 것이라고 편지를 써 두었고 가족들은 준비를 해 두었다는 것이었다. 나는 신부님만큼 기분이 안 좋았고 내가 왜 가지 않았는지 이해할 수 없었다. 그것이 내가 하고 싶어 했던 것이었고, 나는 일이 꼬리에 꼬리를 물고 생겨서 내가 그곳에 못 가게 된 경위를 설명하려고 애썼다. 마침내 신부님은 사실을 알았고 내가 진정으로 가고 싶어 했다는 것을 이해했으며 그 일은 거의 괜찮아졌다.

우리가 이야기를 마쳤을 때, 나는 포도주에 몹시 취해 있었다. **p.28** 그때 대위가 외쳤다. "신부님은 기분이 좋지 않으시다네. 신부님은 여자가 없으면 기분이 좋지 않으시지."

"저는 기분이 좋습니다." 신부님이 말했다.

"신부님은 기분이 좋지 않으셔. 신부님은 오스트리아군이 전쟁에 이기기를 원하신다네." 대위가 계속해서 말했다. 다른 사람들은 귀를 기울였다. 신부님은 고개를 저었다.

"아니에요." 신부님이 말했다.

"신부님은 우리가 절대로 공격하지 않기를 바라셔."

"아니에요. 전쟁이 있다면, 공격도 해야죠."

"공격해야 해. 공격해야 하고 말고!"

신부님이 고개를 끄덕였다.

"신부님을 내버려 둬." 소령이 말했다. "신부님은 좋으시잖아."

"여하튼 신부님이 그 일에 관해 어떻게 하실 수는 없으시잖아." 대위가 말했다.

우리는 모두 일어나서 식당을 나왔다.

제4장

p.29 아침에 근처 정원에 있던 포대가 나를 깨웠다. 나는 창밖을 내다보았다. 포대는 두 번을 더 발포했고 그때마다 공기가 강풍처럼 밀려와 창문을 흔들었다. 정원을 내다보았을 때 나는 트럭이 도로로 나가는 소리를 들었다. **p.30** 나는 옷을 입고 차고로 나갔다.

열 대의 자동차들이 나란히 줄지어 있었다. 그 차량들은 상부가 크고

앞부분이 뭉뚝한 구급차로, 색깔은 회색이고 유개 운반차처럼 만들어진 것이었다. 몇몇 공병들이 마당에 나와 구급차 한 대를 수리하고 있었다.

"적들이 포대를 폭격한 적이 있나?" 내가 공병들 중 한 명에게 물었다.

"아니요, 중위님. 포대는 저 작은 언덕에 의해 보호받고 있습니다."

"다 괜찮은 건가?"

"나쁘지는 않습니다."

"부속품을 구하는 데에는 어려움이 없었나?" 우리가 함께 차를 쳐다보는 동안 내가 공병 병장에게 물었다.

"없었습니다, 중위님."

"주유소는 지금 어디에 있나?"

"같은 장소에 있습니다."

"잘 됐군." 나는 말하고 집으로 돌아와 식당의 식탁에서 커피를 마셨다. **p.31** 창밖으로 아름다운 봄날의 아침이 보였다. 그날 나는 산 속의 주둔 부대를 방문하고 오후가 끝날 무렵에 마을로 돌아왔다.

나는 매우 지저분해졌으므로 씻으려고 내 방으로 올라갔다. 리날디는 휴고의 영문법 책을 가지고 침대 위에 앉아 있었다.

"멋지군." 리날디가 말했다. "나와 함께 바클리 양을 보러 가세."

"그래."

나는 씻고 머리를 빗었고, 우리는 출발했다.

"잠깐 기다리게." 리날디가 말했다. "먼저 한잔 마셔야 할 것 같네." 리날디는 자신의 트렁크를 열고 그랍파 술병을 꺼냈다.

리날디는 두 잔을 따랐다. 그 술은 아주 독했다.

p.32 "한 잔 더?"

"그래." 내가 말했다. 우리는 두 번째 잔을 마셨다. 리날디는 병을 치웠고 우리는 계단을 내려갔다. 마을을 걸어가는 동안은 더웠지만, 해가 지기 시작하고 있어서 기분이 아주 좋았다. 영국인 병원은 전쟁 전에 독일인들에 의해 지어진 커다란 별장이었다. 바클리 양은 정원에서 우리를 기다리고 있었다. 또 다른 간호사가 그녀와 함께 있었다. 우리는 그들 쪽으로 걸어갔다. 우리는 경례를 했다.

"안녕하세요?" 바클리 양이 말했다. "이탈리아 사람이 아니시군요, 그렇죠?"

"네."

리날디는 다른 간호사와 이야기하고 있었다. 그들은 웃고 있었다.

"참 이상한 일이네요. 이탈리아군에 계시다니요."

"진짜 군대는 아니에요. 야전 의무대일 뿐입니다."

p.33 "그래도 아주 이상해요. 왜 그러신 거예요?"

"저도 모릅니다." 내가 말했다. "모든 일에 늘 설명이 있는 것은 아니잖아요. 저 지팡이는 무엇인가요?"

바클리 양은 상당히 키가 큰 편이었다. 바클리 양은 금발이었고 황갈색 피부에 눈은 회색이었다. 나는 바클리 양이 아주 아름답다고 생각했다. 바클리 양은 가죽을 둘러 감은 가는 지팡이를 들고 있었다.

"그 지팡이는 작년에 죽은 어떤 청년의 것이었어요."

"대단히 유감입니다."

"그 사람은 저와 결혼할 예정이었는데, 솜므에서 전사했어요."

"약혼하신 지는 오래되었었나요?"

"8년이요. 우리는 같이 자랐죠."

"그런데 왜 결혼하지 않으셨나요?"

p.34 "모르겠어요." 바클리 양이 말했다. "결혼을 안 하다니 저는 바보였어요. 누구를 사랑해 본 적이 있으세요?"

"아니요." 내가 말했다.

우리는 벤치에 앉았다. 나는 몸을 돌려 바클리 양을 바라보았다.

"머리카락이 예쁘시네요." 내가 말했다.

"마음에 드세요?"

"아주 많이요."

"그 사람이 죽었을 때 몽땅 자르려고 했었어요."

"그러지 마세요."

우리는 다른 간호사와 이야기하고 있는 리날디를 보았다.

"저 아가씨의 이름은 뭐죠?"

"헬렌 퍼거슨이에요. 당신 친구는 의사죠, 안 그래요?"

"네, 아주 유능한 의사죠."

잠시 후 우리는 작별 인사를 하고 헤어졌다.

"바클리 양은 나보다 자네를 더 좋아해." 우리가 돌아올 때 리날디가 말했다. "그것은 분명해. p.35 하지만 퍼거슨 양은 아주 괜찮아."

"아주 괜찮더라." 내가 말했다. 나는 그녀를 주목하지도 않았었다. "그 여자가 마음에 드나?"

"아니." 리날디가 말했다.

제5장

p.36 그날 오후 나는 바클리 양을 다시 만나러 갔다. 나는 수간호사와 우연히 마주쳤는데, 그녀는 바클리 양이 근무 중이라고 말했다.

"전쟁 중이잖아요, 아시겠지만." 수간호사가 말했다.

"압니다."

"당신은 이탈리아군 소속의 미국인이시죠?" 수간호사가 물었다.

p.37 "네, 수간호사님."

"원하신다면 7시 이후에 오시면 바클리 양을 만나실 수 있어요. 하지만 이탈리아 사람들을 많이 데려오지는 마세요."

"점잖은 말을 사용한다고 해도 안 되나요?"

"안 돼요. 멋진 군복을 입었다고 해도 안 돼요."

"안녕하세요." 내가 말했다.

저녁에 나는 바클리 양을 방문하러 돌아왔다. 바클리 양은 정원에 있는 벤치에 앉아 있었고 퍼거슨 양과 함께 있었다. 그들은 나를 보고 기뻐하는 듯했고, 잠시 후 퍼거슨 양은 양해를 구하고 자리를 떴다.

"두 분만 두고 저는 가 볼게요." 퍼거슨 양이 일어나며 말했다.

"가지 마, 헬렌." 바클리 양이 말했다.

"정말 가 봐야 해. 편지를 좀 써야 하거든."

p.38 "좋은 밤 보내세요." 내가 말했다.

"좋은 밤 보내세요, 헨리 씨."

퍼거슨 양이 그 자리를 뜨는 동안 우리는 지켜보았다.

"좋은 분이군요." 내가 말했다.

"네, 아주 좋은 사람이죠. 간호사예요."

"당신은 간호사가 아니신가요?"

"오, 아니에요. 저는 소위 말하는 구급간호봉사대예요."

"차이가 뭐죠?"

"간호사가 되려면 시간이 오래 걸리죠. 구급간호봉사대는 속성이에요."

"그렇군요."

"이탈리아 사람들은 여자들이 전선에 아주 가까이 있는 것을 원하지 않아요. 그래서 우리는 외출도 안 해요."

"그렇다면 제가 이곳으로 오면 되죠."

"오, 그러세요."

"전쟁 이야기는 그만하지요."

"전쟁 이야기를 안 하기가 참 어려워요."

"그래도 그만하지요."

"좋아요."

p.39 나는 어둠 속에서 바클리 양을 쳐다보았다. 나는 바클리 양이 아주 아름답다고 생각했고 그녀의 손을 잡았다. 나는 바클리 양에게 키스하려고 몸을 앞으로 숙였는데 눈이 번쩍하는 얼얼한 섬광이 일었다. 바클리 양이 내 얼굴을 찰싹 때렸던 것이다. 반사 작용으로 내 눈에서 눈물이 나왔다.

"정말 죄송해요." 바클리 양이 말했다. 나는 나에게 어떤 이점이 생겼다고 생각했다.

"그러실 만했지요."

"정말 죄송해요." 바클리 양이 말했다. "당신에게 상처를 주려는 의도는 아니었어요."

바클리 양은 나를 바라보았다. 나는 화가 났지만 체스 게임에서의 말의 움직임처럼 모든 상황을 미리 내다보고 확신이 섰다.

"적어도 우리가 지금은 전쟁에 관해서는 이야기하고 있지 않잖아요." 내가 말했다.

바클리 양은 웃었다.

p.40 "다정하시군요." 바클리 양이 말했다. "당신만 괜찮으시다면 제가 기꺼이 키스해 드릴게요."

나는 바클리 양의 눈을 쳐다보고 그녀에게 힘껏 키스하고 그녀를 꽉 끌어안았다. 나는 바클리 양을 내 몸에 가까이 밀착시켰고 그녀의 심장이 고동치는 것을 느낄 수 있었다. 다음 순간 바클리 양은 내 어깨에 기대어 울고 있었다.

"저에게 잘 대해 주실 거죠?" 바클리 양이 말했다.

나는 이 말이 다소 이상하다고 생각했다. 그럼에도 불구하고 나는 바클리 양의 머리카락을 어루만지고 그녀의 어깨를 토닥거렸다.

"저에게 잘 대해 주셔야 해요." 바클리 양이 나를 올려다보고 말했다. "우리는 이상한 삶을 살게 될 것이니까요."

바클리 양이 마음을 추스른 후, 나는 그녀와 함께 별장의 문 쪽으로 걸었고 그런 다음 집으로 갔다. 별장에 있는 내 방으로 돌아와 보니 리날디가 자기 침대에 누워 있었다.

"바클리 양과는 진전이 있나?"

"우리는 친구야."

제6장

p.41 다음번에 내가 바클리 양을 만나러 갔을 때, 그녀는 정원에 있지 않았다. 나는 바클리 양이 내려올 때까지 병원의 진료실에서 기다렸다. 캐서린 바클리 양이 홀로 내려오는 것을 보았을 때 나는 일어섰다. **p.42** 바클리 양은 아름다워 보였다.

"안녕하세요, 헨리 씨." 바클리 양이 말했다.

"잘 지내셨어요?" 내가 말했다. "여기 앉을까요, 아니면 정원으로 나갈까요?"

"나가시죠. 정원이 훨씬 시원해요."

나는 바클리 양의 뒤를 따라 정원으로 나갔다.

"어디 다녀오셨어요?" 바클리 양이 물었다.

"주둔지에 나가 있었습니다."

"왜 제게 쪽지를 보내지 않으셨죠?"

"겨우 이틀 나가 있었는걸요. 하지만 지금 돌아왔잖습니까."

바클리 양이 나를 올려다보았다.

"그런데 저를 사랑하시나요?"

"네."

"저를 사랑한다고 말씀하셨어요, 안 그런가요?"

"네." 나는 거짓말을 했다. "당신을 사랑합니다." 나는 전에 그런 말을 한 번도 한 적이 없었다.

"저도 당신을 사랑해요. 그래서 그동안 끔찍했어요. 다시 떠나지는 않으실 거죠?"

"떠나겠지만 언제나 돌아올 것입니다."

나는 그녀의 몸을 돌려세웠으므로 바클리 양에게 키스를 할 때 그녀의 얼굴을 볼 수 있었으며, 그녀의 눈이 감겨 있는 것을 보았다. p.43 나는 바클리 양의 감긴 눈에 키스를 했다. 나는 바클리 양이 약간 정신이 나갔을지도 모른다고 생각했다. 그녀가 그렇다고 해도 괜찮았다. 내가 어떤 관계에 빠지든 상관없었다. 매일 밤 남자들이 가득한 별장으로 돌아가는 것보다는 이쪽이 더 나았다.

우리는 평평한 돌 벤치에 앉았고, 나는 바클리 양의 손을 잡았다.

"이것은 우리가 하는 어리석은 게임이에요, 안 그런가요?" 바클리 양이 말했다.

"무슨 게임이요?"

"제가 무엇에 대해 말하는지 모르는 체하지 마세요."

"모르는 체하고 있는 것이 아니에요."

"당신은 좋은 사람이에요." 바클리 양이 말했다. "그리고 당신은 방법을 아는 만큼 게임도 잘하시죠. 하지만 그것은 어리석은 게임이에요."

"늘 다른 사람들이 무슨 생각을 하는지 아시나요?"

p.44 "늘 그런 것은 아니지만, 당신 생각은 알아요. 저를 사랑하는 척하실 필요는 없어요."

"하지만 사랑해요."

"그럴 필요 없을 때는 거짓말하지 마세요. 하지만 당신은 아주 좋은 사람이에요. 저를 다시 보러 와 주시겠어요?"

"물론입니다."

바클리 양은 일어나서 손을 내밀었다.

"안녕히 주무세요."

나는 바클리 양에게 키스를 하려고 했다.

"안 돼요." 바클리 양이 말했다. "저는 몹시 피곤해요."

"키스해 줘요." 내가 말했다.

"몹시 피곤하다니까요."

"키스해 줘요."

우리는 키스를 했지만 바클리 양은 별안간 달아났다.

"안 돼요. 안녕히 가세요, 제발요."

나는 집으로 갔다. 내가 옷을 벗고 있을 때 리날디가 왔다.

"아하!" 리날디가 말했다. "아주 잘 되지는 않나 봐? **p.45** 내가 그 영국 여자와 연관되지 않아서 다행이야."

제7장

p.46 다음날 내가 우리가 있는 산 속 제1주둔지에서 돌아왔을 때는 5시였다. 나는 차를 세차하는 곳으로 나가 샤워를 했다. 그런 다음 내 방 열린 창문 앞에서 바지와 속옷 상의를 입고 앉아서 보고서를 작성했다. 이틀 후면 공세가 시작될 예정이고 나는 플라바로 갈 것이었다.

p.47 그날 저녁 식당에서는 사람들이 너무 말이 많았다. 나는 빨리 식사를 하고 캐서린 바클리 양을 만나러 가야겠다고 작정했다. 그날 밤은 내가 조금이라도 마시지 않으면 우리가 다 같이 전우라고 할 수 없는 분위기여서 나는 포도주를 마셨다. 나는 신부님과 함께 아일랜드 대주교에 관해 이야기했다.

더욱 많은 포도주 잔과 농담이 오고 간 후, 나는 캐서린 바클리 양을 기억해 냈다.

"나는 가 봐야 해." 내가 말했다. 모두들 얼근하게 취했고 즐거워했다.

리날디가 나와 함께 나왔다.

"취한 상태로 그곳에 가면 안 되네."

"나는 안 취했어. 정말이야."

"커피라도 좀 씹지 그래."

"쓸데없는 소리."

"내가 좀 가지고 올게, 친구." 리날디는 볶은 커피콩 한 줌을 가지고 돌아왔다. "그것을 씹게, 친구, 그리고 행운을 빌어. 내가 자네와 함께 가 주지."

p.48 우리는 함께 마을을 이리저리 걸었고 나는 커피를 씹었다. 영국군 별장으로 이어지는 진입로 정문에서 리날디는 작별 인사를 했다.

나는 진입로를 내려가기 시작했다. 나는 뒤돌아보고 리날디가 나를 지켜보는 것을 보았다. 나는 리날디에게 손을 흔들어 인사했다.

나는 별장의 응접실에 앉아서 캐서린 바클리 양이 내려오기를 기다렸다. 누군가가 복도로 내려왔다. 캐서린 양은 아니었다. 그것은 퍼거슨 양이었다.

"안녕하세요." 퍼거슨 양이 말했다. "캐서린이 미안하지만 오늘 저녁에는 당신을 만날 수 없대요."

"아픈 것이 아니라면 좋겠네요."

"건강이 좋은 편은 아니에요."

"제가 걱정하더라고 전해 주시겠어요?"

"네, 그럴게요."

"내일은 캐서린 양을 보러 다시 와도 된다고 생각하시나요?"

p.49 "네, 그럼요."

"대단히 감사합니다." 내가 말했다. "안녕히 주무세요."

나는 별장을 떠났고 갑자기 외롭고 마음이 텅 빈 느낌이 들었다.

제8장

p.50 다음날 오후 우리는 그날 밤에 강 상류에 공격이 있을 것이라는 이야기를 들었다. 시간이 다 됐을 때, 우리는 넉 대의 차량에 타고 출발했다. 나는 첫 번째 차량에 타고 있었고 우리가 영국군 병원 입구를 지날 때, 나는 운전병에게 잠깐 세워 달라고 요청했다. 나는 진입로로 뛰어가 응접실 안으로 들어가서 바클리 양을 불러 달라고 했다.

p.51 "몸이 좀 나아졌는지 보려고 들렀어요." 내가 말했다.

"저는 괜찮아요." 바클리 양이 말했다. "어제는 열이 있었던 것 같아요."

"나는 가야 합니다."

"잠깐 당신과 함께 밖으로 나갈게요."

"괜찮은 것이 확실합니까?" 내가 밖에서 물었다.

"네, 내 사랑. 오늘 밤에 돌아오실 거죠?"

"아니요."

"언제 돌아오세요?"

"내일이요."

바클리 양은 자기 목에서 무언가의 걸쇠를 끄르고 그것을 내 손에 쥐어 주었다.

"성 안토니오예요." 바클리 양이 말했다.

"가톨릭 신자입니까?"

"아니요. 하지만 성 안토니오의 목걸이는 아주 유용하다던데요."

p.52 "당신을 위해 소중히 간직할게요. 잘 있어요."

"조심하세요. 안 돼요, 여기서는 키스하지 마세요."

"알겠습니다."

나는 구급차 좌석으로 올라탔고 우리는 출발했다. 성 안토니오는 작은 흰색 금속 캡슐 안에 있었다. 나는 캡슐을 열고 성 안토니오를 내 손 위에 올려놓았다. 나는 성 안토니오를 다시 캡슐 안에 넣고 금목걸이를 내 목에 걸었다. 그런 다음 나는 성 안토니오에 대해서는 잊고 말았다. 부상을 당한 후, 나는 다시는 성 안토니오를 보지 못했다. 누군가가 아마도 그것을 응급 치료소들 중 한 곳에서 주웠으리라.

우리는 다리를 건널 때 빨리 달렸고 곧 도로 아래쪽 전방에 있는 다른 차량들이 일으킨 먼지를 보았다. 곧 우리는 강가 근처에 있는 구릉지에 있었고 도로가 오르막길이 되면서, 높은 산들의 꼭대기는 여전히 눈으로 덮인 채 북쪽을 향해 솟아 있었다.

p.53 도로는 텅 비어 있었고 우리는 산 속으로 올라간 다음 강가의 계곡으로 내려갔다. 나는 강을 볼 수 있었고, 강물은 맑고 빠르게 흘렀으며 얕았다. 그런 다음 도로가 산등성이를 따라 오르막길이 되면서 나는 또 다른 산등성이를 보았다. 그것들은 백토질로 희고 고랑이 나 있는 것처럼 보이는 꼭대기가 눈으로 덮인 더 높은 산들이었다.

우리가 내려가서 강 옆으로 이어진 주도로에 진입할 때 날은 거의 어두워져 있었다.

제9장

p.54 도로는 붐볐으며 양쪽으로는 옥수숫대와 밀짚 거적 차폐물이 있었다. 우리는 이 거적으로 덮인 터널 안에서 천천히 차를 몰았으며 철도역이 있었던 탁 트인 공간으로 나왔다. 이곳의 도로는 강둑의 수위보다 낮았다.

p.55 움푹 들어간 도로변을 따라 둑에 파놓은 구멍들에는 보병들이 들어가 있었다. 우리가 차를 몰고 갈 때, 나는 해가 지는 반대쪽 산 위쪽에 떠 있는 오스트리아군 관측용 기구들을 보았다. 우리는 벽돌 공장을 지나 차량을 주차했다. 깊게 파 놓은 몇 개의 구멍에는 응급 치료소로서 장비가 갖추어져 있었다.

이곳 벽돌 공장에서 우리는 강둑으로 인해 라이플총 혹은 기관총 사격으로부터 안전했다. 강을 가로지르는 부서진 다리가 있었다. 몇몇 부대가 강을 건널 수 있도록 포격이 시작되면 그들은 또 다른 다리를 놓을 예정이었다.

소령은 콧수염이 난 몸집이 작은 남자였다. 소령은 리비아 전쟁에 참여했었다. 모든 일이 순조롭다면 내가 훈장을 받는 것을 보게 될 것이라고 소령은 말했다. p.56 소령은 나에게 자기와 다른 장교 두 명과 함께 한잔하자고 요청했다. 우리는 럼주를 마시고 친근한 분위기의 대화를 나누었다. 날이 어두워지고 있었다.

나는 몇 시에 공격이 시작될지 물었고 그들은 어두워지자마자 공격할 거라고 말했다. 나는 운전병들에게 갔다. 그들은 이야기를 하며 참호 안에 앉아 있었고 내가 다가가자 말하던 것을 멈추었다. 나는 그들 각자에게 담배를 한 갑씩 주었다. 마네라는 자신의 라이터를 켜고 주변으로 돌렸으며, 나는 내가 들은 것을 그들에게 말해 주었다.

"식사는 어떻게 하나요, 중위님?" 마네라가 물었다. "전투가 시작된 후에는 먹을 기회도 없을 텐데요."

"내가 가서 알아보지." 내가 말했다.

나는 소령의 참호로 돌아갔고 그는 야전 취사장이 곧 마련될 것이며 운전병들은 와서 스튜를 먹을 수 있을 것이라고 말했다. 나는 운전병들에게 돌아가서 그들이 곧 식사를 하게 될 것이라고 말했다. p.57 우리는 벽에 등을 기대고 땅에 앉아 담배를 피웠다.

"누가 공격을 하나요?" 가부찌가 물었다.

"저격병."

"모든 저격병들이요?"

"그럴 거야."

"여기에는 적절한 공격을 할 만큼 부대가 충분히 있지 않아요."

"아마도 진짜 공격이 일어날 곳에서 주의를 돌리려는 것이겠지."

"저격병들은 알고 있나요?"

"그렇지는 않을 거야."

"물론 그들은 모르지." 마네라가 말했다. "알고 있다면 그들은 공격하지 않으려고 할 거야."

"아니, 그들은 공격할 거야." 파시니가 말했다. "저격병들은 바보들이야."

"그들은 용감해." 내가 말했다.

p.58 "그들은 용감해야 하기 때문에 용감한 거야." 마네라가 말했다.

"만약 공격하지 않으면, 헌병대가 총을 쏠 거야. 죽을 가능성이 있더라도 명령을 따라야 해."

"병장이 나가려고 하지 않는 두 명의 장교를 쏘았다는 소리를 내가 지난주에 들었어." 가부찌가 말했다.

"그들 중 한 명은 우리 마을 출신이었지." 파시니가 말했다.

"이제 우리 입 좀 다무세." 마네라가 말했다.

"배가 고픕니다, 중위님." 가부찌가 말했다.

"내가 가서 알아보지." 내가 말했다. 고르디니가 일어나서 나와 함께 밖으로 나왔다.

"제가 어떤 식으로든 도와드리기 위해 할 수 있는 일이 있나요?" 고르디니는 네 명의 운전병들 중 가장 조용한 사람이었다.

"원한다면 나와 함께 가지." 내가 말했다. "우리가 알아보세나."

나는 소령이 텐트 안에 있는 상자 위에 앉아 통화 중인 것을 보았다. 군의관들 중 한 명이 나에게 코냑 한 잔을 주었다. p.59 고르디니는 내 뒤에 서 있었다. 소령이 전화를 끊었다.

"이제 시작이군." 소령이 말했다.

나는 바깥을 내다보았다. 오스트리아군 탐조등들이 우리 뒤에 있는 산 위에서 움직이고 있었다. 그런 다음 갑자기 우리 뒤에 있는 모든 대포들로부터 포격이 시작되었다.

"스튜에 대한 것인데요, 소령님." 내가 말했다.

"여기에는 없네."

커다란 포탄이 떨어져 벽돌 공장 밖에서 터졌다.

"뭐 먹을 것이 있나요?" 내가 물었다.

"파스타가 조금 있네." 소령이 말했다.

"소령님 것을 가져가겠습니다."

소령은 당번병에게 말했고, 그는 뒤쪽으로 나가 커다란 쇠그릇에 담긴 차가운 마카로니와 커다란 치즈 한 덩어리를 가지고 돌아왔다. p.60 나는 고르디니에게 그것들을 주었다.

"포격이 끝날 때까지 기다리는 게 좋아." 소령이 말했다.

"병사들이 먹어야 해서요." 내가 말했다.

"좋을 대로 하게."

밖으로 나가 우리는 벽돌 공장을 가로질러 세 명의 운전병들이 벽에 기대어 앉아 담배를 피우고 있는 참호로 달려갔다.

"어이, 애국자들." 내가 말했다.

고르디니는 나에게 마카로니 그릇을 건넸다.

"먼저 드세요, 중위님."

"아니야." 내가 말했다. "바닥에 그릇을 놓고 우리 모두 먹는다."

"포크가 없는데요."

"제기랄." 내가 영어로 말했다.

나는 치즈를 네 조각으로 잘라 마카로니 위에 얹었다. 나는 손을 마카로니 안에 찔러 넣고 집어 올렸다. 한 덩어리가 풀렸다.

"높이 들어주세요, 중위님."

나는 더 높이 들었고 가닥들이 정리되었다. p.61 나는 그것을 아래로 내려 입 안으로 넣고 빨아들여 끝을 홱 낚아챘다. 나는 씹었고, 그런 다음 치즈를 한 입 베어 물어 씹고 그런 다음 약간의 포도주를 마셨다. 땅을 뒤흔드는 무언가가 밖에 떨어졌다.

"스코다 대포들이군." 고르디니가 말했다.

우리는 계속해서 먹었다. 기차의 시동이 걸리는 듯한 소리가 났고 그런 다음 다시 땅을 뒤흔드는 폭발음이 났다.

"이것은 깊은 참호가 아닌데." 파시니가 말했다.

"저것은 대형 박격포 같은 소리가 났어." 내가 말했다.

"맞습니다, 중위님."

나는 내 몫의 치즈 끝 부분을 먹고 포도주를 한 모금 마셨다. 그런 다음 용광로 문이 활짝 열릴 때처럼 섬광이 있었고, 포효 소리가 났다.

내가 다시 눈을 뜰 수 있었을 때, 나는 땅이 패고 내 머리 앞에 쪼개진 목재 들보가 있는 것을 보았다. p.62 나는 누군가가 울부짖는 소리를 들었다. 나는 움직이려고 애를 써 보았지만 움직일 수가 없었다. 나는 기관총과 라이플총들이 강 건너편에서 발사되는 소리를 들었다. 그때 로켓포와 폭탄 소리가 들렸고, 그런 다음 내 가까이에서 누군가가 "어머니! 오, 어머니!"라고 말하는 소리를 들었다.

나는 주위를 둘러보다가 그 사람을 손으로 건드렸는데, 그는 비명을 질렀다. 그것은 파시니였다. 파시니의 다리는 내 쪽을 향해 있었고 나는 그 다리들이 둘 다 무릎 위로는 으스러져 있는 것을 보았다. 한쪽 다리는 완전히 없어졌고 다른 다리는 힘줄에 붙어 있었다. 파시니는 자신의 팔을 물고서 고통으로 비명을 질렀다.

나는 파시니에게 좀 더 가까이 다가가려고 애썼으나 움직일 수가 없었다. 나는 다시 시도했고 내 다리는 약간 움직였다. 나는 팔과 팔꿈치를 사용해서 뒤로 갈 수 있었다. 파시니는 이제 조용했고, 내가 그에게 갔을 때, 그는 이미 죽어 있었다. p.63 위치를 알아내야 할 다른 세 명이 있었다. 나는 내 다리가 뜨끈하고 축축하며 내 신발 안쪽이 젖어 있고 뜨끈하다는 것을 깨달았다. 나는 내가 포격에 맞았다는 것을 알았다. 나는 손을 무릎에 올렸다. 나의 무릎은 그곳에 없었다. 손을 안으로 넣어 보았더니 내 무릎이 아래로 내려가 정강이에 있었다. 누군가가 내 팔 아래로 손을 넣어 나를 잡았고 또 다른 누군가가 내 다리를 들어 올렸다.

"세 사람이 더 있소." 내가 말했다.

"접니다, 마네라예요. 저희가 들것을 가지러 갔지만 하나도 없었어요. 어떠세요, 중위님?"

"고르디니와 가부찌는 어디에 있나?"

"고르디니는 치료소에서 붕대를 감고 있어요. 가부찌는 중위님의 다리를 잡고 있고요. 제 목을 잡으세요, 중위님. 심하게 맞으셨나요?"

p.64 "다리에. 고르디니는 어떤가?"

"고르디니는 괜찮아요. 대형 박격포 포탄이었어요."

"파시니는 죽었어."

"맞습니다, 파시니는 죽었어요."

치료소 밖에는 우리들 중 상당히 많은 사람들이 어둠 속에서 땅 위에 누워 있었다. 어떤 사람들은 부상을 당했고, 그보다 더 많은 사람들이 죽어 있었다. 내가 임시 치료소에 도착하자마자 마네라가 군의관을 데리고 나왔으며 그는 내 두 다리에 붕대를 감았다. 고르디니는 운전을 할 수가 없다고 마네라가 말했다. 마네라의 어깨는 으스러져 있었고 머리를 다쳤다. 그런 다음 영국군이 세 대의 구급차를 가지고 왔고, 그들은 각각의 구급차에 두 사람씩 실었다. 운전병들 중 한 명이 몹시 창백하고 아파 보이는 고르디니를 데리고 나에게 다가왔다.

"심하게 맞으셨습니까?" 영국인 운전병이 물었다. 운전병은 키가 큰 남자였고 철제 테 안경을 끼고 있었다.

p.65 "다리에."

"심각하지 않았으면 좋겠군요. 담배 드릴까요?"

“고맙네.”

“중위님께서 두 명의 운전병을 잃으셨다고 제게 말해 주더군요.”

“그래. 한 명은 죽었고, 다른 한 명은 자네가 데려온 친구라네.”

“저희가 차량을 가지고 갈까요?”

“그래.”

“저희가 차량을 별장까지 몰고 가겠습니다. 206호던가요, 맞나요?

“그래.”

“멋진 곳이죠. 주변에서 중위님을 뵌 적이 있어요. 중위님은 미국인이라고 하던데요.”

“그래.”

“저는 영국인입니다.”

“알고 있네.”

“중위님의 이 부하 녀석이 제가 중위님을 꼭 뵙기를 원했어요.” 그는 고르디니의 어깨를 툭툭 쳤다. **p.66** “중위님을 이곳에서 모시고 나가는 것에 대해 저는 무슨 일이든 해야겠어요. 제가 저희와 같이 모시고 돌아갈게요.”

그는 임시 치료소를 가로질러 걸어갔다.

“그 친구가 보살펴 드릴 거예요, 중위님.” 고르디니가 말했다.

“자네는 어떤가, 프랑코?”

“저는 괜찮습니다.” 프랑코가 내 옆에 앉았다. 잠시 후 영국인 병사가 들것을 든 두 명의 병사들과 함께 돌아왔다.

“여기 미국인 중위님이 계시네.” 영국인 병사가 완벽한 이탈리아 어로 말했다.

“나는 그냥 기다리겠네.” 내가 말했다. “나보다 훨씬 더 심하게 다친 사람들이 있어.”

“피투성이로 영웅 행세 하지 마세요.” 영국인 병사가 말했다. 그런 다음 이탈리아 어로 “아주 조심스럽게 이분을 들어 올려. 다리에 고통이 무척 심하셔.”라고 말했다. 그들은 나를 들어 올려 임시 치료소로 데리고 갔다. 안에서는 모든 탁자 위에서 수술이 진행되고 있었다. 키 작은 소령은 화를 내며 우리를 바라보았다.

p.67 “제가 미국인 중위님을 맡을게요.” 대위들 중 한 명이 말했다. 그들은 탁자 위로 나를 들어 올렸다. 그들은 내 바지를 벗겼고 대위는 작업을 하는 동안 부관 상사에게 “좌우 허벅다리와 좌우 무릎과 우측 발에 다

수의 외상. 우측 무릎과 우측 발에 심각한 부상. 두피 열상과 두개골 골절 가능성 있음"이라고 구술하기 시작했다.

부관이 서류에서 고개를 들고 바라보며 물었다. "무엇이 상처를 입힌 거죠?"

"무엇에 맞았나?" 대위가 물었다.

"박격포 포탄입니다." 내가 말했다.

"여기 적의 박격포 포탄 파편이 있어." 대위가 계속해서 말했다. p.68 "통증은 아직 시작되지 않았군. 중위에게 브랜디 한 잔 갖다 주게. 그리고 내 생각에 중위는 두개골 골절상을 입은 것 같네. 붕대를 감아 주겠네. 머리를 이리저리 움직이지 말게." 대위가 붕대를 묶었는데, 그의 손은 아주 빨리 움직였고 붕대는 팽팽하게 감겼다. "다 됐네, 행운을 빌겠네."

그들은 나를 들어 올렸고 우리는 밖으로 나갔다. 그들이 나를 영국군 구급차에 실었을 때, 대위가 말했던 통증이 시작되었다. 옆에는 사람이 누워 있는 또 다른 들것이 있었다. 나는 붕대 밖으로 나와 있는 창백해 보이는 그의 코만 볼 수 있었다. 그는 몹시 힘겹게 숨을 쉬었다. 보다 많은 들것들이 들어 올려져 위쪽의 들것걸이에 미끄러져 들어갔다. 키가 큰 영국인 운전병이 와서 들여다보았다.

"아주 조심스럽게 운전하겠습니다." 운전병이 말했다. "여러분이 편안하게 계시면 좋겠습니다." 나는 시동이 걸리는 것을 느꼈고, 운전병이 앞좌석으로 올라타는 것을 느꼈고, 브레이크가 풀리고 클러치를 넣는 것을 느꼈고, 우리는 출발했다.

p.69 얼마 후 나는 무엇인가가 내 팔 위로 똑똑 떨어지는 것을 느꼈다. 처음에 그것은 천천히 떨어졌고, 그런 다음에는 물줄기로 변했다. 나는 운전병에게 소리를 질렀다. 운전병은 차를 세우고 의자 뒤에 난 구멍으로 들여다보았다.

"무슨 일입니까?"

"내 위쪽 들것에 있는 사람한테 출혈이 있어."

구급차가 멈추어 섰다. 갑자기 위에 있는 들것에서 내려오던 핏줄기가 줄어들고 다시 똑똑 덜어지기 시작했다.

"그는 어떤가?" 영군인 운전병이 뒷문을 열고 위쪽 들것에 있는 남자를 쳐다볼 때 내가 물었다.

"죽었습니다." 운전병이 말했다.

p.70 다음 치료소에서 그들은 그 들것을 꺼내고 다른 들것을 집어넣었으며 우리는 가던 길을 계속 갔다.

제10장

p.71 야전병원에 있는 병실에서 나는 오후에 한 방문객이 나를 보러 오고 있다는 말을 들었다. 의사들 중 한 명이 리날디를 데리고 왔을 때 나는 내 발바닥의 가려운 곳을 긁어 달라고 간호병에게 말하고 있는 중이었다. p.72 리날디는 아주 빨리 들어와 나에게 입을 맞추었다. 리날디는 장갑을 끼고 있었다.

"어떤가? 내가 이것을 가지고 왔지……." 그것은 코냑 한 병이었다. 간호병은 의자를 가지고 왔고 리날디는 의자에 앉았다. "그리고 좋은 소식은 자네가 훈장을 받게 될 것이라는 거야. 그들은 자네가 은장 훈장을 타게 해 주고 싶어 하지만 아마 청동 훈장만 타게 해 줄 수 있을 거야."

"왜?"

"왜냐하면 자네가 심하게 부상당했으니까. 만약 자네가 어떤 영웅적인 행동을 했다는 것을 입증할 수 있다면, 자네는 은장 훈장을 탈 수 있을 거야. 영웅적인 행동을 뭐라도 했나?"

"아니." 내가 말했다. "나는 치즈를 먹고 있었어."

"기억해 보게. 전이든 후든 영웅적인 행동을 무언가 했음이 분명할 테니까."

"없어."

"고르디니는 자네가 몇 사람을 등에 업고 옮겼다고 했지만, 제1치료소의 대위는 그것이 불가능하다고 단언하네."

p.73 "나는 누구도 옮길 수 없었어. 나는 움직일 수조차 없었네."

"그것은 중요하지 않아." 리날디가 장갑을 벗으며 말했다. "내 생각에는 우리가 자네에게 은장 훈장을 타게 해 줄 수 있을 것 같네. 다른 사람보다 먼저 의학적으로 도움을 받는 것을 거절하지 않았나?"

"그리 명백하지는 않네."

"그것은 중요하지 않아. 자네가 얼마나 심하게 다쳤는지 보게. 그리고 자네는 용감하고, 언제나 최전선으로 가겠다고 요구하고 있네. 게다가 임무도 성공적이었고."

"강을 건넜나?"

"그래. 그리고 그들은 거의 천 명에 달하는 죄수들을 잡았지. 공보에도 나와 있어. 내가 공보를 자네에게 가져다주겠네."

"바클리 양은 만났나?" 내가 물었다.

"내가 가서 그 여자를 데려오지."

"아니, 그러지 말게." 내가 말했다. "고리지아와 여자들 이야기를 나한테 해 주게."

p.74 "새로운 여자들은 없어. 나는 더 이상 안 간다네."

"전혀?"

"무언가 새로운 일이 있나 보러 잠깐 들르는 정도지. 여자들은 모두 자네를 불러 달라고 하네."

리날디는 코냑 한 잔을 직접 따랐다.

"한잔한다고 자네에게 해가 되지는 않을 거야, 친구." 리날디가 말했다. "마시게."

나는 코냑을 마셨고 온기가 나의 목을 타고 내려가는 것을 느꼈다. 리날디는 또 한 잔을 따랐다.

"자네의 용감한 부상을 위하여." 리날디가 말했다. "은장 훈장을 위하여. 오, 신부님이 자네를 보러 오실 거야. 신부님은 준비를 많이 하시지."

리날디가 일어나서 장갑을 꼈다.

"내가 없는 동안 분별 있게 굴게." 내가 말했다.

"내가 바클리 양을 보내 주지. 잘 있게, 친구. 코냑은 침대 옆에 있네. 빨리 낫게나."

제11장

p.75 신부님이 나를 보러 왔을 때는 땅거미가 질 무렵이었다. 신부님은 작은 구릿빛 얼굴에 당혹스러운 표정을 짓고 어색하게 서 있었다.

"어떠십니까?" 신부님이 물었다. 신부님은 몇 개의 꾸러미를 바닥에 내려놓았다.

p.76 "괜찮습니다, 신부님."

신부님은 앉아서 당혹스러워하며 창밖을 내다보았다. 나는 신부님의 얼굴이 지쳐 보이는 것을 알아챘다.

"저는 잠깐만 있을 수 있습니다." 신부님이 말했다.

"식당은 어땠나요?"

신부님이 미소를 지었다.

"저는 여전히 커다란 놀림감이지요." 신부님이 말했다. "다행히 그 사람들은 모두 무사합니다."

나는 신부님이 그렇게 피곤해 보이는 것에는 익숙하지 않았다.

"식당에 계시는 당신이 그립더군요."

"그곳에 있다면 저도 좋을 텐데요. 저는 언제나 우리 대화가 재미있었어요."

"제가 중위님께 몇 가지 물건을 가지고 왔습니다." 신부님이 꾸러미를 집어 올리며 말했다. "모기장, 베르무트 한 병, 그리고 영국 신문 몇 부예요."

"대단히 고맙습니다. 신문은 어디에서 구하셨어요?"

"그것들을 주문하려고 메스트레로 사람을 보냈지요. 좀 더 가지고 올게요."

p.77 "와 주셔서 감사합니다, 신부님." 나는 베르무트를 두 잔 따라 한 잔을 신부님에게 건넸다. "무슨 일이십니까? 몹시 피곤해 보이시는군요."

"저도 모릅니다. 그냥 기분이 아주 저하되네요."

"전쟁이잖아요."

"네, 저는 전쟁을 혐오합니다. 하지만 언젠가는 끝나겠지요."

"전쟁이 끝나면 무엇을 하실 건가요?"

"가능하면 아브루찌로 돌아갈 것입니다."

신부의 구릿빛 얼굴이 갑자기 아주 행복해졌다.

"아브루찌를 사랑하시는군요."

"네, 아주 많이요."

"그러면 그곳에 가셔야지요."

"제가 그곳에 살고 주님을 사랑하고 그분을 위해 봉사할 수 있다면 행복할 거예요."

나는 침묵을 지켰다.

p.78 "주님을 사랑하지 않으시나요?" 신부님이 물었다.

"아니요. 하지만 저는 그분이 두렵습니다. 그다지 사랑하지는 않고요."

"여인들과 함께 지낸 밤들에 관해 저에게 말씀하신 것 말인데요. 그것은 사랑이 아닙니다. 단지 열정과 욕정일 뿐이죠. 무언가를 사랑할 때는 그것을 위해 무언가 하고 싶어지지요. 그것을 위해 희생하고 싶어집니다. 그것에 봉사하고 싶어지지요."

"그렇다면 저는 사랑하지 않는 거로군요."

"언젠가는 사랑하게 되실 거예요. 그러면 진정으로 행복해지실 테고요."

"저는 언제나 행복했습니다."

"그것은 다릅니다. 그것을 가져보지 않는다면 그것에 대해 알 수 없습니다."

"만약 그것을 가지게 되면 신부님께 말씀드릴게요."

"제가 너무 오래 있었고 말도 많았네요. 식당에 중위님의 안부를 전해드리지요."

"선물 감사합니다."

"안녕히 계세요." 신부님이 내 손을 톡톡 쳤다.

제12장

p.79 어느 날 아침 병실 담당 소령이 다음 날 이동할 수 있을 것 같냐고 나에게 물었다. 나는 그럴 수 있다고 말했다. 나는 내가 아침 일찍 후송될 것이라고 들었다. 소령은 너무 날씨가 더워지기 전인 지금 내가 여행을 해야 한다고 말했다.

p.80 의사들은 나를 보다 좋은 X레이 시설이 있고, 수술 후에 기계로 하는 마사지를 받을 수 있는 밀라노로 후송하기를 간절히 원했다. 나 역시 밀라노로 가고 싶었다. 모든 침대가 공세를 위해 필요했기 때문에 그들은 우리 모두를 내보내고 전선에서 가능한 한 후방으로 멀리 보내고 싶어 했다.

나는 내가 막 설치된 밀라노 소재 미군 병원으로 가게 될 것이라고 들었다. 몇몇 미군 구급차 부대가 이 병원으로 내려올 예정이었고, 이 병원은 미군 부대와 이탈리아군에서 복무하고 있는 다른 미국인들을 돌보게 될 것이었다. 적십자에는 많은 미국인들이 있었다. 미국은 독일에는 선전포고를 했지만, 오스트리아에는 선전포고를 하지 않았다.

이탈리아 사람들은 미국이 오스트리아에도 선전포고를 할 것이라고 확신했고, 그들은 그에 대해 매우 흥분했다. **p.81** 그들은 윌슨 대통령이 오스트리아에 선전포고를 할 것이라고 생각하는지 나에게 물어봤고 나는 머지않아 곧 그런 일이 일어날 것이라고 말했다. 우리 미국인들이 오스트리아의 무엇에 대하여 대항하는지는 나는 알지 못했지만 우리가 독일에 선전포고를 했다면 오스트리아에도 선전포고를 해야 하는 것이 논리적인 것 같았다.

내가 떠나기 전날 밤, 리날디가 소령과 함께 나를 보러 왔다. 우리는 신부님이 나에게 가져다준 베르무트 몇 잔을 나누어 마셨다. 어찌된 셈인지 대화는 나의 삶 쪽으로 흘렀고, 나는 그들에게 내가 할아버지의 돈으로 먹고 살고 있다고 설명했다. 리날디는 또한 캐서린 바클리 양이 밀라노에 있는 병원에 입원할 나를 만나러 갈 계획을 가지고 있으며, 그녀가 그곳으로 용케 보직을 옮긴 것 같다고 말했다. 한 시간 후 그리고 베르무트를 여러 잔 마신 후, 그들은 가려고 일어났다.

p.82 "잘 가게, 친구." 리날디가 나에게 키스하며 말했다. 소령은 내 어깨를 톡톡 두드렸다. 그들은 비틀거리며 나갔다. 나는 내가 몹시 취한 것을 알고 자러 갔다.

우리는 다음날 아침 밀라노로 떠났고 48시간 후에 도착했다. 그것은 끔찍한 여행이었다. 우리는 메스트레의 이쪽 편에 이르기 전에 오랫동안 대피선에 타고 있었으며, 아이들이 나와서 내부를 들여다보았다. 나는 가서 코냑을 한 병 구해 달라고 어린 소년을 보냈으나, 그 아이는 돌아와서 그랍파밖에 구할 수 없다고 말했다. 나는 그것을 구해 달라고 소년에게 말했고, 그 아이가 돌아왔을 때 나는 아이에게 잔돈을 주었다.

내 옆에 있던 남자와 나는 취했고 빈센자를 지날 때까지 잠이 들었다가 그곳에서 잠에서 깨어 온 바닥에 토했다. 그쪽에 있던 남자가 이미 몇 번이나 바닥에 구토를 했었기 때문에 내가 한 짓은 아무 상관없었다.

제13장

p.83 우리는 아침 일찍 밀라노에 도착했고, 그들은 우리를 화물 조차장에 내려 주었다. 구급차 한 대가 나를 미군 병원으로 데려갔다. 그들이 내 들것을 내려놓았을 때, 나는 시장과 문을 연 술집을 보았다. **p.84** 사람들은 길에 물을 뿌리고 있었고, 이른 아침의 냄새가 났다.

병원 안에서는 들것이 엘리베이터 안으로 들어갈 수가 없었고, 그들은 나를 들것에서 내려 엘리베이터로 올리는 것이 나은지 혹은 들것을 계단으로 올리는 것이 나은지 논의했다. 그들이 그것을 논의하는 동안 나는 그들이 말하는 것을 듣고 있었다. 그들은 엘리베이터를 선택했고 이탈리아 사람인 수위가 나를 들것에서 들어 올렸다.

"살살 하게." 내가 말했다.

엘리베이터 안에서는 나의 다리가 구부러져서 고통이 무척 심했다.

"내 다리를 똑바로 펴 주게." 내가 말했다.

"그럴 수 없습니다, 중위님. 충분한 공간이 없어요." 수위는 자기 팔을 내 몸에 둘렀고, 나는 내 팔을 수위의 목에 감았다. 수위의 얼굴에는 땀이 흘러내리고 있었고 그는 툴툴거렸다.

"무거운가?" 내가 물었다.

p.85 "별것 아닙니다."

엘리베이터 문이 열렸고, 우리는 발코니 위에 있었다. 다른 사람들은 나의 들것을 가지고 벌써 도착해 있었다. 놋쇠 손잡이가 달린 일곱 개의 문이 있었다. 들것 운반병들 중 한 명이 초인종을 울리는 버튼을 눌렀다. 우리는 문 안쪽에서 초인종이 울리는 소리를 들었다. 아무도 나오지 않았다.

"다 어디에 있는 거야?" 들것 운반병들이 물었다.

"모르겠는데요." 수위가 말했다. "아래층에서 자거든요."

"가서 누구 좀 데려와요."

수위는 초인종을 울렸고, 잠깐 기다린 다음, 문을 열고 안으로 들어갔다. 수위는 안경을 끼고 있는 나이 든 여자와 함께 나왔다. 그녀의 머리는 풀어져 있었고, 간호사복을 입고 있었다.

p.86 "무슨 소리인지 모르겠어요." 간호사가 말했다. "저는 이탈리아어를 못하거든요."

"제가 영어를 합니다." 내가 말했다. "이들은 저를 어디에 두어야 할지 알고 싶어 해요."

"준비해 놓은 방이 하나도 없어요. 환자를 받기로 되어 있지는 않은데요." 간호사가 머리카락을 걷어 올리고 나를 쳐다보았다.

"그들에게 나를 둘 수 있는 방을 아무거나 그냥 보여 주세요."

"모르겠어요." 간호사가 말했다. "어떠한 환자도 받게 되어 있지 않아서요. 그냥 아무 방에나 당신을 내려 두게 할 수는 없어요."

"아무 방이라도 괜찮습니다." 내가 말했다. "빈방을 찾아봐 주게." 나는 수위에게 이탈리아 어로 말했다.

"따라오시죠." 수위가 말했다. 그들은 나를 긴 복도로 데리고 내려가 어느 방 안으로 옮겼다. 그 방은 새 가구 냄새가 났다. 침대가 하나 있고 거울이 달린 커다란 옷장이 하나 있었다. 그들은 나를 침대에 내려놓았다.

"시트를 씌워 드릴 수가 없어요." 여자가 말했다. p.87 "문이 잠겨 있어서요."

나는 그녀를 무시했다.

"내 주머니에 손을 넣어 내 돈을 꺼내 주게." 내가 수위에게 말했다. 수위는 돈을 꺼냈다. 두 명의 들것 운반병들은 모자를 들고 침대 옆에 서 있었다. "저 사람들에게 5리라씩 주고 자네도 5리라를 가져가게. 내 서류들은 다른 주머니에 있네. 그것들을 간호사에게 주게."

들것 운반병들은 고맙다고 말했다.

"잘 가게." 내가 말했다. "그리고 고맙네." 그들은 다시 경례를 하고 떠났다.

"그 서류들은 내 증세와 이미 받은 치료들을 설명하고 있습니다." 내가 간호사에게 말했다.

간호사가 안경을 통해 그 서류들을 바라보았다.

"저는 이탈리아 어를 못 읽습니다." 간호사가 말했다. "의사의 지시 없이는 어떤 일도 할 수 없어요." p.88 간호사는 울기 시작했고 서류들을 자신의 앞치마 주머니에 넣었다. "미국인이세요?" 간호사가 여전히 울면서 물었다.

"그렇습니다. 그 서류들을 침대 옆 탁자 위에 놔두십시오."

수위는 아직 침대 옆에 서 있었다. 수위는 친해지기 쉬운 얼굴이었고 아주 친절했다.

"자네는 가도 되네." 내가 수위에게 말했다. "당신도 가 봐도 돼요." 내가 간호사에게 말했다. "이름이 뭐죠?"

"워커요."

"가 봐도 좋습니다. 워커 씨. 저는 좀 자야 할 것 같습니다."

내가 깨어났을 때는 햇빛이 덧창을 통해 들어오고 있었다. 나는 목이 말라서 초인종으로 손을 뻗어 버튼을 눌렀다. 문이 열리고 간호사가 들어왔다. 간호사는 젊고 예뻤다.

"안녕하세요." 내가 말했다.

p.89 "안녕하세요." 간호사가 침대로 다가오며 말했다. "의사 선생님을 모셔올 수가 없어요. 의사 선생님은 코모 호수에 계시거든요. 중위님이 오

실 거라는 것을 아무도 몰랐어요. 어디가 아프세요?"

"다리와 발과 머리를 다쳤습니다."

"성함은요?"

"프레데릭 헨리입니다."

"몸을 닦아 드릴게요. 하지만 의사 선생님이 여기 오시기 전까지는 어떤 처치도 해 드릴 수 없어요."

"바클리 양이 여기 있나요?"

"아니요. 여기에는 그런 이름을 가진 사람이 없어요."

"제가 들어왔을 때 울었던 간호사는 누구였나요?"

간호사가 웃었다. "워커 부인이에요. 밤 근무를 서고 있었는데, 중위님이 들어왔을 때 잠들어 있었지요."

우리가 이야기하는 동안 간호사는 내 옷을 벗겼다. p.90 붕대를 제외하고 내 옷이 모두 벗겨졌을 때 간호사는 나를 씻겨 주었다. 내 머리에는 붕대가 감겨 있었고, 간호사는 붕대 가장자리 둘레 전체를 물로 씻어 주었다.

"어디에서 부상을 당하셨어요?"

"플라바 북쪽 이손제에서요."

"많이 아프세요?"

"아니요. 더 이상 아프지는 않아요."

간호사는 방을 나가더니 워커 부인과 함께 돌아왔다. 그들은 함께 여전히 나를 침대에 뉘여 놓은 상태로 침대를 정돈해 주었다. 그것은 나에게는 새로웠고 감탄할 만하다고 생각했다.

"여기 책임자는 누구죠?"

"반 캠펜 양이에요."

"그리고 간호사는 몇 분 계세요?"

"두 명뿐이에요."

"그게 다예요?"

"몇 명 더 올 거예요."

"그들은 언제 여기에 도착합니까?"

"모릅니다. 아픈 분치고는 질문이 아주 많으시군요."

p.91 "저는 아프지 않습니다." 내가 말했다. "부상당한 거지요."

침대를 정돈한 후, 워커 부인은 나가서 병원복 상의를 가지고 돌아왔다. 그들은 그것을 나에게 입혔고 나는 깔끔해진 기분이었다.

"저에게 아주 친절하게 대해 주시는군요." 내가 말했다. 자기 이름이 게이지 양이라고 말한 젊은 간호사는 키득거렸다.

"물 좀 주실래요?" 내가 부탁했다.

"물론이죠. 그런 다음 아침 식사를 하셔도 됩니다."

"배가 고프지는 않습니다. 덧창 좀 열어주시겠어요?

덧창이 열렸고 나는 발코니 쪽 바깥을 내다보았다. 그 너머로 기와지붕을 얹은 집들과 굴뚝들이 보였다. 나는 기와지붕 너머를 바라보았고 흰 구름과 푸른 하늘을 보았다.

"다른 간호사들은 언제 올까요?"

p.92 "왜요? 저희가 잘 보살펴드리지 못하나요?"

"당신은 아주 친절합니다."

"요강을 쓰고 싶으세요?"

"그래 보죠."

그들은 나를 도와 일으켜 주었지만 소용없었다. 나는 도로 침대에 누웠고 발코니 쪽의 바깥을 열린 문으로 내다보았다.

"의사는 언제 올까요?"

"오실 때가 되면요. 저희는 코모 호수에 계신 선생님께 전화를 하려고 계속 시도해 왔어요."

"다른 의사는 없고요?"

"그분이 우리 병원 의사 선생님이세요."

게이지 양은 물 한 주전자와 유리잔 하나를 가지고 왔다. 나는 물을 조금 마시고 다시 잠을 청했다. 나중에 나는 약간의 점심을 먹었고 오후에는 수간호사 캠펜 양이 나를 보러 왔다. 우리는 서로를 마음에 들어 하지 않았다. 캠펜 양은 키가 작고 의심이 많았으며 자기 직책에 비해 지나치게 점잔을 떨었다. 캠펜 양은 많은 질문을 했고 내가 이탈리아군에 소속되어 있는 것을 다소 불명예스럽게 생각하는 듯했다.

p.93 "식사하면서 술을 좀 마실 수 있을까요?" 내가 캠펜 양에게 물었다.

"의사 선생님이 허락하시면요."

"의사가 오기 전까지는 조금도 안 되나요?"

"절대로 안 됩니다."

"의사가 언제라도 곧 오게 할 계획은 세우고 계시는 거죠?"

"전화는 드렸습니다."

캠펜 양이 나가고 게이지 양이 들어왔다.

"왜 반 캠펜 양에게 무례하게 구셨어요?" 게이지 양이 물었다.

"그럴 의도는 아니었습니다. 하지만 그 여자가 점잔을 떨어서요."

"캠펜 양은 중위님이 가부장적이고 무례하다고 생각하셨어요."

p.94 "안 그랬어요. 그리고 의사 없는 병원은 대체 무슨 발상이랍니까?"

"의사 선생님은 곧 오실 거예요. 저희가 코모 호수로 그분께 전화를 드렸답니다."

"그분은 그곳에서 무엇을 하고 계시죠? 수영이라도 하고 계십니까?"

"아니요. 그곳에 진료소가 있어요."

"그냥 다른 의사를 두지 그러세요?"

"자자, 얌전히 계세요. 의사 선생님은 곧 오실 거예요."

나는 수위를 부르러 보냈고 그가 왔을 때 나는 그에게 이탈리아 어로 나에게 친자노(이탈리아산 베르무트) 한 병, 치나티(이탈리아산 적포도주) 한 병과 석간신문을 사다 달라고 말했다. 수위는 나가서 그것들을 신문에 싸서 가져왔다. 수위는 그것들을 풀어 놓고 코르크를 빼냈으며 포도주와 친자노를 침대 밑에 두었다. 나중에 내가 베르무트를 마시고 있는 동안 게이지 양이 에그노그가 담긴 잔을 하나 가지고 왔다. 게이지 양이 들어올 때 나는 친자노 병을 침대의 반대편에 감추었다.

p.95 "반 캠펜 양이 중위님을 위해 여기에 셰리를 넣었어요." 게이지 양이 말했다. "캠펜 양에게 무례하게 구시면 안 됩니다. 캠펜 양은 어리지도 않고, 이 병원은 그녀에게 막중한 책임거리니까요."

"캠펜 양에게 고맙다고 전해 주세요."

"지금 중위님의 저녁 식사를 가지고 올게요."

"괜찮아요." 내가 말했다. "배고프지 않습니다."

게이지 양은 쟁반을 가지고 와서 그것을 침대 탁자 위에 놓았다. 나는 게이지 양에게 감사를 표하고 저녁을 약간 먹었다. 잠시 후, 나는 졸음이 왔고 한밤중에 깨어났다. 날이 밝기 시작하면서 수탉이 울 때까지 나는 그대로 깨어 있었다. 나는 피곤했고 날이 완전히 밝자마자 다시 잠이 들었다.

제14장

p.96 내가 깨어났을 때 방은 햇살로 가득했다. 나는 내가 최전선에 복

귀했다는 생각이 들어 침대에서 기지개를 켰다. 내 다리에 고통이 느껴졌고, 나는 여전히 더러운 붕대가 감긴 다리들을 쳐다보았다. 나는 내가 어디에 있는지 깨달았다. 나는 초인종으로 손을 뻗어 버튼을 눌렀다. 나는 초인종이 홀 아래에서 지이잉 소리를 내고 그런 다음 누군가가 오고 있는 소리를 들었다. p.97 그것은 게이지 양이었다. 밝은 햇살 아래에서 게이지 양은 약간 더 나이 들고 덜 예뻐 보였다.

"안녕하세요." 게이지 양이 말했다. "잘 주무셨어요?"

"네. 대단히 감사합니다." 내가 말했다.

"제가 중위님을 보러 왔을 때 중위님은 이것을 품에 안고 잠들어 계셨어요." 게이지 양은 침대 밑으로 손을 뻗어 베르무트 병을 위로 꺼내 들었다. 그것은 거의 비어 있었다. "왜 저에게 잔을 달라고 하지 않으셨어요?"

"당신이 못 마시게 할 거라고 생각했거든요."

"저는 중위님과 같이 몇 잔 마셨을 거예요."

"당신은 멋진 아가씨로군요."

"혼자 마시는 것은 좋지 않아요." 게이지 양이 말했다. "아무튼 중위님 친구인 바클리 양이 왔어요."

"정말인가요?"

"네. 저는 그 여자가 마음에 들지 않지만요."

p.98 "그 사람을 좋아하게 될 겁니다. 그 사람은 아주 괜찮아요."

게이지 양은 고개를 저었다.

"이쪽으로 조금만 움직여 주시겠어요?" 게이지 양이 말했다. "아침 식사를 하시게 몸을 닦아 드리겠어요." 게이지 양은 천과 비누와 온수로 나를 씻겨 주었다.

"아침 식사 전에 저를 위해 이발사를 불러 주실 수 있어요?"

"이발사를 부르러 수위를 보낼게요." 게이지 양은 나갔다가 돌아왔다. "이발사가 곧 이쪽으로 올 거예요." 게이지 양은 말하고 물이 담긴 대야에 천을 담갔다.

잠시 후 이발사가 수위와 함께 왔다. 이발사는 50세가량 되었고 수염 끝이 위로 향하게 콧수염을 기르고 있었다. 게이지 양은 나를 씻겨 주는 일을 마치고 나갔고 이발사는 비누 거품을 칠하고 내 얼굴을 면도했다. 이발사는 말을 하지 않았다.

"무슨 소식이 있나요? 아무 소식도 모르시오?" 내가 물었다.

"무슨 소식이요?"

p.99 "아무거나요. 마을에서는 무슨 일이 일어나고 있습니까?"

"지금은 전시예요." 이발사가 말했다. "적은 어디에서든 듣고 있지요."

나는 이발사를 올려다보았다.

"가만히 계세요." 이발사가 말하고 면도를 계속했다. "나는 아무 말도 안 할 겁니다."

"당신에게는 무슨 문제가 있는 겁니까?" 내가 물었다.

"저는 이탈리아 사람입니다. 나는 적과는 말하지 않을 겁니다."

나는 내버려 두기로 결정했다. 만약 이발사가 제정신이 아니라면, 면도칼 아래에서 빨리 빠져나올수록 더 좋을 테니까.

면도가 끝났을 때 나는 돈을 지불했고 50첸테시모를 팁으로 주었다. 이발사는 동전을 받는 것을 거절했다.

"됐습니다." 이발사가 말했다. "나는 군인은 아닙니다만, 그래도 이탈리아 사람입니다."

"썩 나가시오."

이발사는 구리 동전 다섯 닢을 침대 옆 탁자에 남겨두고 나갔다. p.100 나는 초인종을 울렸고 게이지 양이 들어왔다.

"수위에게 좀 와 달라고 해 주시겠어요?"

"알겠어요."

수위가 들어왔다. 수위는 웃지 않으려고 아주 힘겹게 애쓰고 있었다.

"저 이발사는 미쳤나?" 내가 물었다.

"아닙니다. 이발사가 실수를 했어요. 이발사는 귀가 많이 안 들리는데 제가 중위님을 오스트리아군 장교라고 말했다고 생각했어요."

"오." 내가 말했다.

"하하하." 수위가 웃었다. "재미있었습니다. 중위님이 꼼짝하기라도 하면 이럴 작정이었대요." 수위는 자신의 집게손가락으로 자기 목을 가로로 그었다.

"하하." 수위가 웃음을 멈추려고 애썼다. "제가 이발사에게 중위님이 오스트리아 인이 아니라고 말했을 때 이발사의 얼굴을 보셨어야 합니다!"

"아주 우습기도 하군." 내가 심통을 내며 말했다. "이발사가 내 목을 잘랐다면 얼마나 웃겼을까. p.101 여기서 나가게."

수위는 나갔고, 나는 그가 홀을 내려가며 웃는 소리를 들었다. 그런 다음 나는 누군가가 복도로 내려오는 소리를 들었다. 나는 문 쪽을 보았다. 캐서린 바클리였다.

캐서린은 침대로 다가왔다.

"안녕하세요, 중위님." 캐서린이 말했다. 캐서린은 젊고 무척 아름다워 보였다. 나는 그처럼 아름다운 사람은 누구도 본 적이 없다고 생각했다.

"안녕하셨습니까?" 내가 말했다. 캐서린을 보았을 때, 나는 그녀를 사랑하게 되었다. 내 안에 있던 모든 것이 뒤집혔다. 캐서린은 아무도 없는지 확인하려고 문 쪽을 바라보았고, 그런 다음 침대 옆에 앉아 몸을 숙이고 나에게 키스를 했다. 나는 캐서린을 끌어당기고 그녀에게 키스했으며 그녀의 심장이 뛰는 것을 느꼈다.

"당신은 사랑스러워요." 내가 말했다. "여행이 힘들었나요?"

"아주 힘들지는 않았어요. 하지만 제가 여기 있는 것은 힘들지도 모르겠네요."

p.102 "당신은 여기 있어야 합니다." 내가 말했다. "오, 당신은 아름다워요." 나는 캐서린에게 넋이 나갔다. 나는 캐서린이 정말로 그곳에 있다는 것을 믿을 수 없어서 그녀를 꽉 껴안았다.

"그러시면 안 돼요." 캐서린이 말했다. "아직 몸도 좋지 않은데."

"나는 괜찮아요. 이리 와요."

"아니요. 당신은 완쾌되지 않았어요."

"괜찮다니까요."

"저를 사랑하세요?"

"사랑해요. 나는 당신에게 미쳐 있어요."

"우리의 심장이 뛰는 것을 느껴 보세요."

"심장은 상관없어요. 나는 지금 당신을 원해요. 당신 때문에 미치겠어요."

"정말로 저를 사랑하세요?"

"그것을 자꾸 묻지는 말고요. 이리 와요. 부탁이에요, 캐서린."

"좋아요. 하지만 잠시만이에요."

"좋아요." 내가 말했다. "문을 닫아요."

"그러시면 안 돼요. 안 된다고요."

p.103 "말하지 마요. 그냥 문을 닫아요."

캐서린이 문을 닫고 돌아오자마자 나는 그녀를 침대로 끌어당겼다.

후에 캐서린이 문을 열고 침대 옆 의자에 앉았다. 격렬함은 사라졌고,

나는 이전에 느꼈던 것보다 더 기분이 좋았다.

"이제 제가 당신을 사랑한다는 것을 믿으시겠어요?" 캐서린이 물었다.

"오, 당신은 사랑스러워요." 내가 말했다. "여기 있어요. 그 사람들이 당신을 내보낼 수는 없어요."

"우리는 더 조심해야 할 거예요. 그것은 미친 짓이었어요. 우리는 그래서는 안 돼요."

"밤에는 할 수 있어요."

"이제 저는 가야 해요, 내 사랑."

"곧 다시 와야 해요."

"올 수 있으면 오겠어요."

"잘 가요."

p.104 "잘 있어요, 내 사랑."

캐서린은 나갔다. 내가 사랑에 빠지기를 원하지 않았던 것을 신은 아신다. 하지만 나는 캐서린 바클리와 사랑에 빠졌고 밀라노에 있는 병원의 병실 침대에 누워 있으며 기분이 아주 좋다는 것을 신은 아신다. 마침내 게이지 양이 들어왔다.

"의사 선생님이 오실 거예요." 게이지 양이 말했다. "선생님이 코모 호수에서 전화하셨어요. 오늘 오후에 여기로 오실 거예요."

제15장

p.105 의사는 전쟁을 혐오하는 것 같은, 체격이 마르고 조용하고 몸집이 작은 남자였다. 의사는 내 넓적다리에서 많은 쇠 파편들을 꺼냈다. 얼마 후 의사는 X레이를 찍는 것이 좋을 것 같다고 말했다.

p.106 X레이는 오스페달레 마지오레에서 찍었고, 그것을 찍은 의사는 유능하고 유쾌했다. 캐서린 바클리는 나와 함께 갔고, 우리는 구급차를 타고 작은 병원으로 돌아왔다. 약 한 시간 뒤에 X레이 원판들이 도착했다. 캐서린 바클리는 그것들을 나에게 보여 주었다. 캐서린은 그것들을 봉투에서 꺼내어 불빛 쪽으로 들어 올렸고 우리는 함께 그것들을 바라보았다.

"그것이 당신의 다리예요." 캐서린이 가리키며 말했다.

"저리 치워 놔요." 내가 말했다. "그리고 이리 와요."

"안 돼요. 가야 해요." 캐서린이 말했다.

캐서린이 나가자마자 세 명의 의사가 병실 안으로 들어왔다. 의료 부문에 실전 경험이 없는 의사들은 서로 동료를 구하는 경향이 있다는 것을 나는 눈치채고 있었다. 맹장을 제대로 떼어내지 못하는 의사는 당신에게 편도선을 제거할 수 없는 의사의 말을 참고하라고 하는 법이다. p.107 이 세 의사들이 바로 그런 의사들이었다.

"이분은 젊은 사람이군요." 입주 의사가 말했다.

"안녕하세요?" 턱수염을 기른 키가 크고 마른 의사가 말했다. X레이 원판을 집어든 세 번째 의사는 아무 말도 하지 않았다.

"붕대를 풀까요?" 턱수염을 기른 의사가 물었다.

"네. 붕대를 풀어 주세요, 간호사." 입주 의사가 게이지 양에게 말했다. 게이지 양은 붕대를 풀었고, 나는 내 다리가 야전병원에서 치료받았을 때보다 훨씬 더 좋아 보이는 것을 보았다.

"깨끗해 보이는군요." 입주 의사가 말했다.

p.108 두 번째 의사와 세 번째 의사는 연수 내과 의사의 어깨 너머를 쳐다보았다.

"한 번 무릎을 움직여 보세요." 턱수염을 기른 의사가 말했다.

"못해요." 내가 말했다.

의사들 중 두 사람이 내 오른쪽 다리를 아주 부드럽게 잡고 다리를 구부렸다.

"그렇게 하면 아픕니다." 내가 말했다.

"원판들을 다시 보여주시겠어요, 선생님?" 턱수염을 기른 의사가 물었다. 세 번째 의사는 턱수염을 기른 의사에게 원판들 중 하나를 건넸다. "왼쪽 다리 사진을 건네주시겠어요?"

"그것이 왼쪽 다리입니다, 선생님." 입주 의사가 말했다.

"오, 그렇군요. 제가 다른 각도에서 보고 있었어요."

그들은 한동안 원판들을 살펴보았다.

"분명한 것 같군요." 턱수염을 기른 의사가 말했다. "시간이 좀 걸리겠어요. 아마 최소한 6개월 정도요."

p.109 "네. 관절 낭액이 다시 만들어져야 해요." 입주 의사가 말했다.

"네. 저런 무릎은 절개할 수 없어요."

"동의합니다, 선생님."

"내가 6개월이나 기다려야 한다고요?" 내가 물었다. "왜죠?"

"무릎이 안전하게 절개될 수 있으려면 6개월이 걸려요."

"맙소사." 내가 말했다.

턱수염을 기른 의사가 내 어깨를 톡톡 두드렸다.

"제가 말할 수 있는 것은 안전한 편을 택하려면 그런 무릎을 수술하기 전에 최소한 6개월을 기다려야 한다는 것입니다." 턱수염을 기른 의사가 말했다. "물론 다른 의견을 구해 보시는 것을 저희는 환영합니다."

"고맙습니다." 내가 말했다.

"천만에요." 턱수염을 기른 의사가 말했다. "빨리 낫기 바랍니다."

p.110 세 의사 모두 나하고 악수를 하고 병실을 나갔다.

"게이지 양." 내가 불렀다. 게이지 양이 들어왔다. "나는 6개월 동안 침대서 지낼 수는 없어요. 다른 의사를 모셔와 저를 보게 해 주실 수 있어요?"

"발렌티니 박사님께 여쭤볼게요."

"그분은 누구이십니까?"

"오스페달레 마지오레의 외과 의사이세요."

두 시간 후 발렌티니 박사가 왔다. 박사는 소령이었고, 그의 얼굴은 햇볕에 그을려 있었고 그의 콧수염 끝은 곧장 치켜 올라가 있었다. 박사는 내내 미소를 짓고 웃었다.

"어떻게 이런 일이 벌어졌나?" 박사가 물었다. "원판들을 좀 보세. 음, 음, 그래. 자네는 아주 건강해 보이는군. 내가 자네를 새로 태어난 것보다 더 낫게 만들어 주겠네."

"그것이 제가 듣고 싶었던 말입니다."

발렌티니 박사가 내 어깨를 두드렸다.

"붕대를 풀어 봐요."

p.111 "발렌티니 박사님, 한잔하시겠어요?"

"한잔이라고? 물론이지. 나는 한 잔보다는 더 마실 거네."

나는 박사에게 친자노 한 잔을 따라 주었다.

"고맙네. 고마워. 다음번에는 내가 코냑을 좀 갖다주지."

"제 무릎은 언제 수술이 가능할 것이라고 생각하십니까?"

"내일 아침. 자네의 위는 비워 두어야 하네. 나는 아래층의 간호사를 만나서 지시를 해 두겠네. 내일 보지. 내가 코냑을 좀 가져다주겠네." 박사는 구릿빛 얼굴에 미소를 띠며 문가에서 손을 흔들었다.

제16장

p.112 캐서린은 그날 밤 나와 함께 지냈다. 나는 밤사이 누군가가 올까 봐 걱정했으나 그들은 모두 잠들었다고 캐서린이 말했다. 내가 아침에 일어났을 때, 캐서린은 가고 없었다. 잠시 후 캐서린은 기운차고 사랑스러운 모습으로 돌아와 침대에 앉았다.

p.113 "우리가 산책을 나갈 수 있다면 좋겠어요." 캐서린이 말했다. "당신의 친구 발렌티니 박사를 위해 당신을 준비시켜 놓자고요."

"오늘 밤에 밤 근무를 할 수 있어요?"

"네. 하지만 오늘 밤에는 저를 원하지 않을 거예요."

"아니, 원할 거예요."

"수술을 받아 보신 적이 없으시군요. 많이 고통스러우실 거예요."

"난 괜찮을 거예요."

"당신은 아플 거예요. 그러면 저는 당신에게 아무것도 아닐 걸요."

"그러면 지금 이리 와요."

"안 돼요." 캐서린이 말했다. "차트를 정리해야 해요, 내 사랑. 그런 다음에 당신을 준비시켜 놓아야 해요." 캐서린은 나에게 키스를 했다. "차트는 준비되었어요. 체온은 정상이네요. 체온은 언제나 정상이에요. 당신은 참 멋진 체온을 가지고 있어요."

p.114 "아마 우리의 아이들도 멋진 체온을 가지고 있을 거예요."

"우리 아이들은 아마도 끔찍한 체온을 가질 거예요."

"발렌티니 박사를 위해 나를 어떻게 준비시켜 놔야 한다는 건가요?"

"당신에게 관장을 시켜야 해요. 그것은 썩 유쾌하지는 않을 거예요."

"당신이 그것을 할 필요가 없으면 좋겠군요."

"저는 다른 누가 당신을 만지는 것을 원하지 않아요. 제가 바보 같지만, 간호사들이 당신을 만지면 저는 화가 나요. 그리고 지금 이곳은 간호사가 너무 많아요. 만일 환자를 더 받지 않으면 그들이 우리를 다른 곳으로 보내 버릴 거예요."

"그러면 나는 당신과 함께 가겠어요."

"바보 같은 소리 마요, 내 사랑. 당신은 아직 움직일 수 없어요. 하지만 어서 나으세요. 그러고 나면 우리는 어디든 갈 테니까요. 전쟁이 빨리 끝났으면 좋겠어요."

"발렌티니 박사가 나를 고쳐줄 거예요."
곧 나는 안팎이 깨끗해졌고 의사를 기다리고 있었다.
p.115 "준비는 다 됐는데 제가 무엇을 해 주기를 원하세요?" 캐서린이 물었다.
"침대로 와요."
"알았어요."
"오, 내 사랑, 내 사랑." 내가 말했다.
"자, 이제 알겠죠." 캐서린이 말했다. "당신이 원하는 것은 제가 무엇이든 해드리잖아요."
"당신은 참 사랑스러워요."
"이제 저는 전부 당신 거예요. 저는 더 이상 제가 아니에요. 저는 그저 당신이 원하는 것을 원할 뿐이에요."

제17장

p.116 수술 후 깨어났을 때, 나는 아팠다. 나는 주위를 둘러보다가 게이지 양을 보았고, 그녀는 "기분이 어떠세요?"라고 말했다.
"괜찮습니다." 내가 말했다.
"박사님이 중위님 무릎 수술을 잘해 주셨어요."
"얼마나 오래 걸렸죠?"
"2시간이요."
p.117 이제 병원에는 세 명의 다른 환자들이 있었다. 한 사람은 말라리아에 걸린 조지아 주 출신으로 체격이 마른 적십자 소속 청년이었다. 말라리아와 황달에 걸린, 뉴욕 출신으로 체격이 마른 청년이 또 한 명 있었고, 유산탄과 고성능 포탄의 결합물에서 기념품으로 신관 뚜껑의 나사를 빼내려고 했던 잘생긴 청년이 있었다.
모든 간호사들이 캐서린 바클리를 무척 좋아했는데, 그녀가 무한정으로 밤 근무를 하려고 했기 때문이었다. 캐서린이 말라리아 환자들을 돌보는 일은 거의 없었고, 신관 뚜껑의 나사를 빼 냈던 청년은 우리 친구였으므로 그는 밤에 절대 초인종을 울리지 않았다.
나는 캐서린을 아주 많이 사랑했고 그녀는 나를 사랑했다. 나는 낮에는 잠을 잤고, 우리가 깨어 있는 낮에는 우리 둘 다 쪽지를 썼고, 그것들을 퍼거슨이 전해 주었다. **p.118** 나는 퍼거슨에게 52사단에 오빠가 한 명, 메소포타미아에 오빠가 또 한 명 있다는 것 외에는 그녀에 대해 아무것도 듣지 못했다. 나는 또한 퍼거슨이 캐서린 바클리에게 아주 잘해 준다는 것을 들어서 알고 있었다.

"우리 결혼식에 오실 거죠, 퍼기?" 내가 한 번은 그녀에게 물었다.

"중위님은 절대 결혼하지 않을 걸요."

"왜요?"

"당신들 두 사람은 결혼하기 전에 싸울 거예요."

"우리는 안 싸워요."

"그러면 중위님이 죽을 테지요. 싸우거나 죽거나잖아요. 그게 사람들이 하는 일이에요. 결혼은 안 하죠. 하지만 두 사람은 잘될지도 몰라요. 하지만 캐서린을 곤란한 처지에 빠지게 하지는 마세요. 캐서린을 곤란에 빠지게 하면 제가 중위님을 죽일 거예요."

"안 그럴게요."

"캐서린을 임신시키지 마세요. 저는 캐서린이 전시 사생아를 갖는 것을 원하지 않아요."

p.119 "당신은 좋은 아가씨예요, 퍼기."

"그리고 캐서린에게 당분간 밤 근무를 하지 말라고 하셔야 해요. 캐서린은 몹시 지쳐 가고 있어요. 또한 반 캠펜 양이 당신이 아침 내내 자는 것에 대해 의심을 하게 되었어요."

"저는 캐서린이 밤 근무를 쉬기를 원해요."

"아니, 중위님은 안 그래요."

"그런다니까요."

"저는 믿지 않아요. 하지만 당분간 중위님이 캐서린이 밤 근무를 못하게 만든다면 저는 중위님을 대단히 높이 평가할 거예요." 그 말과 함께 퍼거슨은 내 쪽지를 가지고 나갔다.

그날 오후 나는 초인종을 울렸고 잠시 후 게이지 양이 들어왔다.

"무슨 일이죠?" 게이지 양이 물었다.

"그냥 당신과 이야기를 하고 싶었을 뿐이에요. 바클리 양이 당분간 밤 근무를 쉬어야 한다고 생각하지 않으세요? 몹시 지쳐 보이더군요. 왜 바클리 양이 그렇게 오래 근무를 서야 하는 거죠?"

p.120 게이지 양이 재미있다는 듯이 나를 바라보았다.

"저는 당신 편이에요." 게이지 양이 말했다. "저에게는 그런 식으로 말씀하지 않으셔도 돼요."

"무슨 뜻입니까?"

"바보같이 굴지 마세요. 용건은 그게 다예요?"

"베르무트 한 잔 드실래요?

"좋아요, 딱 한 잔만이요."

게이지 양은 한 잔을 따랐다.

"당신이 잔으로 마셔요." 내가 말했다. "제가 병으로 마실게요."

"건배." 게이지 양이 말했다.

"제가 늦잠 자는 것에 대해서 반 캠펜 양이 뭐라고 하던가요?"

"수간호사님은 그냥 화가 난 거예요. 당신을 '특권층 환자'라고 부르면서요."

"그 여자는 지옥에 갈지도 몰라요."

"못된 사람은 아니에요." 게이지 양이 말했다. "그냥 나이가 많고 까다로울 뿐이죠. 그리고 수간호사님은 당신을 전혀 좋아하지 않아요."

"압니다."

p.121 "그래도 저는 중위님이 마음에 들어요. 그리고 저는 중위님 편이에요. 그것을 잊지 마세요. 아직 그것을 모르시겠지만, 언젠가는 알게 되실 거예요."

캐서린 바클리는 그 주에 세 번의 밤 근무를 쉬었다. 캐서린이 돌아왔을 때는 마치 우리가 각자 오랫동안 여행을 떠났다가 다시 만난 것 같았다.

제18장

p.122 내가 수술을 받고 회복되는 동안 우리는 밀라노에서 즐거운 시간을 가졌다. 내가 외출할 수 있을 만큼 건강이 좋아졌을 때, 우리는 마차를 타고 공원에 갔다. 나는 마차와 천천히 가고 있던 말과 내 옆에 앉아 있던 캐서린을 기억한다. 내가 목발을 짚고 돌아다닐 만큼 건강이 좋아졌을 때, 우리는 비피나 그랑 이탈리아로 저녁을 먹으러 가서 갤러리아의 야외 테이블 앞에 앉았다.

p.123 저녁 식사 후 우리는 다른 음식점과 철제 셔터가 내려진 가게들을 지나며 갤러리아 사이를 산책하곤 했다. 우리는 대개 샌드위치를 파는

작은 가게에 들렀는데, 그곳에서는 햄과 양상추 샌드위치와 아주 작은 갈색의 윤기 나는 롤로 만든 안초비 샌드위치 등을 팔았다. 우리는 밤중에 배가 고플 때 먹을 수 있도록 샌드위치를 샀다. 그런 다음 우리는 대성당 앞 갤러리아 밖에 있는 무개마차를 타고 병원으로 돌아오곤 했다.

병원에서는 수위가 대개 목발을 가지고 도와주러 나왔다. 나는 마부에게 돈을 주곤 했고, 그런 다음 우리는 엘리베이터를 타고 위층으로 올라가곤 했다.

p.124 캐서린은 언제나 간호사들이 사는 아래층에서 내렸고, 나는 계속 올라가서 목발을 짚고 홀에서 내려 내 방으로 갔다. 때때로 나는 옷을 벗고 침대에 들었으며, 때로는 발코니에 앉아 지붕 위의 제비들을 구경하면서 캐서린을 기다렸다.

모든 환자들이 잠들고 캐서린이 환자들이 호출을 하지 않을 것을 확신할 때 캐서린은 들어왔다. 나는 캐서린의 머리카락을 묶은 핀들을 풀어 그것들을 우리 둘 주변에 늘어놓는 것을 아주 좋아했다. 그것은 나에게 마치 우리가 한 텐트 안에 혹은 폭포수 뒤에 있는 것처럼 느끼게 해 주었다. 캐서린은 아름다운 머리카락에 사랑스러운 얼굴을 지니고 있었다. 우리는 함께 누워 있곤 했고, 나는 손가락 끝으로 캐서린의 뺨과 이마를 만지고 "피아노 건반처럼 부드러워요."라고 말하곤 했다.

우리는 서로에게 캐서린이 밀라노로 온 첫날에 결혼했노라고 말했다. **p.125** 나는 법적으로 혼인한 상태이기를 바랐지만, 캐서린은 만약 우리가 결혼한다면 그들이 자기를 멀리 보내 버릴 것이라고 말했다. 아이를 가질까 봐 걱정되었기 때문에 나는 우리가 결혼하기를 원했으나 우리끼리는 우리가 결혼했고 크게 걱정하지 않는 체했다.

"나는 당신을 위해서 우리가 결혼하면 좋겠어요." 내가 말했다.

"저는 당신이에요. 우리는 한 사람이에요. 따로따로가 아니에요."

"나는 여자들은 언제나 결혼하고 싶어 한다고 생각했어요."

"내 사랑, 저는 결혼했어요. 당신과 결혼한 거예요. 게다가 저는 이미 한 번 결혼하려고 기다린 경험이 있어요."

"그 일에 대해서는 이야기하고 싶지 않아요."

"제가 당신 말고 누구도 사랑하지 않는 것을 아시잖아요. 다른 누군가가 저를 사랑했던 것을 신경 쓰시면 안 돼요."

p.126 "신경 쓰여요."

"죽은 사람을 질투하시면 안 돼요."

"그 일에 대해서는 이야기하고 싶지 않다고 했잖아요."

"저는 당신이 이 여자 저 여자와 함께 지냈다는 것을 알지만, 그것이 저에게는 중요하지 않아요."

"우리가 은밀히 결혼할 수는 없을까요?"

"교회나 국가에 의해서가 아니라면 결혼할 방법이 없어요. 제가 종교를 가지고 있다면 제게 중요한 의미를 가질 테지만 저는 종교가 없어요."

"하지만 나에게 성 안토니오를 주었잖소?"

"그것은 행운을 빌어 주기 위한 것이었죠. 그것은 누군가 다른 사람으로부터 받은 선물이었어요."

"나는 행운이 필요하게 될 거예요. 머지않아 곧 최전선으로 돌아가야 하니까."

"당신이 가기 전까지는 그것에 대해서는 생각하지 마요. 저는 행복해요, 내 사랑, 그리고 우리는 즐거운 시간을 보내고 있어요. 저는 오랫동안 행복하게 지내지 못했어요. 당신을 처음 만났을 때 저는 거의 제정신이 아니었어요. 이제 우리는 행복하고 서로를 사랑하고 있어요. p.127 우리 그냥 행복해져요. 제가 하는 일 중에 당신 마음에 들지 않는 것이 있으세요? 제가 무엇을 해 드리기를 바라세요? 제 머리를 풀고 싶으세요?"

"침대로 와요."

"먼저 제가 가서 환자들을 살펴보게 해 주세요."

제19장

p.128 여름 한철이 그렇게 지나갔다. 무더웠다는 것과 신문에 많은 승전보가 실렸다는 것 외에는 나는 그 나날들에 대해 많이 기억하지 못한다. 나는 무척 건강했고 내 다리는 빨리 회복되었다.

머지않아 나는 목발을 짚었고, 그런 다음에는 지팡이를 짚고 걸었다. p.129 그런 다음 나는 오스페달레에서 물리 치료를 받기 시작했다. 나는 오후에 그곳에 갔고 그런 후에는 카페에 들러 차를 한잔 마시면서 신문을 읽었다. 나는 마을을 돌아다니지 않았다. 내가 원하는 전부는 캐서린을 보는 것이었다. 캐서린과 함께 있지 않을 때에는 그냥 시간만 죽이고 있었다.

나는 대개 아침에 잠을 잤고, 오후에는 이따금 경마장에 갔는데, 이 때문에 물리 치료에 늦었다. 때때로 나는 영미 클럽에 가서 창문 앞에 있는 깊이 푹 들어가는 가죽 쿠션 의자에 앉아 잡지를 읽었다. 내가 목발을 떼어 버렸을 때 그들은 내가 캐서린과 함께 외출하도록 내버려 두지 않았는데, 간호사가 간병이 필요한 것처럼 보이지 않는 환자와 함께 목격되는 것이 꼴사나웠기 때문이었다. **p.130** 하지만 퍼거슨이 따라나서면 우리는 때때로 저녁 식사를 하러 나가곤 했다.

무더운 여름이었고, 나는 밀라노에 있는 많은 사람들을 알았지만, 늘 오후 시간이 다 끝나자마자 병원으로 돌아가고 싶은 마음이 간절했다. 전선에서는 우리 편이 카르소 고원으로 진격하고 있었고, 플라바 맞은편의 쿡을 점령했고 바인시짜 고원을 점령하는 중이었다. 서부 전선에서는 그다지 잘하고 있지 못했다. 전쟁은 아주 오랫동안 계속될 것 같았다.

어느 날 오후 나는 클럽을 떠나 조심스럽게 계단을 내려가 비아 만조니로 올라갔다. 그랑 호텔 밖에서 나는 경마장에서 돌아오던 노신사 마이어즈 씨와 그의 부인을 만났다. 부인은 검은색 공단 옷을 입은 가슴이 풍만한 여자였다. 마이어즈 씨는 키가 작고 나이가 많았으며 백발의 콧수염을 기르고 있었다. 마이어즈 씨는 지팡이를 짚으며 서투르게 걸었다.

p.131 "안녕하시오?" 마이어즈 부인이 말했다. 나는 부인과 악수를 했다.

"안녕하시오?" 마이어즈 씨가 말했다.

"경마는 어떠셨어요?" 내가 물었다.

"굉장했지. 세 명의 승자를 맞혔다오." 마이어즈 부인이 말했다.

"마이어즈 씨는요?" 나는 마이어즈 씨에게 물었다.

"괜찮았지. 나는 승자를 한 명 맞혔네. 자네도 우리와 함께 나갔어야 하는데."

마이어즈 씨가 말을 하면, 그가 당신을 쳐다보고 있지 않다거나 당신을 다른 누군가로 오해하고 있다는 인상을 갖게 된다.

"그럴게요." 내가 말했다.

"당신을 보러 병원에 가려던 참이었다오." 마이어즈 부인이 말했다. "내 아들들에게 줄 것이 있거든. 당신들은 모두 내 사랑스러운 아들들이라오."

p.132 "부인을 보게 되어 환자들이 기뻐할 거예요." 내가 말했다. "저는 돌아가야겠어요."

"내 사랑스러운 아들들에게 안부 전해 주시구려."

"알았어요. 안녕히 가세요." 나는 말했다.

나는 거리를 내려갔다. 코바에서 나는 캐서린에게 줄 초콜릿 한 상자를 샀고 여점원이 그것을 포장하는 동안 술집으로 다가갔다. 나는 마티니를 딱 한 잔만 마시고 값을 치렀고, 밖에 있는 계산대 위에서 초콜릿 상자를 집어 들고 병원 쪽으로 돌아왔다.

스칼라 극장에서부터 시작되는 거리 위쪽의 작은 술집 밖에서 나는 내가 아는 몇 사람, 그러니까 부영사, 성악을 공부하는 두 사람, 그리고 이탈리아군에 있는 샌프란시스코 출신의 이탈리아 인 에토레 모레티를 만났다. 나는 그들과 한잔했다. 성악가들 중 한 사람은 엔리코 델크레도라는 가명으로 노래를 하는 사람으로 이름이 랠프 시몬즈였다. 나는 그가 얼마나 노래를 잘하는지는 몰랐지만, 랠프는 언제나 자신이 아주 커다란 일을 일으키기 직전이라고 말했다. p.133 랠프는 뚱뚱하고 마치 건초열이 있는 것처럼 코와 입 주위가 헐어 보였다. 랠프는 피아센자에서 노래를 하고서 돌아온 것이었다. 랠프는 토스카를 불렀고, 그의 말에 따르면 그 노래는 굉장했다.

"여기에서는 언제 노래하실 건가?" 내가 물었다.

"가을에 스칼라 극장에서 공연할 거야."

"관객들이 아마 자네에게 벤치를 던질걸." 에토레가 말했다. "모데나에서 관객들이 랠프에게 벤치를 던지게 된 경위를 들었나?"

"얼토당토않은 거짓말이야."

"내가 그 자리에 있었다네." 에토레가 말했다. "나도 직접 벤치 여섯 개를 던졌는걸."

"자네는 딱 샌프란시스코에서 온 이탈리아 놈이야."

"관객들은 랠프가 가는 곳은 어디에서든 그에게 벤치를 던진다네." 에토레가 말했다. "랠프가 이탈리아 어를 발음하지 못해서야."

p.134 "저 녀석은 멍텅구리야." 에두아르도 조반니라는 가명으로 노래를 하는 테너 에드거 손더즈가 말했다. "할 줄 아는 말이라곤 벤치를 던진다는 것밖에 없으니."

"그것은 자네들 둘이 노래하면 모든 사람들이 어떻게 해야 할지 아는 것이잖아." 에토레가 말했다. "그런 다음 미국에 돌아가면 자네들은 스칼라 극장에서의 자네들의 '승리'에 관해 거짓말을 하겠지. 관객들이 스칼라 극장에서 첫 곡조차도 그럭저럭 부르지 못하게 할 텐데."

"나는 10월에 스칼라 극장에서 토스카를 부를 거야." 시몬즈가 말했다.

"우리도 꼭 가야겠지, 그렇지 않나, 맥?" 에토레가 부영사에게 말했다. "저 녀석들은 누군가 자기들을 보호해 줄 사람이 필요할 거야."

"어쩌면 미군이 그들을 보호해 줄지도 몰라." 부영사가 말했다.

"자네가 은장 훈장을 탈 거라는 얘기가 들리더라." 에토레가 나에게 말했다. "어떤 종류의 감사장을 받게 되는 거야?"

p.135 "받게 될지 어떨지는 확실하지도 않아."

"자네는 받을 거야. 오, 이봐, 그러면 코바의 아가씨들이 자네가 멋지다고 생각할 거야. 그 아가씨들은 모두 자네가 혼자서 200명의 오스트리아군 병사들을 죽였다고 생각할 거야."

"자네는 훈장을 몇 개나 가지고 있나, 에토레?" 부영사가 물었다.

"저 녀석은 모든 훈장을 다 탔어." 시몬즈가 말했다. "그들의 심벌이야."

"청동 훈장 두 개와 은장 훈장 세 개를 탔지." 에토레가 말했다.

"저 녀석은 아주 여러 차례 심하게 다쳤어." 시몬즈가 덧붙였다.

"장교가 된 지 얼마나 되었지, 에토레?" 내가 물었다.

"2년. 나는 머지않아 곧 대위가 될 거야. 자네는 중위가 된 지 얼마나 되었나?"

p.136 "거의 3년이 되어 가."

"자네는 이탈리아 어를 잘 모르니까 대위가 될 수 없는 거야." 에토레가 말했다. "자네는 말은 하지만 읽고 쓰는 것은 잘 못하지. 왜 미군에 들어가지 않았나?"

"어쩌면 들어갈지도 몰라."

"나도 들어갈 수 있으면 좋겠군. 오, 이봐, 미군에서는 대위가 얼마나 받지, 맥?"

"내 생각에는 약 250달러쯤일 거야."

"맙소사! 250달러가 있으면 뭐든지 할 수 있겠군! 자네는 빨리 미군에 들어가는 것이 좋겠네, 프레드. 나도 들어갈 수 있는지 좀 알아봐 줘."

"알았어."

"가자, 심." 손더즈가 일어나며 말했다.

"알았어."

"나도 가야 해." 내가 말했다. 6시 15분 전이었다. p.137 "차오, 에토레. 사고 치지 말게나."

"언제 전선으로 돌아갈 거야?"

"머지않아 곧."

"자, 또 보세."

나는 병원으로 가는 지름길로 이어지는 뒷길을 따라 내려갔다. 에토레는 스물세 살이었다. 에토레는 샌프란시스코에서 삼촌 손에 자랐으며 전쟁이 선포되었을 때는 토리노에 있는 자기 아버지와 어머니를 방문하고 있었다. 에토레는 진정한 영웅이었으나, 자신이 만나는 사람은 모두 지루하게 만들었다. 캐서린은 에토레를 참을 수 없어 했다.

"아시다시피 우리에게도 영웅들은 있어요." 캐서린이 말했다. "하지만 그들은 말이 많지 않아요."

"에토레는 괜찮은데."

"그렇게 우쭐거리지 않고 저를 정말정말 지루하게 만들지 않는다면 저도 그 사람이 괜찮다고 생각할 거예요."

"에토레는 나도 지루하게 하기는 해요."

p.138 우리는 발코니에 나가 이야기를 하고 있었다. 밖에는 비가 내리기 시작했고 우리는 비가 지붕을 쿵쿵 두드리는 소리를 들었다.

"오늘 다른 사람은 누구를 또 만났어요?" 캐서린이 물었다.

"마이어즈 씨와 그의 부인이요."

"그분들은 이상한 부부예요."

"남편은 고향에 돌아오기 전까지는 감옥에 있었다더군요. 그 사람이 늙어서 머지않아 죽을 테니까 내보내 준 거예요."

"그런데 그분은 밀라노에서 영원토록 행복하게 살고 있잖아요. 부인이 이곳으로 몇몇 물건들을 가지고 오세요."

"비가 심하게 내리네요."

"언제나 저를 사랑해 주실 거죠, 그럴 거죠?"

"그래요."

"그러면 비가 오더라도 차이는 없겠죠?"

"없어요."

"저는 비가 무서워요."

"왜요?" 쉴 새 없이 내리는 비는 나를 졸리게 했다.

p.139 "저도 모르지만 저는 언제나 비를 무서워했어요."

"왜요?"

"잘 모르겠어요."

"말해 봐요."

"그러고 싶지 않아요."

"말해 봐요."

"싫어요."

"말해 달라니까요."

"좋아요. 왜냐하면 때때로 제가 빗속에 죽어 있는 것이 보여서 비가 무서운 거예요. 그리고 때로는 당신이 빗속에 죽어 있는 것을 보기도 해요."

캐서린은 울기 시작했다. 나는 캐서린을 안아 주었고 그녀는 우는 것을 그쳤다. 하지만 밖에는 비가 그치지 않았다.

제20장

p.140 어느 날 우리는 헬렌 퍼거슨과 포탄 신관 폭발로 눈에 부상을 입고 병원으로 실려 온 크로웰 로저스라는 청년과 함께 경마장에 갔다.

우리 넷은 한 대의 무개 마차에 타고 산 시로로 나갔다. 날씨가 좋은 날이었고 우리는 공원을 통과하여 도로가 먼지투성이인 마을 밖으로 나갔다. **p.141** 그곳에는 철제 담장과 풀이 무성하게 자란 커다란 정원이 있는 별장들이 있었다. 경마장 트랙으로 들어가는 마차들이 많았다. 우리는 마차에서 내려 프로그램을 사고 경주마 대기소로 걸어갔다.

특별관람석은 낡고 나무로 만들어져 있었으며, 마권 매표소는 관람석 아래에 있었다. 우리는 마이어즈 씨 부부와 만났다. 내야에는 울타리를 따라 한 무리의 군인들이 있었고, 경주마 대기소는 사람들로 가득 채워졌다. 우리는 우리가 아는 몇몇 사람들을 보았고 퍼거슨과 캐서린에게 자리를 잡아주고 말들을 구경했다.

그곳에는 자줏빛을 띤 검은 말 한 마리가 있었고, 크로웰은 그 색깔로 염색된 것이라고 단언했다. 우리는 그 말을 보았고 그 말은 의심스러워 보였다. **p.142** 우리는 그 말을 프로그램에서 찾아보았고, 그 말은 자팔락이라는 이름의 검은색 거세마로 명부에 올라 있었다. 이 경마는 경주에서 우승한 적이 없는, 천 리라 이상의 값어치가 넘는 말들을 위한 것이었다. 캐서린은 그 말의 색이 바뀌었다고 확신했다. 우리는 모두 그 말에 걸어야 한다는 데 동의했고 100리라를 함께 걸었다. 프로그램은 그 말이 35대 1의 이익을 줄 것이라고 제시했다. 크로웰은 건너가서 마권을 샀다.

자팔락이 경주에서 우승했다.

"굉장하지 않아요?" 캐서린이 말했다. "우리는 3천 리라 이상을 갖게 될 거예요."

"그들이 배당금을 지불하기 전까지 자주색 염색이 지워지지 않으면 좋겠어요." 크로웰이 말했다.

"마이어즈 씨가 저 말에 돈을 걸었는지 궁금하네요." 캐서린이 말했다.

"우승한 말에 거셨나요?" 내가 마이어즈 씨에게 소리쳤다. 마이어즈 씨는 고개를 끄덕였다.

"나는 안 걸었다오." 마이어즈 부인이 말했다. "당신들은 어떤 말한테 걸었어요?"

p.143 "자팔락이오."

"정말이오? 그 녀석한테는 35대 1의 배당금이 걸렸잖아요!"

"배당금을 많이 지불해 주지는 않을 거야." 마이어즈 씨가 말했다.

"프로그램에 35대 1이라고 표시되어 있었어요." 내가 말했다.

"배당금을 많이 지불해 주지는 않을 거라니까. 마지막 순간에 그 말에 많이 걸었거든. 켐프톤과 그 패거리들이. 두고 보게. 2대 1의 배당조차도 안 될 걸."

"그러면 우리는 3천 리라를 못 받겠네요." 캐서린이 말했다. "저는 이런 사기성 경주는 마음에 안 들어요!"

"내려가서 한잔하고 얼마나 배당받을지 알아봐요." 크로웰이 말했다. 우리는 내려가서 마이어즈 씨가 옳았다는 것을 알았다. 그들은 2대 1에도 못 미치는 배당금을 지불하고 있었다.

우리는 특별관람석 밑에 있는 술집으로 갔고 우리가 아는 두세 명의 예의 바른 이탈리아 사람들과 부영사인 맥애덤스 씨와 우연히 마주쳤다. p.144 그들은 우리가 아가씨들과 합류했을 때 우리를 따라잡았다. 이탈리아 사람들은 여간 예의 바르지 않았고 우리가 돈을 걸려고 다시 내려간 사이에 맥애덤스 씨는 캐서린과 이야기를 나누었다. 우리는 마이어즈 씨와 마주쳤고 그와 같은 말에 100리라를 걸었다. 나는 기분이 몹시 좋은 상태였고 우리는 다른 두 명의 이탈리아 인들과도 친해졌는데, 그들은 각자 우리와 함께 한잔 하고 아가씨들에게 돌아갔다. 이 이탈리아 사람들 또한 아주 공손해서 우리가 전에 만난 두 사람의 예의범절과 다를 바 없었다. 머지않아 아무도 앉을 수가 없었다.

우리의 말이 우승했으나 배당금은 조금도 받지 못했다. 마이어즈 씨는 화가 났다.

"자네들은 20리라를 벌기 위해 200리라를 걸어야 하는군!" 마이어즈 씨가 말했다. "시간 들일 가치가 없는 일이야."

나는 경주마 대기소로 내려가려고 일어났다.

"저도 함께 내려가겠어요." 캐서린이 일어서며 말했다. p.145 이탈리아 사람들도 모두 일어섰다. 우리는 아래층으로 내려가 경주마 대기소 쪽으로 나갔다.

"이런 것을 좋아하세요?" 캐서린이 말했다.

"그래요. 나는 즐거운 시간을 보내고 있어요."

"저는 이렇게 많은 사람들과 함께 있는 것이 견딜 수가 없어요."

"그러면 이 바깥에 있으면서 울타리에서 경주를 구경합시다."

"그것이 좋겠어요. 우리가 들어본 적 없고 마이어즈 씨가 걸지 않을 말에 걸어요."

"알았어요."

우리는 '나를 위한 빛'이라는 이름의 말에 걸었고 이 말은 출전마 5마리 중 4등을 했다. 우리는 울타리에 기대어 말들이 지나가는 것을 구경했다.

"우리 둘만 있을 때가 더 좋지 않으세요?"

"맞아요." 내가 말했다.

"우리가 다른 사람들과 함께 있을 때 저는 무척 외로웠어요. p.146 하지만 당신의 즐거움을 망치게 두지는 않을 거예요, 내 사랑. 당신이 원할 때 언제든 돌아가요."

"아니요. 여기 있으면서 한잔합시다."

캐서린의 기분이 더 나아지자마자 우리는 돌아갔다. 우리는 다른 사람들을 다시 만나서 기분이 좋았고, 즐거운 시간을 보냈다.

제21장

p.147 9월에 날씨는 훨씬 서늘해졌다. 이탈리아 전선에서는 전황이 몹시 악화되고 있었다. 이탈리아군은 산 가브리엘레를 점령할 수 없었다. 바인시짜 고원에서의 전투는 끝났고, 그 달 중순경에는 산 가브리엘레 점령을 위한 전투 역시 거의 끝이 났다. p.148 에토레는 전선으로 다시 파견되

었다. 더 이상 경마는 없었다. 크로웰은 미국으로 송환당했다.

어느 날 오후 나는 이발소에 들러 면도를 하고 병원으로 돌아왔다. 나의 다리는 훨씬 나아졌다. 나는 샛길을 따라 걸어가면서 절뚝거리지 않으려고 연습했다. 어떤 노인이 아케이드 아래에서 반면 영상을 오려 내고 있었다.

"하나 가질래요, 중위님?" 노인이 물었다.

"좋지요." 내가 말했다.

"모자를 벗으세요."

"계속 쓰고 있고 싶은데요."

"멋져 보이지 않을 텐데요." 노인이 말했다. "하지만 더 군인답겠네요."

노인은 검은 종이에서 오려 내고, 그런 다음에 흰색 카드에 옆얼굴을 풀로 붙여 그것들을 나에게 건넸다.

p.149 "얼마죠?" 내가 물었다.

"공짜예요." 노인은 손사래를 쳤다.

"받으세요." 나는 동전 몇 개를 꺼냈다.

"아니에요. 중위님을 위해 만든 거예요. 애인에게 드리세요."

"정말 감사합니다."

나는 병원으로 돌아왔고 나를 기다리고 있는 몇 통의 편지들을 발견했다. 명령서가 와 있었다. 내가 전선으로 복귀하기 전에 3주간의 요양 휴가를 더 갖게 될 예정이라는 것이었다.

나는 그날 오후에 캐서린에게 내게 온 편지에 대해 말해 주었다.

"3주 동안 여행이라도 가야겠네요." 캐서린이 말했다.

"어디로?"

"어디든지요. 아무도 우리를 모르는 어딘가로요."

p.150 캐서린은 낙담한 것 같았다.

"무슨 일이에요?" 내가 물었다.

"아무것도 아니에요."

"무언가 잘못되었다는 것을 알아요. 말해 봐요, 내 사랑."

"걱정 끼치고 싶지 않아요."

"그러지 않을 거예요."

"확신하세요? 저는 걱정하지 않지만, 당신이 걱정할까 봐 두려워요."

"그냥 말해 봐요."

"임신 3개월이에요, 내 사랑. 걱정하시는 것은 아니죠, 그렇죠? 제발 걱정하지 마세요."

"알겠어요."

"정말이요?"

"그럼요. 나는 걱정 안 해요. 실은 기분이 아주 좋아요."

"이제 우리가 갈 장소를 골라요. 10월에는 어디든 아름다울 거예요. 우리는 즐거운 시간을 보내게 될 거예요, 내 사랑, 그리고 당신이 전선에 계시는 동안 저는 당신에게 매일 편지를 쓰겠어요."

p.151 나는 코냑을 한 잔 따라 그것을 마셨다.

"한잔하겠소?" 내가 물었다.

"아니요. 한잔하는 일은 늘 당신을 즐겁게 만들지만 저는 어지럽게 만들기만 하거든요."

나는 또 한 잔을 따랐다.

"저는 가서 환자들을 살펴보는 것이 좋겠어요." 캐서린이 말했다. "나중에 다시 올게요."

"나는 신문이나 볼게요." 내가 말했다.

제22장

p.152 다음날은 춥고 비가 왔다. 내가 오스페달레 마지오레에서 돌아오고 있을 때는 비가 세차게 내렸다. 나는 마른 옷으로 갈아입고 브랜디를 약간 마셨지만, 브랜디는 맛이 좋지 않았다. 나는 밤새 시름시름 앓았다.

"황달에 걸렸군." 입주 의사가 말했다. p.153 "중위 눈의 흰자위를 봐요."

게이지 양이 보았고, 내 눈의 흰자위는 노란색이었다. 나는 2주 동안 앓았고, 그런 이유 때문에 캐서린과 나는 요양 휴가를 함께 보낼 수 없었다.

어느 날 내가 황달로 누워 있을 때, 반 캠펜 양이 병실로 들어와 침대 밑을 살펴보다가 그곳에서 빈 병들을 보았다. 나는 한 무더기의 병들을 수위더러 아래로 내려놓게 했었는데 캠펜 양이 그 병들을 밖으로 내가는 것을 본 것이 분명했으며 더 찾으러 올라온 것이라는 생각이 들었다.

"이것들은 모두 브랜디 병들이군요, 안 그래요?" 반 캠펜 양이 물었다.

"아마도요."

"저는 중위님이 황달에 걸려 동정하고 있었어요. 동정은 중위님께 쓸데

없는 것이군요."

"고맙습니다."

"중위님이 전선으로 복귀하는 것을 원하지 않는다고 비난받을 리는 없어요. p.154 하지만 알코올 중독으로 스스로를 황달에 걸리게 하는 것보다 무언가 지적인 것을 찾으려고 하셨다면 좋을 텐데요."

"무엇으로라고요?"

"알코올 중독이요. 들으셨잖아요. 일단 건강해지면 전선으로 복귀하셔야 해요. 스스로 초래한 황달은 중위님에게 요양 휴가를 가질 자격을 주지 않아요."

"황달에 걸려본 적 있어요, 반 캠펜 양?"

"제가 직접 걸려 본 적은 없지만, 그동안 많이 보았지요."

"환자들 중 어떤 이들은 황달에 걸리는 것을 즐겼던 듯하군요?"

"전선으로 복귀하는 것보다는 훨씬 나으니까요."

"반 캠펜 양." 내가 말했다. "당신은 자해를 해서 스스로 불구가 되려고 시도한 사람을 본 적이 있소?"

캠펜 양은 내 질문을 무시했다. 캠펜 양은 그 질문을 무시하거나 병실에서 나가거나 해야 했다. p.155 캠펜 양은 나를 오랫동안 싫어해 와서 이번이 나를 괴롭힐 기회였기 때문에 병실을 나가고 싶어 하지 않았다.

"저는 많은 남자들이 자해한 부상을 통해 전선에서 탈출하는 것을 봤어요."

"그것은 내가 한 질문이 아니오. 나 역시 자해한 부상은 본 적이 있소. 나는 자해를 해서 스스로 불구가 되려고 시도한 사람을 본 적이 있느냐고 물었소."

캠펜 양이 병실을 떠났고, 그런 다음 잠시 후에 게이지 양이 들어왔다.

"무슨 일이 있었던 거예요? 반 캠펜 양이 몹시 화가 났어요."

"캠펜 양은 내가 전선으로 복귀하는 것을 회피하려고 술을 마셔 내가 황달에 걸렸다고 생각해요."

"헉." 게이지 양이 말했다. "중위님이 술을 마신 적이 없다고 제가 증언할게요. p.156 모두 중위님이 전혀 술을 마시지 않았다고 증언할 거예요."

"캠펜 양이 술병들을 보았어요."

"그 병들을 치우라고 제가 여러 차례 말씀드렸잖아요. 그것들이 어디에 있죠?"

"침대 밑에요."

"여행 가방은 있으세요?"

"아니요. 저 배낭을 쓰세요."

게이지 양은 병들을 꾸려서 문 쪽으로 나가려고 했다.

"수위에게 그것들을 내다 놓으라고 할게요." 게이지 양이 말했다.

"잠깐만요." 반 캠펜 양이 말했다. 캠펜 양은 문가에 서 있었다. "제가 가지고 가지요, 감사합니다." 수위가 캠펜 양과 함께 있었다. "그것들을 가져가 주세요." 캠펜 양이 말했다. "보고서를 쓸 때 그것들을 의사 선생님께 보여드리고 싶어요."

캠펜 양은 홀을 내려갔고, 수위가 배낭을 들고 따라갔다.

나는 군사법원에 회부되는 것이 두려웠지만, 나는 단지 내 휴가를 잃었을 뿐이었다.

제23장

p.158 나는 내가 전선으로 복귀하기로 예정된 날 밤에 캐서린을 만났다. 우리는 함께 거리를 걸어 다녔고 총포상 앞에서 걸음을 멈추었다.

"잠깐 들어가 봅시다." 내가 말했다. "권총을 잃어버렸거든요. 새것을 하나 사야 해요."

나는 중고 권총 한 자루와 여분의 탄창과 탄약통 한 상자를 구입했다.

p.159 나는 탄약통과 권총 값을 지불하고, 탄창을 채워 제자리에 놓고, 권총을 빈 권총집에 넣고, 탄약통으로 여분의 탄창을 채우고 그것들을 권총집에 있는 가죽 구멍에 넣었다.

우리는 총포상을 나와 거리를 가로질러 다른 쪽 길로 걸어 올라가기 시작했다.

"훨씬 기분이 좋군요." 캐서린이 말했다. "전에는 기분이 안 좋았어요."

"함께 있으면 우리는 언제나 기분이 좋잖아요."

"우리는 영원히 함께 있을 거예요."

"그래요, 내가 자정에 기차에 탈 것이라는 것을 빼면."

"피곤하세요?" 캐서린이 물었다.

"아니요. 당신은?"

"저는 걷는 것을 즐기고 있어요. 당신과 함께 걷는 것은 재미있어요."

p.160 "하지만 너무 오래 걷지는 맙시다. 어디 안에 들어갑시다." 내가 말했다.

"방을 하나 잡아요. 당신하고만 있고 싶어요."

비가 내리기 시작했으므로 우리는 역까지 마차를 탔다. 오랫동안 마차를 탔다.

"저녁은 어떡할까요?" 캐서린이 물었다.

"룸서비스로 할 거예요."

호텔에서, 나는 내가 들어가서 접수원에게 말하는 동안 캐서린에게는 마차에서 기다리라고 했다. 방은 많았다. 나는 마차 쪽으로 도로 나와서 마부에게 요금을 지불했고, 캐서린과 나는 함께 걸어서 들어갔다.

접수원은 엘리베이터 쪽으로 향하는 우리에게 머리를 숙여 절했다. 접수원은 우리와 함께 엘리베이터에 올라탔고 우리에게 방을 보여 주었다.

"저녁 식사 메뉴를 올려 주시겠소?" 내가 말했다.

"알겠습니다." 접수원이 말했다. 접수원은 머리를 숙이고 나갔다.

p.161 나는 창문으로 가서 줄을 잡아당겨 두꺼운 플러시 천으로 만든 커튼을 닫았다. 캐서린은 샹들리에를 바라보며 침대에 앉아 있었다. 캐서린은 모자를 벗었고 그녀의 머리는 불빛 아래에서 반짝였다. 그녀는 슬픈 것 같았다.

"이리 오세요." 캐서린이 미소를 지으며 말했다.

나는 가서 그녀의 이마에 키스를 했다.

"당신은 언제나 착한 내 여자예요."

"저는 언제나 당신 여자예요." 캐서린이 말했다.

식사를 한 후 우리는 기분이 좀 더 나아졌다. 커피를 마시고 난 후에는 방이 우리의 방처럼 느껴졌다. 병원에 있는 내 병실이 우리의 집이었는데 이제는 이 방이 우리의 집이었다.

"예쁜 방이에요." 캐서린이 말했다.

나는 포도주 한 잔을 따랐다.

"나는 포도주가 아주 좋아요." 내가 말했다. "인생의 모든 나쁜 일들을 잊게 해 주거든요."

p.162 "근사해요." 캐서린이 말했다. "하지만 술이 우리 아버지를 아주 병들게 했어요."

"당신 아버지에 대해 이야기를 해 봐요."

"아버지는 편찮으세요. 당신은 우리 아버지를 뵐 필요가 없을 거예요. 당신은 아버지가 안 계세요?"

"계부가 있어요."

"저를 좋아하실까요?"

"당신이 만날 필요는 없을 거예요."

내 머리는 갑자기 아주 맑고 냉철해졌으며 사실을 말하고 싶었다.

"어디에서 우리 아이를 낳을 거예요?"

"아직 잘 모르겠어요. 하지만 제가 찾을 수 있는 가장 좋은 장소일 거예요. 저는 걱정하지 마세요, 내 사랑. 당신 걱정만 하세요."

"얼마나 자주 편지를 쓸 거예요?"

"매일 쓸게요."

"우리 가야 할 것 같소. 기차를 놓칠지도 몰라요."

"알았어요, 내 사랑."

"나는 우리의 멋진 새집을 떠나기 싫어요."

"걱정 마세요. 당신이 돌아오면 아름다운 당신 집을 갖게 될 거예요."

제24장

p.164 나는 계산서의 금액을 지불하고 웨이터에게 우리에게 마차를 하나 잡아 달라고 부탁했다. 우리는 웨이터가 빗속에서 길을 건너가는 것을 지켜보았다.

"기분이 어때요, 캐트?" 내가 물었다.

"졸려요."

마차가 오고 웨이터는 내려서 우산을 펴고 호텔 쪽으로 다가왔다. **p.165** 우리는 문에서 웨이터를 만났고 밖으로 나가 그의 우산 밑으로 들어가 연석에 있는 마차 쪽으로 젖은 길을 내려갔다.

웨이터는 우리가 마차에 들어갈 때까지 우산을 들고 서 있었으며 나는 그에게 팁을 주었다.

우리는 거리를 달려 내려가 왼쪽으로 돌았으며, 그런 다음 역 앞쪽에 이르렀다. 짐꾼 한 명이 역의 대기소 아래에서 나왔다.

"아니요." 내가 말했다. "고맙지만 당신이 필요 없소." 나는 이미 병원의 수위에게 내 수하물을 기차에 두고, 나를 위해 좌석을 하나 잡을 수 있게 한 병사에게 돈을 지불하도록 수위에게 준비시켜 놓은 터였다.

"여기에서 작별 인사를 해요." 내가 캐서린을 돌아보며 말했다.

"제가 들어가는 것을 원하지 않으세요?"

"그래요. 잘 있어요, 캐트."

p.166 "저를 병원까지 데려다 주라고 마부에게 말해 주시겠어요?"

나는 마부에게 병원의 주소를 말해 주었다.

"안녕." 내가 말했다. "당신과 우리 아기를 잘 보살펴요."

"잘 가요, 내 사랑."

"잘 있어요." 내가 말했다. 나는 빗속으로 나갔고 마차는 떠났다. 그런 다음 나는 역을 통과하여 기차 쪽으로 승강장을 내려갔다.

수위가 승강장에서 나를 기다리고 있었다. 나는 수위를 따라 기차 안으로 들어갔고, 통로를 따라 가서 문을 통과하여 객차로 들어갔다. 나의 배낭과 더플 백은 수위의 머리 위 수하물 선반에 있었다. 복도에는 많은 사람들이 서 있었고, 우리가 들어갔을 때 객차 안의 사람들이 모두 우리를 쳐다보았다.

기차 안에는 충분한 자리가 없었고 모두가 적대적이었다. p.167 내 자리를 잡아 놓기 위해 수위에게 돈을 받은 어떤 병사가 나에게 자리를 내주려고 일어났다. 누군가가 내 어깨를 톡톡 두드렸다. 나는 몸을 돌렸다. 그것은 턱에 붉은 상처가 있는 아주 키가 크고 마른 대위였다. 대위는 복도 유리창으로 나를 보고 안으로 들어온 것이었다.

"뭡니까?" 내가 물었다. 나는 그와 얼굴을 마주 보려고 몸을 돌렸다. 객차 안에 있는 모두가 우리를 지켜보고 있었다.

"자네 그러면 안 돼." 대위가 말했다. "누군가에게 당신 자리를 잡아 놓게 하면 안 되지."

"글쎄요, 벌써 한 일입니다."

"자네는 그럴 권리가 없어. 나는 자네가 오기 전에 두 시간 동안 여기 있었단 말이야."

"무엇을 원하십니까?"

"그 자리."

p.168 나는 객차에 있는 모든 사람들이 나에게 반감이 있는 것을 느낄 수 있었다. 나는 그들을 비난하지 않았다. 대위가 옳았다.

"앉으십시오, 대위님." 내가 말했다. 나에게 자리를 맡아주었던 병사가 자리에서 비켰고 키 큰 대위가 앉았다. "내 짐을 가져다주게." 나는 병사에게 말했다. 우리는 복도에서 나왔다. 기차는 만원이었고 내가 좋은 자리를 찾을 기회는 없었다. 나는 수위와 병사에게 10리라씩 주었다. 나는 그들에게 작별 인사를 했고 우리는 악수를 했으며 그들은 떠났다. 그들 둘 다 찝찝한 기분이었다.

기차가 역을 떠날 때 기차 안에서는 우리 모두가 복도에 서 있었다. 나중에 나는 복도 바닥에서 잠을 잤다. 나는 밤새 잤고, 브레스치아와 베로나에서 더 많은 사람들이 올라탈 때 잠깐 잠에서 깨었다. 사람들은 모든 복도의 바닥에서 잤고, 기차는 언제나 붐볐다.

제25장

p.169 나는 군용 트럭을 타고 우디네에서 고리지아로 달렸다. 나는 시장 관저 앞에 있는 커다란 광장에서 트럭에서 내렸고, 운전병은 나의 배낭을 내려주었으며 나는 그것을 매고 두 개의 더플 백을 흔들거리며 별장으로 걸어갔다.

p.170 별장에서 나는 소령이 벽에 지도와 타자로 친 서류가 붙어 있는 휑한 방 안의 탁자 앞에 앉아 있는 것을 발견했다.

"어이." 소령이 말했다. "좀 괜찮은가?" 소령은 전보다 더 나이 들어 보였다.

"네, 고맙습니다." 내가 말했다. "이곳은 어떻습니까?"

"형편없는 여름이었네." 소령이 말했다. "훈장은 받았나?"

"네." 나는 배낭을 내려놓았다. "제가 무엇을 하면 좋을까요?"

"의료 차량은 여기 없네. 여섯 대가 북쪽 카포레토에 있지. 카포레토를 아나?"

"네." 내가 말했다. 나는 그곳을 골짜기에 종루가 있는 작고 하얀 마을로 기억했다.

"바로 거기에서 운영되고 있다네. 전투는 끝났지만 많은 병사들이 아프다네."

"다른 차량들은 모두 어디에 있습니까?"

"두 대는 산 위에 있고 네 대는 바인시짜 고원에 있어. **p.171** 자네가 원한다면 가서 네 대의 차를 맡아도 되네. 지노가 그곳에 올라가 있은 지

오래 되었지. 자네는 그곳에 올라갔다 온 적이 없지, 그렇지?"

"없습니다."

"형편없었네. 우리는 차량 세 대를 잃었어."

"들었습니다."

"맞아. 리날디가 자네에게 편지를 썼지."

"리날디는 어디에 있습니까?"

"이곳 병원에 있네. 가서 씻고 자네 친구 리날디를 만나 보게나."

나는 내 방으로 가서 가방을 풀고 침대에 누웠다. 나는 지쳤고 발은 아팠다. 바깥은 어두워지고 있었다. 나는 캐서린에 관해 생각했고 리날디를 기다렸다. 나는 밤에 자기 전을 제외하고는 캐서린에 관해서 생각하지 않겠다고 결심했다. 하지만 나는 지쳤고 할 것이 아무것도 없어서 누워서 그녀에 대해 생각했다. p.172 그때 리날디가 들어왔다. 리날디는 약간 더 야위어 보였으나 더도 말고 덜도 말고 똑같았다.

"어이, 친구." 리날디가 말했다. 나는 일어나 앉았다. 리날디가 다가와서 나를 끌어안았다. "자네 무릎 좀 보세."

"바지를 벗어야겠군."

"그럼 벗게, 친구. 밀라노에서 의사들이 어떤 일을 했는지 보고 싶군."

나는 일어나서 바지를 벗고 무릎 붕대를 끌어 내렸다. 리날디는 바닥에 앉아 내 무릎을 앞뒤로 구부려 보았다. 리날디는 손가락으로 상처를 죽 훑고 양손의 엄지손가락으로 슬개골을 누르고 무릎을 손가락으로 살살 움직였다.

"그것보다 무릎을 더 움직일 수는 없나?"

"못 해."

"그러면 자네를 돌려보낸 것은 범죄야. 그들은 자네를 더 쉬게 해야 해."

"전보다는 훨씬 좋아졌어."

p.173 "자네는 물리 치료가 더 필요해."

"나는 괜찮아."

"친구, 이것은 내가 자네보다 더 잘 아는 거야." 리날디가 일어나 침대에 앉았다. "무릎은 괜찮을 거야." 리날디가 무릎 검사를 마쳤다. "전부 말해 보게."

"말할 것은 아무것도 없어." 내가 말했다. "한 일도 별로 없어."

"자네는 유부남처럼 말하는군." 리날디가 말했다. "무슨 일인가?"

"아무 일도 아니야." 내가 말했다. "자네야말로 무슨 일이 있나?"

"이 전쟁이 나를 죽이고 있어." 리날디가 말했다. "몹시 우울하다네."

"내가 가고 없는 동안 멋진 시간을 보낸 것이 분명해. 말해 봐."

"여름과 가을 내내 나는 수술을 하고 있었어. **p.174** 내내 일만 하지. 힘든 일은 나에게 모두 준다니까. 나는 훌륭한 외과 의사가 될 거야, 친구. 그래도 괜찮았어. 내가 수술을 하고 있을 때는 생각을 할 필요가 없으니까. 나는 생각하는 것을 싫어해. 전쟁 때문이지. 알지? 하지만 이제 친구, 모두 끝이야. 나는 더 이상 수술은 하지 않지만 지옥에 있는 듯한 기분이야. 전쟁은 끔찍해. 하지만 이제 자네가 나를 기운 나게 해 주려고 여기 왔잖아. 레코드판은 가지고 왔나?"

"그래."

그것들은 내 배낭 속의 마분지 상자에 있었다. 나는 피곤해서 그것들을 꺼내야 된다는 것도 신경 쓰지 않았었다.

"괜찮나, 친구?" 리날디가 물었다.

"끔찍한 기분이야."

"이 전쟁은 끔찍하지." 리날디가 말했다. "자자. 한잔하고 기운 내자. 그러면 괜찮아질 거야."

"나는 못 마셔. 황달에 걸렸거든."

p.175 "오, 자네는 심각하게 손상된 간을 가지고 밀라노에서 돌아왔군."

"오, 빌어먹을, 한잔하세. 취하고 싶지는 않아. 딱 한 잔만 하겠네."

리날디는 방을 가로질러 세면대로 미끄러지듯 가더니 두 개의 잔과 코냑 한 병을 가지고 돌아왔다.

"맛 좋은 오스트리아제 코냑일세." 리날디가 말했다. "산 가브리엘레에서 도로 가져왔지."

우리는 술을 마셨다. 리날디가 웃었다.

"나는 자네를 취하게 하고 자네의 간을 꺼내어 튼튼한 이탈리아 인의 간을 집어넣고 다시 자네를 사내로 만들어 주겠네."

나는 코냑을 더 달라고 잔을 내밀었다. 이제 밖은 어두워지고 있었다. 코냑 잔을 붙잡고, 나는 가서 창문을 열었다. 비는 그쳤다.

"코냑을 창밖으로 버리지 말게." 리날디가 말했다. "못 마시겠거든 그냥 나를 주게."

p.176 "지옥에나 가게." 내가 말했다. 나는 리날디를 다시 보게 되어 기

뺐다. 리날디는 2년 동안 나를 곯렸고, 나는 언제나 그것을 좋아했다. 우리는 서로를 완벽하게 이해했다.

"사랑에 빠진 거야?" 리날디가 물었다. 나는 창가 벽에 기대어 서 있었다.

"그래."

"바클리 양과?"

"그래. 바클리가 내 아이를 가졌네."

"바클리 양은 자네에게 잘해 주나?"

"그래."

"나는 전부 다 알고 싶네. 그러니까 그녀가……?"

"리날디." 내가 말했다. "제발 입 다물게. 내 친구가 되고 싶다면 더 이상 말하지 말게나."

"나는 자네 친구가 되고 싶은 것이 아니야, 친구. 나는 자네의 친구라고."

"그럼 입 다물게."

"알겠어. 어떤 상황인지 알겠군."

나는 침대로 가서 리날디 옆에 앉았다. p.177 리날디는 나를 이해했다.

"자네 애인을 위하여." 리날디가 미소를 지으며 말했다. 리날디가 잔을 내밀었다.

"그래."

"그녀에 관해서는 어떤 상스러운 말도 하지 않겠네. 자자, 내려가서 뭘 좀 먹자고."

나는 씻고 머리를 빗었으며 우리는 아래로 내려갔다. 리날디는 약간 얼근하게 취했다. 식사가 완전히 준비되어 있지 않았으므로 리날디는 코냑 병을 가지러 다시 위층으로 올라갔다. 나는 식탁에 앉았고, 리날디는 술병을 가지고 돌아와서 우리 잔에 각각 코냑을 한 잔씩 따랐다.

나는 절반을 마셨다. 홀에서, 나는 당번병이 외치는 소리를 들었다. "수프요! 수프가 나왔습니다!"

소령이 들어와서 앉았다.

"이 사람들이 다인가?" 소령이 물었다. 당번병은 수프 그릇을 내려놓고 국자로 접시 가득 수프를 퍼 주었다.

p.178 "신부님이 오시지 않는다면 이 사람들이 전부입니다." 리날디가 말했다. "이 친구가 여기 있는 줄 안다면 신부님은 여기 계실 텐데요."

"신부님은 여기 오실 거야." 소령이 말했다. "자네가 여기 있다고 소식을 남겨두었거든."

"식당의 법석거리던 소리가 그립네요." 내가 말했다.

"너무 조용하군." 소령이 말했다.

"시끄러워질 것입니다." 리날디가 말했다.

신부님이 왔을 때는 우리가 스파게티 식사를 끝내가고 있었다. 신부님은 이전과 똑같았고 몸집이 작고 구릿빛인 데다가 체격은 탄탄했다. 나는 일어났고 우리는 악수를 했다.

"앉으십시오." 소령이 말했다. "늦으셨네요."

"안녕하세요, 신부님." 리날디가 영어 단어를 사용해서 말했다. 그들은 그 말을 대위에게서 배웠는데, 대위는 영어를 약간 하고 신부님을 놀리기를 좋아했다.

"안녕하세요, 리날디." 신부님이 말했다.

"잘 지내셨나요?" 신부님이 나에게 물었다.

"잘 지냈어요." 내가 말했다. "어떻게 지내셨어요?"

p.179 "술 좀 드세요, 신부님." 리날디가 도중에 끼어들었다.

"좋습니다." 신부님이 정중하게 말했다. 리날디는 잔을 채웠다.

리날디가 신부님을 놀리고 싶어 하는 것은 분명했는데, 아마도 대위가 없기 때문인 듯했다. 신부님은 나를 돌아보고 미소를 지었다. 이제 놀리는 것이 신부를 괴롭히지 않는다는 것을 나는 알 수 있었다.

"신부님을 곯려 먹던 그 선량한 옛 친구들은 다 어디에 있지? 카발칸티는 어디에 있어? 브룬디는? 케사레는 어디에 있는 거야? 지원도 없이 나 혼자 이 신부님을 곯려야 하는 거야?"

"그분은 마음씨 좋은 신부님이시네." 소령이 말했다.

"마음씨 좋은 신부님이시죠." 리날디가 말했다. "하지만 아무리 그래도 신부님이에요. 저는 식당 분위기를 옛날처럼 만들고 싶어요. 이 녀석을 즐겁게 해 주고 싶다고요. 망할 신부님을 위해, 건배, 신부님."

p.180 소령은 리날디를 보고 그가 취했다는 것을 알아챘다.

"망할 너희들을 위해 건배." 리날디가 말했다. "그리고 빌어먹을 모든 전쟁들을 위해 건배."

"이 친구가 스트레스를 많이 받아서 피곤한 모양이군." 소령이 나에게 말했다.

"휴가를 얻으셔야 하겠어요." 신부님이 말했다.

소령은 신부님에게 몰래 고개를 저었다. 리날디는 신부를 바라보았다.

"제가 휴가를 얻어야 한다고 생각하세요?"

소령이 다시 신부님에게 고개를 저었다. 리날디는 여전히 신부님을 쳐다보고 있었다.

"싫으시다면 그럴 필요 없어요."

"지옥으로 꺼져 버려." 리날디가 말했다. "그들은 언제나 나를 없애려고 해. 매일 밤 그들이 나를 제거하려고 한다고. 나는 그들과 싸워 쫓아 버릴 거야. 그래서 내가 아픈 게 뭐 어때서? 그래, 내가 그것에 걸렸지만, 모두 그것에 걸려 있는걸. 군대 전체가 그것에 걸려 있지. 먼저 작은 뾰루지가 나지. 그런 다음 양 어깨 중간에서 발진을 보게 돼. 그런 다음에는 아무것도 볼 수 없지. p.181 하지만 걱정 마세요, 마음씨 착한 우리 신부님. 신부님은 절대 안 걸리실 테니까요. 이 친구는 걸리겠지만, 신부님은 안 걸린다고요."

당번병이 후식을 가지고 들어왔다. 리날디는 조용했다. 리날디는 괜찮아 보였다. 우리는 잡담을 나누고 커피를 마신 후 모두 나와 홀로 들어갔다.

"자네는 신부님과 이야기하고 싶어 했잖아. 나는 마을로 가야겠어." 리날디가 말했다. "안녕히 계세요, 신부님."

"안녕히 가세요, 리날디." 신부님이 말했다.

"또 보세, 친구." 리날디가 말했다.

"그래." 내가 말했다. "빨리 돌아오게." 리날디는 대답하지 않고 문 밖으로 나갔다.

"저 친구는 몹시 지치고 과로한 상태야." 소령이 말했다.

제26장

p.182 소령은 자기 사무실로 들어갔고 나는 신부님을 위층 내 방으로 초대했다. 나는 리날디의 침대에 누웠고 신부님은 내 침대에 앉았다. 방은 어두웠다.

"정말로 어떠세요?" 신부님이 물었다.

"좋습니다. 오늘 밤에는 단지 피곤한 것뿐이에요."

"저도 피곤합니다. 전쟁에 지쳐 있지요. 하지만 머지않아 전쟁은 끝날 것 같습니다. p.183 저는 느낄 수 있어요."

"무슨 뜻입니까?"

"모두 온화해졌거든요. 소령님처럼요."

"저도 같은 느낌이에요." 내가 말했다.

"여름은 끔찍했어요." 신부님이 말했다. 신부님은 내가 떠났을 때보다 이제 더 확신하고 있었다. "얼마나 끔찍했는지 믿지 못하실 거예요. 그리고 저는 그것이 더 오래가지는 않을 것 같습니다."

"그러면 무슨 일이 일어날까요?"

"양측이 전투를 중단하겠죠."

"저도 그러기를 바랍니다." 내가 말했다.

"그런 일이 일어나지 않을 것 같나요?"

"쌍방이 즉각 전투를 중단할 것 같지는 않군요."

"아마 중위님 말이 맞을 것입니다. 너무 기대가 크죠. 하지만 사람들 마음에 변화가 있는 것이 보여서 저는 전쟁이 지속될 거라고 생각하지 않아요."

"이번 여름에는 누가 전투에서 이겼나요?"

"이긴 쪽은 없어요."

p.184 "오스트리아군이 이겼어요." 내가 말했다. "그들이 그럭저럭 산가브리엘레를 방어했으니까요. 그들이 이겼으니까 그들은 전투를 중단하지 않을 거예요. 이기고 있을 때는 누구든 중단하지 않거든요."

"중위님이 제 희망을 짓밟으시는군요."

"저는 그냥 솔직해지려는 것입니다."

"그러면 중위님은 전쟁이 절대로 끝나지 않을 것이라고 생각하세요? 아무것도 변하지 않을 것이라고요?"

"모르겠습니다. 단지 오스트리아군이 이기고 있을 때는 전투를 중단하지 않을 것이라고 생각합니다. 우리는 지고 있을 때 그냥 크리스천이 될 뿐이죠."

신부님은 아무 말도 하지 않았다.

"우리는 지고 있기 때문에 지금 모두 다 더 온순한 것입니다." 내가 계속해서 말했다.

"저는 여전히 믿고 싶고 무슨 일이든 일어나기를 기도합니다. 아무튼 아주 오래 있어서 죄송합니다. 중위님은 분명히 몹시 피곤하실 거예요. 하지만 중위님과 이야기 하는 것은 즐겁습니다."

"다시 이야기를 나누게 되어 아주 좋았어요."

우리는 일어나서 어둠 속에서 악수를 나누었다.

p.185 "저는 내일 아침 일찍 전선으로 갈 겁니다."

"돌아오시면 뵙겠습니다."

제27장

p.186 리날디가 들어왔을 때 나는 잠에서 깼으나 우리는 말하지 않았고 나는 다시 잠이 들었다. 아침에 나는 리날디가 일어나기 전에 옷을 갈아입고 나갔다.

나는 전에 바인시짜 고원을 본 적이 없었고, 내가 부상을 당한 강가 지역 너머 오스트리아군이 있던 경사면을 올라가는 것은 이상했다. p.187 집들은 심하게 부서져 있었으나 주변 상황은 매우 질서정연했고 어디에든 표지판이 있었다. 우리는 지노를 발견했고 그는 우리에게 커피를 주었으며 후에 나는 그와 함께 가서 다양한 사람들을 만나고 모든 주둔지들을 안내받았다.

지노는 우리 맞은편 전선에는 지금 크로아티아 사람들과 몇몇 마자르 사람들이 있다고 나에게 말해 주었다. 우리 부대는 여전히 공격 태세에 있었다. 오스트리아군의 공격이 있을 경우에는 이를 알릴 무선도 없고 후퇴할 장소도 없었다. 고원에서 뻗어 나온 낮은 산맥들을 따라 훌륭한 방어진지들이 있었지만, 방어를 위해 그 진지들을 편성하는 것에 관해서는 아무것도 실행된 것이 없었다.

p.188 나는 산악전의 가치를 믿지 않는다고 지노에게 말했다.

"자네는 항상 움직일 수 있는 기동력을 갖춰야 해." 내가 말했다. "산은 그다지 기동성이 있지 않아. 또한 사람들은 언제나 내리막길을 향해 사정거리에서 벗어나 사격을 하지. 만약 측면을 빼앗기면, 정예 부대원들은 가장 높은 산악 지대에 남게 되지. 산악 지대를 빼앗아 방어하는 것은 끝내야 해. 하지만 정말로 무슨 일이 시작되면, 모두 산을 떠나 내려와야 해."

지노와 나는 오랫동안 대화하는 것을 끝내지 않았다. 어떤 시점에서 지노는 나에게 식량이 부족해졌다고 말했다.

"나는 한 번도 배불리 먹어본 적이 없어." 지노가 말했다. "하지만 나는 많이 먹고 굶주려 본 적은 없어. 최전선의 연대들은 꽤 많은 음식들을 보급받지만 지원 부대들은 그렇게 많이 보급 받지 못하고 있어. 어딘가에서 무언가가 잘못되고 있어. 모든 병사들에게 충분한 식량이 있어야 해."

p.189 "식량 중 일부가 보급되어서는 안 될 곳에 보급되고 있는 것이 분명해."

"그래, 그들은 최전방 대대에 가능한 많은 식량을 지급하지만, 후방 대대들은 그리 많은 식량을 받지 못하고 있어. 식량이 부족한 것은 병사들에게는 매우 안 좋아. 식량이 사고방식에 만드는 차이에 주목한 적 있나?"

"그래." 내가 말했다. "식량 때문에 전쟁에서 승리할 수는 없지만 전쟁에서 패배하게 만들 수는 있지."

"패한다는 이야기는 하지 마세. 패하는 것에 대해서도 이미 충분히 말이 많으니까. 이번 여름에 한 일이 헛되이 끝날 리는 없어."

나는 아무 말도 하지 않았다. 나는 '신성한'이니 '영광스러운'이니 '희생'이니 그리고 '헛되이'라는 말에는 늘 당혹스러웠다. 나는 그러한 단어들이 종종 전쟁에서 사용되는 것을 들었으나 나는 신성한 것이라곤 아무것도 본 적이 없었다. p.190 영광스러운 것들에는 영광이 없었고 희생은 쓸모없었다. 듣기에 견딜 수 없는 말들이 많아서 결국 지명만이 위엄을 갖게 되었다. 지노는 애국자였으므로 이따금 그러한 단어들을 사용했다. 하지만 지노는 좋은 친구였고 나는 그가 애국자라는 것을 이해했다. 지노는 태생적으로 애국자였다. 지노는 고리지아로 돌아가려고 나를 바인시짜 고원으로 데려간 페두찌와 함께 차를 타고 떠났다.

그날 하루 종일 폭풍이 불었다. 밤에는 바람이 강해졌고 새벽 3시에는 비가 더 세차게 내리면서 폭격이 있었고 크로아티아군이 산간의 초원을 가로질러 최전선으로 침투해 들어왔다. 그들은 비가 오는 가운데 어둠 속에서 싸웠고 제2선으로부터 나온 반격이 그들을 후퇴시켰다. 많은 포격이 있었고, 나는 빗속에서 이리저리 날아가는 많은 로켓포를 보았다. p.191 기관총과 라이플총의 포화는 영원처럼 보이는 것을 위해 그치지 않았다. 적들은 다시 오지 않았고 점점 조용해졌다. 비바람의 돌풍 사이로 나는 북쪽으로의 대규모 폭격 소리를 들을 수 있었다.

많은 사람들이 그날 밤에 부상을 당했다. 부상자들이 진지 안으로 들어왔고, 일부는 들것으로 일부는 걸어서 그리고 일부는 들판을 가로질러 온 병사들의 등에 업혀 실려 왔다. 그들은 모두 흠뻑 젖고 겁에 질려 있었다. 우리는 두 대의 구급차를 들것 대상자들로 채웠고 내가 두 번째 차량의 문을 닫고 그것을 잠갔을 때, 얼굴 위로 떨어지는 비가 눈으로 바뀐 것이 느껴졌다. p.192 눈송이는 비와 함께 묵직하고 빠르게 내리고 있었다.

새벽에 여전히 폭풍은 불었지만 눈은 그쳤다. 날이 밝자마자 또 한 번의 공격이 있었으나, 그것은 성공적이지 못했다. 우리는 하루 종일 공격이 있을 것이라고 예상했지만 해가 지기 시작할 때까지 공격은 없었다. 내가 마을 뒤쪽의 들판에서 총이 발사되는 소리와 포격 소리를 들었을 때는 날이 어두워지고 있었다.

나중에 우리는 남쪽에 대한 공격이 성공적이지 못했다고 들었다. 적들은 그날 밤에 공격하지 않았지만 우리는 그들이 북쪽까지 뚫고 들어갔다는 말을 들었다. 밤에 우리는 후퇴를 준비하라고 들었다. 나중에 주둔지의 대위가 오고 나서 우리에게 새로운 명령이 내려졌으며, 바인시짜 전선은 무슨 일이 일어나더라도 확보되어야 한다고 말했다. 대위는 오스트리아군이 카포레토를 향해 27군단을 돌파했다고 말했다.

p.193 "만약 그 개자식들이 적들이 돌파하게 두었다면 우리는 끝장이야." 대위가 말했다.

"공격하고 있는 것은 독일군들이야." 군의관들 중 한 명이 말했다. '독일군'이라는 단어는 두려움의 대상이었다. 우리는 독일군과는 어떠한 관련도 맺고 싶지 않았다.

"15개의 독일군 사단이 있지." 군의관이 계속해서 말했다. "그들은 돌파했고, 머지않아 우리는 앞뒤로 차단당할 거야."

"그래서 저는 여기 있어야 하는 겁니까 아니면 떠나야 하는 겁니까?" 내가 물었다.

"가장 최근의 명령은 우리가 여기에 있어야 한다는 거야. 자네는 부상병들을 이곳에서 치료 후송소로 소개시켜 주게."

"때때로 우리는 치료 후송소에서 야전병원까지도 소개시키지요." 내가 말했다. "말씀해 보십시오……. 제가 후퇴에 참여해 본 적이 없어서……. 만약 후퇴가 있다면 우리가 어떻게 모든 부상병들을 철수시켜야 합니까?"

p.194 "우리는 할 수 있는 한 많이 태우고 나머지는 남겨두지."

"차량에는 무엇을 싣나요?"

"의료 장비들."

"알겠습니다." 내가 말했다.

후퇴는 그 다음날 밤에 시작되었다. 우리는 독일군과 오스트리아군이 북쪽에서 아군을 돌파했으며 치비달레와 우디네를 향해 산간 골짜기들을 내려가고 있다고 들었다. 후퇴는 조직적이었고, 비에 젖고 침울했다. 밤에는 붐비는 길을 따라 천천히 가며 우리는 모두 전선으로부터 이동하는, 빗속을 행군하는 부대, 대포, 짐마차를 끄는 말, 노새, 트럭을 지나쳤다. 그것은 진군과 똑같았다.

우리는 다음날 한낮에 고리지아에 도착했다. 비는 그쳤고, 마을은 거의 텅 비어 있었다. **p.195** 그들은 여자들을 트럭에 싣고 있었다. 모두 일곱 명의 여자들이 있었고 그들은 모자를 쓰고 외투를 입고 있었고 작은 여행 가방들을 가지고 다니고 있었다. 그들 중 둘은 울고 있었고, 또 다른 한 명의 여자는 우리에게 미소를 짓고 혀를 내밀고 위아래로 날름거렸다.

우리가 별장 진입로로 들어갔을 때 나는 뛰어내렸다.

"차량을 밖으로 내놓고 공병들에게 차량을 살펴보게 하게." 내가 운전병에게 말했다. "오일을 갈고 차동 장치를 점검하도록. 기름을 채워 놓은 다음 잠을 좀 자두게."

"네, 중위님."

별장은 텅 비어 있었고, 리날디와 소령은 창문에 나에게 쪽지를 남겨두었다. 나는 홀에 쌓여 있는 서류들을 차에 싣고 포르데노네로 전진하라는 지시를 받았다. **p.196** 공병들은 이미 떠나고 없었다. 나는 차고로 갔다. 내가 그곳에 있는 동안 두 대의 다른 차량이 들어왔고 운전병들이 내렸다. 비가 다시 오기 시작했다.

"저는 정말 졸립니다. 플라바에서 이곳까지 오며 세 번이나 잠이 들었어요." 피아니가 말했다. "저희가 어떻게 하면 좋겠습니까, 중위님?"

"우리는 오일을 갈고, 기름을 치고, 가솔린을 채운 다음 현관에 차를 대고 그들이 남겨둔 물건들을 실을 거야."

"저희는 곧바로 떠날 건가요?"

"아니, 우리는 세 시간 잔다."

"그 말씀을 들으니 기쁘군요." 보넬로가 말했다. "저는 깨어 있는 상태로 운전할 수가 없었어요."

"자네의 차는 어떤가, 아이모?" 내가 물었다.

"괜찮습니다."

"오일 가는 것을 도와주겠네."

"괜찮습니다, 중위님." 아이모가 말했다. "저 혼자 할 수 있습니다. 중위님은 가서 짐을 챙기세요."

p.197 "내 짐은 이미 챙겼네." 내가 말했다. "나는 가서 그들이 우리에게 남겨 놓은 짐들을 꺼내겠네. 준비가 되자마자 곧 차들을 돌려오게."

그들은 별장의 현관 앞으로 차를 돌려 왔고 우리는 복도에 쌓여 있던 병원 장비들을 차량에 실었다.

"부엌에 불을 피우고 옷들을 말리게." 내가 말했다.

"저는 옷을 말리는 것은 상관없어요." 피아니가 말했다. "잠을 자고 싶어요."

"나는 소령님 침대에서 자야지." 보넬로가 말했다.

"나는 어디에서 자든 상관없어." 피아니가 말했다.

"소령님 방에는 두 대의 침대가 있네." 내가 말했다. "자네들 둘은 그곳에서 자게. 내가 자네들을 깨워 주겠네."

p.198 "중위님이 너무 오래 주무시면 오스트리아군이 저희를 깨울 겁니다, 중위님." 보넬로가 말했다.

"늦잠은 안 잘 거네." 내가 말했다. "아이모는 어디에 있나?"

"부엌에 들어갔습니다."

"자러 가게." 내가 말했다.

나는 부엌으로 갔다. 아이모는 가스레인지에 불을 지폈고 물 주전자를 올려놓고 있었다.

"파스타를 좀 요리할까 생각 중이었어요." 아이모가 말했다. "잠에서 깨면 모두들 배고파 할 겁니다."

"피곤하지 않나, 바르톨로메오? 자네는 좀 자 둬야 해." 내가 말했다. "우리는 치즈와 통조림 고기를 먹으면 돼."

"이것이 더 나아요." 바르톨로메오가 말했다. "저 두 멍청이들에게는 무언가 뜨거운 것이 좋을 겁니다. 좀 주무세요, 중위님."

"한잔하겠나, 바르톨로메오?"

"떠날 때 할게요, 중위님. 지금은 제게 전혀 도움이 되지 않을 거예요."

"세 시간 후에 자네가 일어났을 때 내가 자네를 부르지 않으면, 나를 깨워 주게, 알겠지?"

p.199 "저는 시계가 없습니다, 중위님."

"소령님의 방 벽에 시계가 있네."

"알겠습니다."

나는 눕자마자 잠이 들었고 세 시간 후에 일어났다. 우리는 출발하기 전에 부엌에서 식사를 했다. 아이모는 양파와 통조림 고기가 들어간 스파게티를 한 양푼 가득 만들었다. 우리는 식탁에 둘러앉아 별장의 포도주 저장실에 남겨졌던 포도주들 중에서 두 병을 마셨다. 밖은 아직 어두웠으며 비가 내리고 있었다.

"제가 우리가 각자 포도주 한 병씩 가지고 차에 타도록 조치해 놓았습니다." 아이모가 말했다.

"자네 잠은 조금이라도 잤나?" 내가 물었다.

"조금 잤습니다. 저는 많이 자지 않아도 됩니다."

"내일 우리는 왕의 침대에서 잘 거야." 보넬로가 말했다. 포도주는 보넬로를 몹시 기분 좋게 만들어 주고 있었다.

p.200 우리는 차에 우리의 짐을 싣고 우디네를 향해 떠났다.

제28장

p.201 우리가 마을을 빠져나간 지 얼마 안 되어 도로는 후퇴하는 부대들로 심하게 정체되었다. 몇 시간 후 우리는 전혀 이동하지 못하고 있었다. 나는 내려서 트럭과 마차 사이로 그리고 말들의 젖은 목덜미 아래로 가면서 앞서 걸었다. **p.202** 내 눈에 보이는 한, 차량들로 이루어진 전체 종대는 이동하지 못했다.

하지만 꼼짝 못하는 차량들 너머 반대편에서 나는 부대들이 이동하는 것을 보았다. 나는 우리의 차로 돌아왔다. 나는 이러한 정체가 우디네까지 늘어져 있을지도 모른다고 생각했다. 피아니는 핸들에 엎어져 잠들어 있었다. 나는 피아니 옆으로 올라탔고 나도 역시 잠이 들었다.

몇 시간 후 나는 우리 앞에 있는 트럭의 기어가 돌아가는 소리를 들었다. 나는 피아니를 깨웠고 우리는 출발해서 몇 야드를 이동하고, 그런 다음 멈추어 섰다가 가고, 그런 다음 멈추어 섰다. 차량 행렬이 밤에 다시 정체되어 출발하지 않을 때까지 우리는 이렇게 몇 시간을 계속 이동했다. 나는 내려서 아이모와 보넬로를 보려고 다른 차들로 갔다. 보넬로는 두 명의 공병 병장들을 자기 차의 좌석에 태우고 있었다. 내가 차 문을 열자 그들은 경직되어 버렸다.

"이 사람들은 다리에 무슨 조치를 취하기 위해 남겨졌습니다." 보넬로가 말했다. **p.203** "자기 부대를 찾지 못해서 제가 태워 주었습니다."

"중위님의 허락을 구하지 않은 것에 대해 사과드립니다, 중위님."

"허락하지." 내가 말했다.

"중위님은 미국인이셔." 보넬로가 말했다. "누구든 태워 주실 거야."

병장들 중 한 명이 미소를 지었고, 다른 병장은 내가 북미나 남미에서 온 이탈리아 사람인지 물었다.

"이탈리아 인이 아니시라니까. 미국인이셔."

병장들은 그 말을 믿지 않는 듯했다. 나는 그들을 떠나 아이모에게 돌아왔다. 아이모는 소녀 두 명을 좌석에 태우고 뒤쪽 구석에 앉아 담배를 피우고 있었다.

"이런, 이런." 내가 말했다. 아이모는 웃었다.

"이 소녀들에게 말 좀 걸어 보세요, 중위님." 아이모가 말했다. "저는 못 알아듣겠어요. 이봐!" 아이모는 소녀들 중 한 명의 넓적다리를 친근한 방식으로 꼬집었다. p.204 소녀는 숄을 몸에 단단히 두르고 아이모의 손을 치웠다. "이봐!" 아이모가 말했다. "중위님께 너희들 이름과 여기에서 무엇을 하고 있는지 말씀드려."

소녀가 화가 나서 나를 쳐다보았다. 다른 소녀는 바닥을 내려다보았다. 나를 바라본 소녀는 내가 알아들을 수 없는 사투리로 말했다. 소녀는 열여섯 살 정도로 보였다.

"동생?" 내가 다른 소녀를 가리키며 물었다.

소녀는 고개를 끄덕이고 미소를 지었다.

"그래." 나는 말하고 소녀의 무릎을 톡톡 두드렸다. 나는 내가 소녀를 건드렸을 때 그녀가 경직되는 것을 느꼈다. 소녀의 동생은 한번 올려다보지도 않았다. 동생은 한 살쯤 어려 보이는 듯했다. 아이모는 자신의 손을 언니인 소녀의 넓적다리에 올려놓았고 그녀는 그 손을 다시 치워 버렸다. 아이모는 웃었다.

"좋은 사람." 아이모가 자신을 가리켰다. "좋은 사람." 아이모는 나를 가리켰다. "걱정 마." p.205 소녀는 화가 나서 아이모를 바라보았다. 두 소녀는 야생조류 같았다.

"이 아이는 저를 좋아하지도 않으면서 왜 저와 함께 차에 탄 것일까요?" 아이모가 물었다. "제가 이 아이들에게 몸짓을 하자마자 바로 차에 올라탔거든요." 아이모는 언니인 소녀에게 몸을 돌렸다. "걱정하지 마." 아이모가 말했다. "우리는 너희를 건드리지 않을 거야." 소녀의 눈은 몹시 겁에 질려 아이모를 쳐다보았다. 소녀는 숄을 더 단단히 끌어당겼다. "차는 완전히 꽉 찼어." 아이모가 말했다. "우리는 너희를 건드리지 않을 거야." 소녀의 입술이 부르르 떨리더니 눈물이 포동포동한 뺨으로 흘러내렸다. 소녀는 흐느껴 울기 시작했다.

"제가 이 아이를 겁준 것 같군요." 아이모가 말했다. "그럴 뜻은 없었는데." 아이모는 자신의 배낭에서 치즈 두 덩어리를 꺼냈다. "여기 있어." 아이모가 그 치즈를 소녀들에게 건네며 말했다. "그만 울어."

언니는 고개를 젓고 계속해서 울었으나 동생은 치즈를 가져가 먹기 시작했다. **p.206** 얼마 후 동생이 자기 언니에게 두 번째 치즈 조각을 주었고 그들은 둘 다 먹었다.

"언니는 괜찮을 거야." 아이모가 말했다.

갑자기 어떤 생각이 아이모에게 떠올랐다.

"처녀?" 아이모가 옆에 있는 소녀에게 물었다. 두 소녀는 격렬하게 끄덕였다. 언니인 소녀는 사투리로 뭐라고 말을 했다.

"괜찮아." 아이모가 말했다. "괜찮아."

내 차로 돌아오면서 나는 소녀들이 얼마나 예쁜지에 대해 생각했다. 퇴각지는 두 예쁜 처녀들에게 전혀 알맞은 장소가 아니었다. 나는 피아니가 나를 깨울 때까지 차에서 두어 시간을 더 잤다. 나는 캐서린에 관한 꿈을 꾸었다.

"다시 이동하기 시작했습니다." 피아니가 내 어깨를 살살 흔들며 말했다.

나는 내 손목시계를 보았다. 새벽 3시였다. 나는 내 포도주 병을 향해 뒷좌석으로 손을 뻗었다.

p.207 "잠꼬대를 하시더군요." 피아니가 말했다.

날이 밝기 전에 우리는 다시 정체되었고 약 한 시간 후에 우리는 다시 이동하기 시작했다. 낮 동안의 진행 속도를 보고 나는 우리가 우디네에 도착하기를 바라기라도 한다면 주도로에서 벗어나 시골을 가로질러 가야 할 것임을 알았다.

우리가 양옆에 산울타리가 쳐진 두 개의 밭 사이로 북쪽으로 이어진 작은 도로를 우연히 만났을 때, 나는 우리가 그 길을 택하는 것이 낫다고 생각하고 보넬로와 아이모에게 말해 주려고 다른 차들로 서둘러 돌아갔다.

"그 길이 아무 데로도 이어져 있지 않다면 다시 돌아오면 돼." 내가 말했다.

"이 사람들은 어떻게 할까요?" 보넬로가 물었다. 두 공병 병장들은 보넬로 옆의 좌석에 앉아 있었다. 그들은 면도를 하지 않은 상태였으나 그럼에도 불구하고 이른 아침에는 군인처럼 보였다.

p.208 "우리가 진흙탕에 빠지면 그들이 차를 미는 것을 도와줄 거야." 내가 말했다. 나는 아이모에게 돌아가 우리가 시골을 가로질러 가 볼 거라고 말해 주었다.

"다리는 어떠십니까, 중위님?"

"괜찮아. 자네는 어떤가?

"괜찮아요. 하지만 무척 배가 고파요, 중위님." 아이모가 말했다.

"저 도로 위쪽에 무언가가 있을 테니까 그곳에 차를 세우고 식사를 하세."

약간 아래쪽으로 샛길을 내려갔을 때 우리는 인적이 없는 한 농가와 마주쳤다. 나는 도로를 뒤돌아보고 그 농가가 평원보다 약간 높은 곳에 있음을 알았고, 우리는 시골 전체를 볼 수 있었다. 두 명의 병장은 집 안을 뒤졌고 그들 중 한 명은 손에 시계를 들고 나왔다.

"그것을 있던 곳에 갖다 두게." 내가 말했다. 병장은 나를 쳐다보았고 집 안으로 돌아가더니 시계 없이 돌아왔다.

p.209 "자네 동료는 어디에 있나?" 내가 물었다.

"화장실에 갔습니다." 병장은 구급차 안으로 돌아갔다. 병장은 우리가 자기를 두고 갈까 봐 두려워하는 것 같았다.

"아침 식사는요, 중위님?" 보넬로가 물었다.

"그래. 식사를 하자." 피아니와 보넬로는 집 안으로 들어갔다.

"이리 와." 아이모가 소녀들에게 말했다. 아이모는 그들이 내리도록 도와주려고 손을 내밀었다. 언니는 고개를 저었다. 그들은 병사들과 함께 인적이 없는 어떤 집으로 들어가지 않으려고 했다.

우리는 농가로 들어갔다. 농가는 크고 어두웠으며, 보넬로와 피아니는 부엌에 있었다.

"먹을 것이 많이 있지 않아요." 피아니가 말했다. p.210 "대부분을 싹 가져가 버렸어요."

보넬로는 커다란 치즈를 육중한 부엌 식탁 위에서 얇게 썰었다.

"치즈는 어디에 있었나?"

"지하실 안에요. 피아니가 약간의 포도주와 사과도 찾아냈어요."

"그거 훌륭한 아침 식사군." 내가 말했다.

두 명의 공병 병장들이 들어왔다.

"치즈 좀 드시오, 병장님들." 보넬로가 말했다.

"저희는 가야 합니다." 병장들 중 한 명이 치즈를 먹고 포도주를 마시며 말했다.

"우리는 곧 떠날 거야. 걱정 말게." 보넬로가 말했다.

"우리는 우선 먹어야 해." 내가 말했다.

"네. 하지만 시간은 귀중합니다." 다른 병장이 말했다.

"이 나쁜 녀석들은 이미 다 먹은 모양입니다." 피아니가 말했다. 병장들은 피아니를 노려보았다. 그들은 우리를 싫어했다.

p.211 "길을 아십니까?" 병장들 중 한 명이 나에게 물었다.

"아니." 내가 말했다. 그들은 서로 걱정스럽게 쳐다보았다.

"우리는 정말로 출발해야 합니다." 첫 번째 병장이 말했다.

"그럴 거야." 내가 말했다. 나는 적포도주 한 컵을 더 마셨다. 치즈와 사과와 함께 먹으니 포도주는 아주 맛이 좋았다.

"치즈를 가지고 오게." 내가 말하고 밖으로 나갔다. 보넬로가 커다란 포도주 항아리를 들고 나왔다.

"그것은 너무 커." 내가 말했다. "포도주로 수통들을 채우게."

보넬로는 수통들을 채웠고 포도주 중 일부는 마당의 포석에 넘쳐흘렀다. 그런 다음 보넬로는 항아리를 집어 들고 그것을 그냥 문 안에 두었다.

"이렇게 하면 오스트리아 놈들이 문을 때려 부수지 않고도 찾을 수 있을 거야." 보넬로가 말했다.

p.212 "가세." 내가 말했다. "피아니와 내가 선두에 서지."

두 명의 공병 병장들은 이미 보넬로 옆자리에 앉아 있었다. 소녀들은 치즈와 사과를 먹고 있었고 아이모는 담배를 피우고 있었다. 우리는 출발하여 좁은 샛길로 내려갔다.

제29장

p.213 다음날 정오쯤에 나는 우리가 우디네에서 약 10킬로미터 정도 떨어져 있다고 파악했다. 그때쯤 비는 그쳐 있었으나, 아이모의 차는 진흙탕에 빠지게 되었다. 우리의 유일한 선택권은 바퀴 앞의 흙을 파내고 그런

다음 차가 다시 앞으로 움직일 수 있을 때까지 미는 것이었다. p.214 우리는 모두 길로 내려가 차 주위에 모였다. 두 명의 공병 병장들은 바퀴를 살펴보았다. 그런 다음 말 한 마디 없이 그들은 길 아래쪽으로 떠났다. 나는 그들을 쫓아갔다.

"돌아오게." 내가 말했다. "우리를 도와 차를 꺼내게."

"우리는 가겠습니다." 한 사람이 말했다.

"돌아와서 우리를 도우라고 말했잖은가." 내가 말했다.

"우리는 가야 합니다." 다른 병장이 말했다. 그들은 서둘러 떠나려고 했다. 그들은 나를 쳐다보지도 않았다.

"돌아와서 우리를 도와 차를 꺼내라. 명령이다." 내가 말했다.

"우리는 계속 가야 합니다." 첫 번째 병장이 말했다. "중위님은 우리에게 명령을 내리실 수 없습니다. 중위님은 우리의 장교가 아니니까요."

그들은 몸을 돌려 길 아래쪽으로 향했다.

"멈춰." 내가 말했다. 그들은 진흙투성이 길 아래로 계속 이동했다. p.215 "멈추라고 명령한다." 내가 소리쳤다. 그들은 약간 더 빨리 이동했다. 나는 권총집에서 권총을 꺼내어 말을 더 많이 했던 한 사람을 겨냥하고 발사했다. 나는 빗맞혔고 그들은 달리기 시작했다. 나는 세 번을 더 쏘았고 한 사람을 쓰러뜨렸다. 다른 병장은 들판으로 도망쳤다. 나는 그를 향해 쏘았다. 권총은 비어서 딸깍 소리를 냈고 나는 다른 탄창을 장전했다. 보넬로가 나섰다.

"제가 가서 그 개자식을 끝장내겠습니다." 보넬로가 말했다. 나는 보넬로에게 권총을 건넸고 그는 공병 병장이 길에 얼굴을 박고 누워 있는 곳으로 내려갔다. 보넬로는 몸을 숙이고 권총을 그 작자의 머리에 대고 두 번 방아쇠를 당겼다. 그런 다음 그 병장의 다리를 잡고 그를 길가로 끌고 가 산울타리 옆에 뉘여 놓았다.

우리는 이후 1시간을 차를 진흙 밖으로 꺼내려고 애쓰며 보냈다. p.216 소용이 없었다.

"어떻게 하죠, 중위님?" 보넬로가 물었다.

"차를 두고 간다." 내가 말했다. "아이모의 처녀들은 어쩌지?"

"그 소녀들은 뒷자리에 태우면 돼요." 피아니가 말했다. "아무튼 멀리 갈 것은 아니니까요."

나는 구급차 뒷문을 열었다.

"안에 타." 내가 말했다. 소녀들은 안에 올라타서 구석에 앉았다. 그들은 총을 발사한 것을 알아차리지 못한 것 같았다. 나는 피아니 옆 좌석에 올라탔고 우리는 출발했다. 우리는 들판을 가로질러 반대쪽 도로로 가려고 했으나 그럴 수가 없었다. 차에게는 땅이 너무 부드럽고 질었다. 차들이 마침내 그리고 완전히 서 버렸을 때 우리는 차량들을 들판에 버리고 우디네를 향해 걷기 시작했다.

주요 간선 도로를 향해 뒤쪽으로 이어진 도로에 도착하자 나는 두 소녀에게 도로 아래쪽을 가리켰다.

p.217 "저곳으로 내려가." 내가 말했다. "저기에 사람들이 있을 거야." 나는 소녀들에게 각각 10리라짜리 지폐 한 장씩을 주었다. "저기로 가." 내가 가리키며 말했다. "친구들! 가족!"

우리는 소녀들이 우리를 걱정스럽게 뒤돌아보며 숄을 단단히 두르고 도로를 내려가는 것을 보았다. 세 명의 운전병들은 웃었다.

"제가 저 소녀들과 같이 가면 저에게 얼마를 주시겠어요, 중위님?" 보넬로가 물었다.

"오스트리아군이 저 소녀들을 잡는다면 혼자 있는 것보다 사람들과 있는 편이 나아." 내가 말했다.

우리는 우디네 쪽으로 걷기 시작했다.

"자네는 오늘 사람을 죽였어, 보넬로." 아이모가 말했다. "고해할 때 뭐라고 할 거야?"

"나는 이렇게 말할 거야. '저를 축복해 주세요, 신부님. 제가 병장을 한 명 죽였거든요.'"

p.218 우리 모두 웃었다.

"저 친구는 무정부주의자예요." 피아니가 말했다. "교회는 안 다녀요."

"자네도 무정부주의자잖아." 보넬로가 말했다.

"자네가 정말로 무정부주의자인가?" 내가 물었다.

"아니요, 중위님. 저희는 사회주의자예요. 우리는 이몰라 출신이지요, 그곳에 가본 적 있으세요?"

"아니." 내가 말했다.

"그곳은 아름다운 곳이랍니다, 중위님. 전쟁이 끝나고 그곳에 오시면 저희가 좋은 시간을 보내시도록 구경시켜 드릴게요."

"어쩌다가 사회주의자가 되었나?"

"저희는 늘 사회주의자였어요."

"이몰라로 오세요, 중위님. 저희가 중위님도 사회주의자로 만들어 드릴게요."

길이 오르막길이 되었을 때 우리는 말하는 것을 중단했다.

제30장

p.219 나중에 우리는 물 높이가 높은 강을 만났다. 강둑을 따라 축축한 진흙투성이의 땅을 제외하고는 아무것도 없었다. 우리는 둑으로 올라갔고 마침내 철교를 보았다.

p.220 "아름다운 다리로군요." 아이모가 말했다. 그것은 대개 말라 있는 강바닥인 것을 가로지르는 아무 장식도 없는 긴 철교였다.

"그들이 다리를 폭파하기 전에 서둘러 건너는 것이 좋겠어." 내가 말했다.

"다리를 폭파하려고 남아 있는 사람은 아무도 없어요." 피아니가 말했다. "모두 가 버리고 없어요."

"아마도 폭발물이 설치되어 있을 겁니다." 보넬로가 말했다.

"내가 먼저 건너지." 내가 말했다. "한 사람으로 폭파되도록 폭발물이 설치되어 있지는 않을 거야. 한 번에 한 명씩 가지."

나는 다리를 건너기 시작했다. 나는 지뢰선이나 폭약의 흔적이 있는지 철로를 보았으나 아무것도 보이지 않았다. 앞에 비에 젖은 시골을 가로질러 비 사이로 우디네가 보였다. 나는 다리를 건너 뒤를 돌아보았다. 강 바로 위에 또 하나의 다리가 있었다.

내가 지켜볼 때 차량 한 대가 그 다리를 건넜다. 다리의 양 옆은 아주 높아서 차량의 몸체는 일단 다리 위에 올라가자마자 보이지 않았다. p.221 하지만 나는 운전병과 승객들의 머리를 보았다. 그들은 모두 독일군 철모를 쓰고 있었다. 그런 다음 그 차는 다리를 건너 나무들과 길 위에 버려진 차량들 뒤로 사라졌다. 나는 다리를 건너는 아이모와 다른 사람들에게 서두르라고 손을 흔들었다. 나는 내려가서 철둑 옆에 몸을 웅크렸다. 아이모는 곧 나와 합류했다.

"독일군 차가 위쪽 다리를 건넜네."

"맙소사."

다른 사람들이 왔고 우리는 모두 철둑 뒤로 진흙 속에 몸을 웅크렸다.

"우리가 차단되었다고 생각하세요, 중위님?" 아이모가 물었다.

p.222 "확실하지는 않아."

"한잔하시죠." 피아니가 말했다. "우리가 차단당했다면 한잔하는 것이 낫겠어요." 피아니가 자신의 수통 마개를 열었다.

"보세요! 보세요!" 아이모가 도로 쪽을 가리키며 말했다. 석교 맨 위쪽을 따라 우리는 독일군 철모가 움직이는 것을 보았다. 그들이 다리를 떠날 때 우리는 그들을 보았다. 그들은 오토바이 부대였다. 막대 폭탄이 그들의 허리띠에 매달려 있었다. 그들의 철모와 회색 군복은 젖어 있었고 그들은 앞쪽과 양옆을 보며 편안하게 오토바이에 타고 있었다. 그들은 스물네 명 이상은 되었다. 머지않아 그들은 도로 위로 사라졌다.

"맙소사." 아이모가 말했다.

"그놈들은 독일 놈들이에요, 오스트리아 놈들이 아니고요." 피아니가 말했다.

"왜 여기에 저들을 저지하기 위한 사람이 없지?" 내가 말했다. "왜 그들이 다리를 폭파하지 않지? 왜 이 철둑을 따라 기관총이 배치되어 있지 않는 거야?"

p.223 나는 화가 났다. 나는 피아니의 수통에서 포도주를 한 입 가득 마셨다.

"이동하세." 내가 말했다.

우리는 얼마 동안 철로를 따라 걸었다.

"내려와! 내려와!" 아이모가 말했다. 우리는 철둑 옆으로 뛰어내렸다. 길을 따라 지나가는 또 다른 무리의 오토바이 부대가 있었다. 나는 철둑 가장자리를 살피고 그들이 지나가고 있는 것을 알았다.

"그들은 우리를 보았지만, 총을 쏘지 않았어요." 아이모가 말했다.

"그들은 우리를 원하지 않아." 내가 말했다. "그들은 다른 무언가를 쫓고 있어."

우리는 우리 길을 계속 갔다. 철로는 이제 간선 도로에서 벗어나 남쪽으로 향했으며 우리는 도로를 따라 무엇이 지나가는지 볼 수 없었다. 운하 위의 짧은 다리가 폭파되어 있었으나 우리는 남아 있는 다리로 올라가 건넜다. p.224 우리는 우리 앞에서 포격 소리를 들었다.

우리는 운하 너머의 철로에 도착했다. 철로는 들판을 가로질러 마을을 향해 곧바로 뻗어 있었다.

그때 샛길에서 우리를 향해 총알이 한 방 발사되었다.

우리는 철둑 아래쪽으로 달렸다. 운전병들은 나보다 앞에 있었다. 두 방의 총알이 더 빽빽한 덤불에서 나왔고 아이모는 철로를 건너다가 다리가 걸려 얼굴을 처박고 쓰러졌다. 우리는 반대편으로 아이모를 끌어내려 그를 뒤집어 보았다. 우리 셋은 빗속에서 아이모 주변으로 몸을 웅크렸다. 아이모는 아래쪽 목덜미를 맞았고, 탄환은 위쪽 방향으로 조준되어 오른쪽 눈 아래로 나왔다. 아이모는 거의 즉사했다. 피아니는 아이모의 머리를 내려놓고 응급 붕대 조각으로 그의 얼굴을 닦아 주었다.

"그들은 독일군이 아니었어." 내가 말했다. "그쪽에 독일군이 있을 리 없어."

p.225 "이탈리아 인들이에요!" 피아니가 말했다. 보넬로는 아무 말도 하지 않았다. 보넬로는 아이모 옆에 앉아 있었다. 피아니는 아이모의 모자를 들고 그것을 그의 얼굴 위에 놓았다.

"우리는 독일인들보다 이탈리아 인들로부터 더 위험에 빠져 있어." 내가 말했다. "후방 부대는 모든 것을 두려워하고 있는 반면에 독일군은 자기들이 추적하는 것을 정확히 알고 있지."

"이제 우리는 어떡하죠?" 피아니가 물었다.

"우리는 어두워질 때까지 누워 있는 것이 좋겠어. 우리가 남쪽에 도착할 수 있으면 모두 무사할 텐데."

우리는 철둑의 북쪽으로 내려갔다. 나는 진흙에 누워 있는 아이모를 돌아보았다. 아이모는 아주 작았고 그의 팔들은 옆구리에 붙어 있었다. 아이모는 확실히 죽은 것처럼 보였고, 나는 내가 그를 얼마나 좋아했는지 깨달았다. 내 주머니에는 아이모의 서류가 있었고, 나는 그의 가족에게 편지를 쓰기로 작정했다. p.226 들판을 가로질러 앞쪽에서 우리는 농가를 한 채 보았다. 그 집은 텅 비어 있었다. 우리는 주변을 둘러보았지만, 먹을 것을 아무것도 찾을 수 없었다.

"우리는 헛간에서 좀 자 둬야 해." 내가 말했다. "뭐 먹을 것을 좀 찾을 수 있을 것 같나, 피아니, 그리고 그곳으로 좀 가지고 오겠나?"

"해 보죠." 피아니가 말했다.

"저도 찾아볼게요." 보넬로가 말했다.

"좋아." 내가 말했다. "내가 가서 헛간을 점검하겠네."

집과 마찬가지로 헛간은 대체로 텅 비어 있었으나, 우리가 깔고 잘 충분한 건초가 있었고, 농가에서보다는 주변 전망이 더 좋았다. 피아니는 잠시 후 긴 소시지, 무언가 들어 있는 단지와 포도주 두 병을 겨드랑이에 끼고 왔다.

"보넬로는 어디 있나?" 내가 물었다.

"보넬로는 떠났습니다, 중위님." 피아니가 말했다. "전쟁 포로가 되기로 작정했어요."

p.227 나는 아무 말도 하지 않았다.

"우리가 죽게 될까 봐 두려워했어요."

나는 아무 말도 하지 않았다.

"우리는 어쨌든 전쟁의 가치에 믿음이 없습니다, 중위님."

"왜 보넬로와 함께 가지 않았나?" 내가 물었다.

"저는 중위님을 떠나고 싶지 않았습니다."

"보넬로는 어디로 갔나?"

"모릅니다, 중위님. 그냥 떠났어요."

"알았네." 내가 말했다. "먹지."

우리는 건초에 앉아 소시지를 먹고 포도주를 마셨다.

"자네는 이 창문으로 밖을 내다보게, 피아니." 내가 말했다. "나는 저 창문으로 가서 내다보겠네."

나는 어두워질 때까지 내가 있는 창문 밖을 지켜보았다. 나는 피아니에게 건너가서 그를 깨웠다.

"어두워지면 이동하세." 내가 말했고, 우리는 출발했다.

p.228 그날 밤에는 아무 일도 일어나지 않았고, 새벽 5시쯤에 우리는 우리가 차량과 부대로 붐비는 어느 도로 옆을 따라 걷고 있는 것을 알았다. 갑자기 나는 아이모가 죽지 않았다면 후퇴가 전혀 위험하게 느껴지지 않았을 것이라는 생각이 들었다.

"보넬로는 바보였네요." 피아니가 말했다.

"자네 말이 옳아."

"보넬로를 어떻게 하실 겁니까, 중위님?"

"모르겠네."

"보넬로를 그냥 적군에 잡힌 포로로 보고하실 수는 없나요?"

"모르겠네."

"아시다시피 전쟁이 계속된다면, 그들이 보넬로의 가족을 괴롭힐 거예요."

"전쟁은 계속되지 않을 거야." 어떤 병사가 말했다. "우리는 집으로 가는 중이야. 전쟁은 끝났어."

"모두들 집으로 가는 중이야." 또 다른 병사가 말했다.

p.229 "어서요, 중위님." 피아니가 말했다. 피아니는 그들을 따라잡고 싶어 했다.

"중위님? 누가 중위야? 장교들을 끌어내려라!"

피아니가 내 팔을 잡았다.

"중위님을 이름으로 부르는 것이 낫겠어요." 피아니가 말했다. "저들이 문제를 일으키려고 하거나 실제로 일으킬지도 몰라요. 저들이 몇몇 장교들을 총살시켰어요."

동이 트기 전에 우리는 타글리아멘토 제방에 도착했고 범람한 강을 따라 모든 차량들이 건너가는 다리로 내려갔다. 우리는 다리를 건너는 대규모의 사람들 무리에 섞여 들어갔다. 모두 조용했고, 빽빽한 사람들 무리는 아주 천천히 이동했다. 피아니는 혼잡 속에서 다소 앞에 있었다. 우리는 거의 건넌 상태였다.

다리 맨 끝에는 장교들과 이탈리아 헌병들이 양쪽에 서 있었다. p.230 우리가 그들에게 가까이 갔을 때, 나는 그들 중 한 명이 대열에서 어떤 남자를 가리키는 것을 보았다. 헌병 한 명이 그를 쫓아가서 그의 팔을 잡고 끌고 나왔다. 헌병은 그를 도로에서 끌어냈다. 우리가 더 가까이 갔을 때, 나는 그들 중 한두 명이 나를 쳐다보는 것을 보았다. 그런 다음 한 명이 나를 가리키더니 뭐라고 말했다. 나는 헌병 한 명이 내 쪽으로 오는 것을 보았고, 그가 내 옷깃을 잡는 것을 느꼈다.

"나한테 무슨 문제가 있소?" 나는 말하고 헌병의 얼굴을 쳤다. 곧 나는 대여섯 명의 헌병들에게 진압되었다.

"무슨 일이 벌어지고 있는 것이오?" 내가 물었다.

"다른 놈들과 함께 이 자를 뒤로 데려가." 첫 번째 장교가 말했다. "이 자는 억양이 다른 이탈리아 어를 한다."

"네 놈도 마찬가지다, 이 멍청한 자식아." 내가 말했다.

그들은 나를 강둑 옆 들판에 난 도로 아래쪽에 있는 장교들의 열 뒤로 데려갔다. 우리가 그들을 향해 다가갔을 때, 총알이 발사되었다. p.231 네 명의 장교들이 함께 서 있었는데, 그들 앞에는 한 남자가 양옆에 헌병을 한 명씩 끼고 있었다. 다른 네 명의 헌병들은 라이플총에 기대어 심문하는 장교들 근처에 서 있었다. 나는 그 장교들이 심문하고 있는 남자를 보았다. 그는 내가 그들이 다리에서 끌고 가는 것을 보았던 그 중령이었다.

"소속 사단은?"

그가 대답했다.

"연대는?"

그가 대답했다.

"왜 당신 연대와 함께 있지 않나?"

그가 대답했다.

"장교는 자기 소속 부대와 함께 있어야 한다는 것을 모르시오?"

그는 안다고 했다.

p.232 "야만인들이 신성한 조국의 땅을 밟게 허용한 것은 당신 같은 사람들이오."

"당신은 전에 후퇴한 적이 없소?" 중령이 물었다.

"이탈리아군은 절대로 후퇴해서는 안 됐소."

우리는 빗속에서 그 자리에 서서 귀를 기울였다.

"나를 쏠 거면 더 이상 심문은 하지 말고 당장 쏴 주시오." 중령이 말했다. "심문이 한심하오." 중령이 성호를 그었다. 장교들은 서로 이야기했다. 한 사람이 종이 위에 무언가를 적었다.

"부대 이탈 죄로 사형에 처한다." 그가 말했다.

두 명의 헌병이 중령을 강둑으로 데려가서 그의 머리를 쏘았다. 헌병들 중 몇 명은 새로 온 사람들을 쳐다보고 있었다. 다른 헌병들은 죽은 중령을 쳐다보고 있었다. 나는 머리를 확 숙이고 두 사람 사이를 밀치고 강을 향해 달렸다. p.233 나는 텀벙 하는 소리를 내고 뛰어들었다. 물은 몹시 차가웠으나 가능한 한 물속에 있었다. 위로 떠오른 순간, 나는 숨을 들이쉬고 다시 잠수했다. 옷을 많이 껴입고 군화를 신은 채 물에 잠겨 있기는 쉬웠다.

두 번째로 솟아올랐을 때, 나는 내 앞에 있는 나무토막을 보고 그것으로 손을 뻗어 한 손으로 잡았다. 나는 그 뒤에 머리를 감추고 그 너머를 쳐다볼 엄두는 내지도 못했다. 나는 달리고 있을 때와 처음으로 공기를 마시러 나왔을 때 총성을 들었다. 몇 분 후 더 이상 총성을 듣지는 못했다. 나무토막은 물살에 흔들렸고 이제 나는 그것을 양손으로 잡았다. 나는 아주 빠르게 이동하고 있었고, 나무토막을 붙잡고 그것에 내 몸을 맡겼다.

제31장

p.234 차가운 물속에서 고통스러운 시간을 오래 보낸 후에, 나는 마침내 용케 강둑으로 나오는 데 성공했다. 주위에 아무도 없는 것을 확인한 후, 나는 도랑의 둑을 따라 나 있는 덤불 옆에 앉아 군화를 벗고 물을 쏟아냈다. 나는 외투를 벗고, 안쪽 주머니에서 모두 젖어 버린 서류와 돈이 들어 있는 지갑을 꺼내고 그런 다음 외투를 쥐어짰다. p.235 나는 바지를 벗어 그것도 짰고, 그런 다음 셔츠와 속옷도 벗어서 짰다. 나는 몸을 문질러 닦아내고 나서 다시 옷을 입었다.

외투를 다시 입기 전에, 나는 소매에서 중위 계급장을 오려 내어 그것들을 돈과 함께 주머니 안에 넣었다. 나는 3천 리라가 조금 넘는 돈을 가지고 있었다. 그들이 내 권총을 가지고 갔으므로 나는 내 권총집을 외투 속에 찼다. 비가 내리면서 날씨는 추워졌다. 나는 도로로 나왔다. 앞쪽에서 나는 몇몇 부대가 도로를 내려오는 것을 보았다. 나는 길 한쪽을 따라 절뚝거리며 걸었고 그들은 나를 주목하지 않았다. 나는 계속해서 도로를 내려갔다.

나는 그날 베네치아 평원을 횡단했다. p.236 그 평원은 대개 구릉 없이 평평한 시골이었고, 내가 바다에 가까이 갈수록 도로의 수는 점점 줄어들었다. 철로와 우연히 마주쳤을 때 나는 기차가 지나가기를 기다렸다. 몇 시간 후 기차가 왔다. 기차는 아주 길고 엔진은 기차를 아주 천천히 가게 했으므로 나는 내가 기차에 올라탈 수 있을 거라고 확신했다. 나는 기차가 지나가는 것을 조심스럽게 지켜보았고 그런 다음 캔버스 천으로 덮인 낮은 무개화차 한 량이 다가오는 것을 보았다. 나는 뛰어올라 뒤쪽에 있는 후방 손잡이를 잡아당겼다.

나는 캔버스 천이 얼마나 단단히 묶여 있는지 쳐다보았다. 그것은 가장자리 아래쪽이 밧줄로 묶여 있었다. 나는 칼을 꺼냈고, 밧줄을 잘라 내 팔 아래에 끼웠다. 빗속에서 단단히 묶여 있는 캔버스 천 아래에는 딱딱한 불룩한 짐이 있었다. 나는 앞을 올려다보았다. 앞에 있는 화물 차량에는 경비병이 있었으나 그는 앞을 바라보고 있었다. 나는 캔버스 천 아래로 몸을 숙였다. 내 이마는 무언가에 아주 세게 부딪혔고, 나는 얼굴에 흐르는 피를 느꼈으나 안으로 기어가서 납작하게 누웠다. p.237 그런 다음 몸을 돌려 캔버스 천을 도로 아래쪽으로 묶었다.

나는 내가 대포들이 있는 캔버스 천 아래에 있다는 것을 깨달았다. 대포들은 깨끗하게 기름이 칠해진 냄새가 났다. 나는 누워서 캔버스 천 위로 떨어지는 빗소리와 철로 위를 달리는 차량의 덜컹거리는 소리에 귀를 기울였다. 작은 불빛이 들어왔고, 나는 누워서 대포들을 바라보았다. 이마의 혹은 부어올랐고, 나는 가만히 누워 피가 응고되게 한 다음 베인 곳을 제외하고 말라붙은 피를 떼어냈다.

나는 손수건이 없었으므로 손가락으로 더듬어 말라붙은 피가 있던 곳을 캔버스 천에서 똑똑 떨어진 빗물로 씻어 냈다. 그런 다음 내 외투의 소매로 핏자국을 말끔히 닦았다. 나는 수상쩍어 보이고 싶지 않았다. p.238 나는 대포들이 필시 메스트레로 갈 것이라는 것과 그들이 이 대포들을 관리할 것이기 때문에 그들이 그곳에 도착하기 전에 빠져나가야 할 것임을 알고 있었다. 그들에게는 잃어버릴 대포가 없었다. 나는 몹시 배가 고팠다.

제32장

p.239 나는 몸이 비에 젖고 춥고 배가 고팠다. 나는 돌아누워 팔베개를 하고 엎드려 누웠다. 나의 무릎은 뻣뻣했으나 어떤 식으로든 나를 방해하지는 않았다. 발렌티니 박사가 대단히 자기 일을 잘한 것이었다. 나는 캐서린에 대해 생각했으나 내가 그녀를 만날 수 있을지 아직 확신하지도 못하는 때에 그녀에 대해 생각한다면 정신을 놓게 될 것임을 알고 있었다. p.240 나는 캐서린에 대해 생각하지 않거나 조금만 생각하려고 애썼다.

나는 차량들과 내가 잃은 부하들을 생각했다. 나는 최선을 다했으나 그들 모두를 잃었다. 그리고 이탈리아 헌병들은 나를 죽이려고 했다. 나는 더 이상 군대에 의무감이 느껴지지 않기 시작했다. 하지만 화가 나지는 않았다. 나는 이탈리아군에 반감은 없었다. 나는 세상의 모든 행운을 그들에게 빌어 주었다. 하지만 그것은 이제 더 이상 나의 공연은 아니었고, 단지 이 지긋지긋한 기차가 메스트레에 도착하고 나는 식사를 하고 생각하는 것을 중단하게 되기를 바랄 뿐이었다.

피아니는 그들에게 내가 총살당했다고 말할 것이었다. 그들은 자기들이 쏜 사람들의 주머니를 뒤져서 서류들을 가져갔다. 그들은 내 서류들을 갖지 못했으므로 나를 익사한 것으로 공식 기록을 만들지도 몰랐다. 나는 미국에서는 어떤 소식을 들을지 궁금했다. 나는 아주 배가 고팠다. 나는 신부님이 어떻게 되었는지 궁금했다. **p.241** 그리고 리날디도. 그리고 소령도. 글쎄, 나는 이제 그들을 보지 못할 것이었다. 그들 중 누구도 다시 보지 못할 것이었다. 내 인생의 그 부분은 끝났다. 나는 리날디가 걱정되었다. 어쨌든 시간 맞추어 약만 먹는다면 그것은 심각한 질병은 아니라고들 했다. 하지만 리날디는 걱정할 터였다.

나는 생각하고 싶지 않았다. 나는 식사를 하고 싶었다. 나는 캐서린과 함께 먹고 마시고 자고 싶었다. 어쩌면 오늘 밤에라도. 아니다. 그것은 불가능했다. 하지만 내일 밤 우리는 근사한 식사와 시트를 나누어 쓰고 함께가 아니면 절대 다시 떠나지 않을 것이다. 우리는 꽤 빨리 이동해야 할 것이다. 캐서린은 나와 함께 갈 것이었다. 나는 캐서린이 갈 것임을 알았다. 우리는 언제 갈 것인가? 그리고 어디로? 그것은 생각해 볼 일이었다. 날이 어두워지고 있었다. 나는 누워서 우리가 갈 수 있는 곳들을 생각해 보았다. 아주 많은 장소들이 있었다.

제33장

p.242 밀라노에서 나는 미군 병원의 수위한테서 캐서린이 헬렌 퍼거슨과 함께 스트레사 마을로 떠났다고 들었다. 나는 수위에게 내 방문을 비밀로 지켜 달라고 부탁하고 마차를 탔다. 나는 마부에게 내가 아는 사람들 중 한 사람인 성악을 공부하고 있던 시몬즈의 주소를 주었다.

p.243 시몬즈는 포르타 마젠타 방향의 마을에서 멀리 떨어진 곳에 살았다. 내가 그를 만나러 갔을 때 시몬즈는 여전히 잠을 자고 있었다.

"자네는 몹시 빨리 일어나는군, 헨리." 시몬즈가 침대에 일어나 앉아 담배에 불을 붙이며 말했다.

"도움이 필요하네, 심." 내가 말했다. "내가 어떻게 해야 스위스로 건너갈 수 있는지 아나?"

"이탈리아 인들은 자네를 이탈리아 밖으로 내보내 주지 않을 거야."

"알아. 하지만 스위스는 어떤가? 그들은 어떻게 할까?"

"아무 짓도 안 하겠지. 자네는 스위스에서 어디로든 갈 수 있어. 나는 자네가 어디로 갈 것인지 당국에 그냥 말해야 할 것이라고 생각하네. 왜지? 헌병을 피해 도망 중인가?"

"아직은 아니야."

"이봐 헨리. 내가 어떻게 해 주기를 바라나?"

p.244 "자네는 나랑 몸집이 비슷해. 나가서 민간인 옷을 좀 사다 주겠나? 나도 옷은 있지만 그것들이 전부 로마에 있어서 말이야."

"로마는 불결한 곳이지. 그곳에서 무엇을 하고 있었나?"

"건축을 공부하고 있었다네."

"옷을 살 필요는 없네. 자네가 원하는 옷은 전부 자네한테 주지. 옷방으로 들어가게. 원하는 옷을 다 가져가. 자네 어디로 가려고?"

"먼저 스트레사에 가야 하네."

"이상적이군. 스트레사에서 그냥 배를 저어 스위스로 가면 되네."

나는 창밖을 내다보았다.

"내려가서 마차를 보내겠네." 내가 말했다.

"도로 올라오면 나와 아침 식사를 하세."

나는 내려가서 마부에게 돈을 지불했다.

제34장

p.245 민간인 옷을 입으니 나는 가면무도회 의상을 입고 있는 듯한 느낌이 들었다. 하지만 스트레사로 가는 기차에 올라타자마자 나는 신경 쓰지 않았다. 단지 캐서린이 보고 싶을 뿐이었다.

내가 그들이 있는 호텔에 도착했을 때 캐서린과 헬렌 퍼거슨은 저녁 식사를 하고 있었다. p.246 퍼거슨이 말을 하고 있었지만 내가 들어갔을 때 그녀는 말을 멈추었다.

"세상에." 퍼거슨이 말했다.

"안녕." 내가 말했다.

"당신이군요!" 캐서린이 말했다. 캐서린은 매우 기뻐하는 것 같았다. 나는 캐서린에게 키스를 하고 식탁에 앉았다.

퍼거슨은 나를 보게 되어 아주 기쁜 것 같지는 않았다.

"저를 보게 되어 반갑지 않으신가요?" 내가 미소를 지으며 퍼거슨에게 물었다.

"네, 기쁘지 않아요. 중위님은 여름 내내 연애를 하고 이 아가씨를 임신시키더니 살짝 떠났어요. 그리고 이제 중위님이 또 살짝 떠날 것 같아요."

나는 캐서린에게 미소를 지었고 그녀도 나에게 미소를 지었다.

"우리는 함께 슬쩍 떠날 거야." 캐서린이 말했다.

"두 사람 다 똑같아." 퍼거슨이 말했다. "네가 창피하다, 캐서린 바클리. p.247 너는 수치도 모르고 명예도 모르고 저 사람처럼 엉큼해."

"그만해, 퍼기." 캐서린이 말하고 그녀의 손을 토닥였다. "우리가 서로를 좋아하는 것을 알면서."

캐서린은 용케 헬렌 퍼거슨을 진정시켰고, 우리 셋은 함께 저녁 식사를 했다.

그날 밤 호텔에서 나는 마침내 내가 집에 있고 혼자가 아니라고 느꼈다. 나는 캐서린을 안고 그녀의 가슴이 뛰는 것을 느끼면서 내가 한 사람의 일부라고 느꼈다. 나는 나의 군 생활이 끝났으며, 그녀와 함께 떠나고 싶다고 말했다.

나는 그날 아침에 내가 일어났던 때가 기억난다. 캐서린은 자고 있었고 햇살이 창문을 통해 안으로 들어오고 있었다. 나는 창문으로 다가갔다. p.248 아래쪽으로는 정원이 있었는데, 지금은 아무것도 없었지만, 아름답게 정돈되어 있었고, 자갈길, 나무들, 연못 옆의 돌담과 저 너머 산을 등지고 햇빛을 받고 있는 호수가 있었다. 나는 창밖을 내다보며 서 있었고 돌아봤을 때는 캐서린이 일어나 나를 바라보는 것이 보였다.

"내가 범죄자인 것 같아요." 내가 말했다. "나는 탈영했어요."

"내 사랑, 어리석게 굴지 마요. 그냥 이탈리아군대일 뿐이잖아요."

나는 웃었다.

"당신은 훌륭한 여자예요." 내가 말했다.

"그리고 당신은 훌륭한 남자가 되어 우리가 어서 스위스로 갈 방도를 찾을 거예요."

제35장

p.249 캐서린은 퍼거슨을 보러 갔고 나는 바에 앉아 신문을 읽었다.

"그레피 백작이 손님에 관해 물어보고 계셨어요." 바텐더인 에밀리오가 말했다.

"누구?"

p.250 "그레피 백작님이요. 손님이 간밤에 이곳에 오셨을 때 여기 계시던 연세가 좀 많으신 분을 기억하십니까?

"그분이 여기 계신가?"

"네, 질녀분과 함께 여기 계십니다. 손님이 여기 계시다고 제가 그분께 말씀드렸어요. 백작님은 손님과 당구를 치고 싶어 하십니다."

"백작님이 어디 계신가?"

"산책 나가셨습니다."

"당구 실력은 어떠신가?"

"훌륭하십니다. 백작님은 대부분의 사람들을 이기시지요. 손님이 여기 계시다고 말씀드렸을 때 백작님은 무척 기뻐하셨습니다. 당구를 같이 칠 사람이 아무도 없거든요."

그레피 백작은 아흔네 살이었다. 백작은 백발에 콧수염을 기르고 훌륭한 예의범절을 지닌 노인이었다. 백작은 오스트리아와 이탈리아 양국의 외교관을 지냈으며 그의 생일잔치는 밀라노의 큰 사교행사였다.

나는 캐서린과 헬렌 퍼거슨과 함께 저녁 식사를 하기 전에 죽여야 할 시간이 있었으므로 함께 낚시를 가자고 에밀리오를 초대했다. p.251 그 후에 나는 캐서린과 퍼거슨과 함께 간단한 저녁 식사를 했고 그레피 백작을 만나러 갔다.

나는 당구장에서 백작을 발견했다. 나를 보았을 때 백작의 얼굴은 환해졌고 그는 손을 내밀었다.

"당신이 이곳에 계셔서 참으로 기쁘군요." 백작이 말했다. "저와 게임을 해 주러 오시다니 참 친절하십니다."

"저를 불러 주셔서 대단히 감사합니다."

"건강은 어떠십니까?"

"저는 아주 좋습니다. 백작님은요?"

"항상 좋지요. 하지만 늙어가고 있어요. 이제 나이의 신호가 파악됩니다."

"그럴 리가요."

우리는 샴페인 병을 따고 당구를 쳤다. 백작은 전쟁에 관해 이야기하고 싶어 했지만, 나는 상세한 대답을 해 주지 않았다.

p.252 몇 게임 치고 나서 우리는 푹신한 가죽 의자에 앉았고, 얼음 통 속에 담긴 샴페인과 술잔이 우리 사이의 탁자 위에 있었다.

"당신은 인생에서 가장 귀중한 것이 무엇인가요?" 백작이 나에게 물었다.

"제가 사랑하는 사람입니다."

"저도 그렇습니다. 왜냐하면 그 아이가 내가 가진 전부니까요. 그리고 생일잔치를 하기 위해서도요." 백작이 웃었다. "당신이 나보다 더 현명하군요. 당신은 생일잔치를 하지는 않잖아요."

우리는 둘 다 샴페인을 마셨다.

"좀 더 마실까요?" 백작이 물었다.

"제 애인에게 돌아가야 합니다."

"정말 한잔 더 안 하시겠어요?"

"네."

백작은 일어섰다.

"아주 건강하고 아주 행복하시기를 빕니다."

p.253 "고맙습니다. 오래오래 사시기 바랍니다."

"고맙습니다. 그리고 명심하세요. 사랑이란 종교적인 감정이라는 것을요. 그것을 잊지 마세요."

제36장

p.254 그날 밤 나는 폭풍우 소리에 잠에서 깨었다. 그런 다음 누군가가 문을 두드리는 소리를 들었다. 나는 캐서린을 방해하지 않으려고 아주 조용히 문으로 가서 문을 열었다. 에밀리오였다. 에밀리오는 외투를 입고 젖은 모자를 들고 있었다.

"무슨 일인가, 에밀리오? 자네 곤란한 일이 생겼나?"

p.255 "아니요. 중위님이 그래요, 중위님. 그들이 아침에 중위님을 체포하러 올 거예요."

"정말인가?"

"네. 이제 어떻게 하실 거예요? 두려워할 것이 아무것도 없다면 체포는 별것도 아니에요. 하지만 전시에 체포되는 것이 늘 좋은 법만은 아니지요."

"나는 체포되고 싶지 않아."

"그러면 스위스로 가셔야 해요."

"어떻게?"

"제 보트를 타고요."

"하지만 밖에 폭풍우가 부는데." 내가 말했다.

"폭풍우는 거의 끝났어요. 폭풍우는 심하지만, 중위님은 괜찮으실 거예요. 하지만 지금 당장 가셔야 해요, 짐을 꾸리고 부인에게 옷을 입히세요.

제가 나머지 짐을 챙겨 드릴게요."

에밀리오는 가방들을 가져갔고 자기 보트가 있는 부두에서 만나자고 우리에게 말했다. p.256 내가 우산을 들어 캐서린에게 씌워 주며 우리는 그곳으로 갔다. 우리가 그곳에 도착했을 때, 호수는 바위에 면하여 거무스름했다. 에밀리오는 늘어선 나무들 옆에서 나왔다.

"중위님의 가방은 보트 안에 있습니다." 에밀리오가 말했다.

"보트 값은 치르고 싶네." 내가 말했다.

"얼마나 가지고 계십니까?"

"그리 많지는 않네."

"그러면 돈은 나중에 주세요. 괜찮습니다."

"얼마나?"

"주고 싶으신 만큼이요."

"얼마인지 말해 주게."

"500프랑만 보내 주세요."

"알겠네."

"여기 샌드위치가 조금 있습니다." 에밀리오가 나에게 꾸러미를 건넸다. "그리고 브랜디 한 병과 포도주 한 병이 있어요." 나는 그것들을 내 가방에 넣었다. "어디로 가는지 아세요?"

p.257 "호수 상류로."

"그러면 얼마나 먼지도 아세요?"

"루이노를 지나야지."

"루이노, 카네로, 카노비오, 트란자노를 지나세요. 브리사고에 도달해야 비로소 스위스에 계시는 겁니다. 몬테 타마라를 지나가셔야 해요. 멈추지 않으면 아침 7시에는 그곳에 도착하실 겁니다."

"그렇게 먼가?"

"35킬로미터예요."

나는 보트에 올라타고 캐서린이 타는 것을 도와주었다.

"호텔비는 남겨두셨어요?" 에밀리오가 물었다.

"그래. 방 안에 있는 흰 봉투 안에 있네."

"알겠습니다. 행운을 빕니다, 중위님."

"행운을 비네. 전부 다 고맙네."

에밀리오가 몸을 숙여 우리 배를 밀어 주었다.

제37장

p.258 우리가 스위스에 도착했을 때, 우리는 둘 다 완전히 기진맥진했다. 우리는 에밀리오가 우리에게 준 것은 전부 먹고 마셨지만, 두 사람 다 몹시 배가 고팠다. 우리는 호수 안으로 배를 끌고 들어갔고, 나는 우리가 스위스에 있다고 확신했다. 나는 이제 호수에서 아주 가까이 나 있는 도로를 보았고, 도로에 있는 카페에서 병사 한 명이 나오고 있는 것을 보았다. p.259 그는 회색과 녹색으로 된 군복을 입고 독일군처럼 철모를 쓰고 있었다. 그가 우리를 보았다.

"병사에게 손을 흔들어 봐요." 내가 캐서린에게 말했다. 캐서린은 손을 흔들었고 병사는 미소를 짓고 손을 흔들어 주었다. 나는 노 젓는 속도를 줄였다. 우리는 마을의 선창가를 지나가고 있었다.

"우리가 브리사고에 있는 것 같아요." 내가 말했다.

"그러면 상륙해서 아침을 먹을까요?"

"그럽시다."

우리는 보트를 어느 덤불에 숨기고 가방은 보트에 두었다. 우리는 육지로 발을 디뎠고 함께 스위스에 있었다.

"참 아름다운 나라예요." 캐서린이 말했다.

"아름답지 않소?"

"가서 아침 먹어요!"

우리는 병사가 나온 카페 안으로 들어가서 깨끗한 나무 탁자에 앉았다. p.260 우리는 몹시 흥분해 있었다. 훌륭한 달걀 토스트로 아침 식사를 하고 나서 곧이어 우리는 보트로 돌아왔다. 어떤 병사가 보트 옆에 서 있었다.

"이것은 당신들의 보트인가요?" 그가 물었다.

"네."

"어디에서 오셨습니까?"

"호수 상류에서요."

"저와 동행해 주실 것을 요청해야 하겠군요."

"가방은 어떡하고요?"

"가지고 오십시오."

우리는 세관으로 끌려갔고 그곳에서는 아주 마르고 군인다운 중위 한 명이 우리를 심문했다.

"당신들의 국적은 어떻게 되오?"

"미국인과 영국인입니다."

"여권을 보여주시오."

우리는 중위에게 여권을 보여 주었다. 중위는 그것들을 오랫동안 조사했다.

"왜 보트를 타고 이 길로 스위스에 온 것이오?"

p.261 "나는 운동선수입니다." 내가 말했다. "노 젓는 것은 특히 내가 좋아하는 것입니다. 기회가 있을 때마다 나는 노를 젓습니다."

"왜 이곳에 왔소?"

"겨울 스포츠를 위해서입니다."

"이곳은 겨울 스포츠를 위한 곳이 아니오."

"압니다. 저는 겨울 스포츠를 할 수 있는 곳으로 가고 싶어요."

"이탈리아에서는 무엇을 했소?"

"건축을 공부했습니다. 하지만 전쟁이 터져서 더 이상 공부할 수 없었지요."

"당신들을 로카르노로 보내야 할 것 같소." 중위가 말했다. "마차를 잡을 수 있고 병사 한 명이 동행할 것이오."

"알겠습니다." 내가 말했다. "보트는 어떻게 되죠?"

"그것은 몰수될 것이오. 돈은 얼마나 있소?"

p.262 "2천 5백 리라요."

중위는 아주 깊은 인상을 받았다. "당신은요, 부인?"

캐서린은 천 리라가 약간 넘는 돈을 가지고 있었다. 중위는 기분이 좋았다. 우리에 대한 중위의 태도는 호의적으로 바뀌었다.

"만약 겨울 스포츠를 위해 이곳에 오셨다면, 벵겐이 적당한 장소요." 중위가 말했다. "우리 아버지가 벵겐에 호텔을 가지고 있소. 그곳으로 가셔야 하오."

"잘됐군요." 내가 말했다. "성함을 말씀해 주시겠어요?"

"내가 카드에 자세한 사항을 적어 드리겠소." 중위가 아주 정중하게 나에게 카드를 내밀었다.

"그 병사가 당신들을 로카르노까지 데려다 줄 것이오. 로카르노에서는 당신들에게 비자나 경찰 허가증을 줄 것이 확실하오."

중위의 말이 맞았다. 로카르노에서 우리에게는 임시 비자가 주어졌다. 그것은 우리가 여권과 쓸 돈을 소지하는 것을 도와주었다. 그러나 비자는 언제든 철회될 수 있었으며, 우리는 어디를 가든 경찰에 보고를 하기로 되어 있었다.

p.263 비자를 얻은 후 우리는 근사한 호텔을 발견하고 투숙 절차를 밟았다. 우리는 기진맥진했으나 둘 다 스위스에 무사히 도착한 것에 몹시 기뻐했다.

제38장

p.264 그해 가을이 아주 깊어가도록 눈은 오지 않았다. 우리는 산의 경사면 쪽 소나무 숲에 있는 갈색 통나무집에서 살았고, 밤에는 서리가 내려서 아침이면 화장대 위에 둔 두 개의 물 주전자에 있는 물 위로 얇은 얼음이 끼었다. 구팅겐 부인이 이른 아침에 방으로 들어와 창문을 닫고 높이가 높은 난로에 불을 지폈다.

p.265 소나무 장작은 우지끈 소리를 내고 불꽃을 튀겼으며 그런 다음에는 불꽃이 난로 안에서 으르렁거렸다. 구팅겐 부인이 두 번째로 방으로 들어왔을 때, 그녀는 불을 지피기 위한 커다란 장작들과 뜨거운 물이 담긴 물 주전자를 가지고 왔다. 일단 방이 따뜻해지자 구팅겐 부인은 아침 식사를 가지고 왔다. 침대에 앉아 아침 식사를 하면서, 우리는 호수 건너 프랑스 쪽에 있는 산들을 볼 수 있었다. 산꼭대기에는 눈이 쌓여 있었다.

바깥의 농가 앞에는 산 위로 도로 하나가 나 있었다. 바퀴 자국과 산마루가 서리로 얼어붙어 단단했고 도로는 숲을 지나 초원이 있는 산 위로 완만하게 올라갔다. p.266 숲 가장자리의 초원에 있는 헛간과 오두막들은 계곡 너머로 보였다. 계곡 밑바닥에는 호수로 흘러가는 시내가 하나 있었다. 계곡을 가로질러 바람이 불면, 바위들 사이로 흐르는 시냇물 소리가 들렸다.

때때로 우리는 도로를 벗어나 소나무 숲을 지나가는 오솔길로 트레킹을 했다. 숲 바닥은 부드러웠는데, 서리가 도로처럼 길을 단단하게 만들지 않았기 때문이었다. 우리는 또한 도로가 딱딱하게 굳은 것은 신경 쓰지 않았는데, 신발 바닥과 뒤꿈치에 징이 박혀 있기 때문이었다. 하지만 그것이 숲에서 걷는 것처럼 기분 좋지는 않았다.

집 앞에서는 산이 호수를 따라 있는 작은 평원 쪽으로 가파르게 뻗어 내려갔다. 우리는 햇살을 받으며 집의 현관에 앉아 산허리로 뻗어 내린 구불구불한 길을 보았다. 낮은 산의 측면에 있는 계단식으로 된 포도밭의 포도나무는 이제는 모두 죽어 있었다. p.267 호수에는 두 그루의 나무가 있는 섬이 하나 있었고, 그 나무들은 보트의 돛처럼 보였다.

산은 험준하고 호수의 반대편은 경사가 급했다. 호수 끝 아랫자락에는 로네 계곡의 평원이 있었는데 이곳은 두 산맥 사이에 평평한 곳이었다. 계곡 위쪽 산맥이 잘라낸 곳은 당 뒤 미디였다. 그것은 높은 눈 덮인 산이었으나 너무 멀리 있어서 그림자를 드리우지는 못했다.

우리는 아주 햇빛이 잘 들 때에만 현관에서 아침 식사를 먹었다. 나머지 시간에는 소박한 목재 벽과 구석에 큰 난로가 있는 위층의 작은 방에서 먹었다. p.268 우리는 마을에서 책과 잡지들을 구입했다. 난로가 있는 작은 방은 우리의 거실이었다. 우리는 두 개의 안락의자와 책과 잡지들을 놓아둘 탁자를 가지고 있었고, 응접실 탁자에서 카드놀이를 했다.

구팅겐 부부는 아래층에 살았고, 때때로 우리는 그들이 저녁에 이야기하는 것을 들었는데 그들 역시 함께 아주 행복해했다. 구팅겐 씨는 급사장이었고 구팅겐 부인은 같은 호텔에서 급사로 일했었다. 그들은 이 집을 사려고 함께 돈을 저축했다. 그들에게는 역시 취리히에 있는 호텔에서 급사장이 되려고 공부하고 있는 아들이 하나 있었다. 아래층에는 그들이 포도주와 맥주를 파는 가게가 있었고, 때때로 저녁에 우리는 밖에서 길에 마차가 서고 사람들이 포도주를 마시러 가게로 들어오려고 계단을 밟고 올라오는 소리를 듣곤 했다.

p.269 어느 날 나는 캐서린에게 우리가 결혼을 해야 한다고 제안했다.

"싫어요." 캐서린이 말했다. "나는 지금 당장은 너무 못났어요. 일단 내가 아기를 낳고 체중이 좀 빠지면 결혼해요."

크리스마스를 단 사흘 앞두었을 때에야 비로소 눈이 왔다. 어느 날 우리가 아침에 일어났더니 모든 것이 하얬다.

"스키를 탈 수 있으면 좋을 텐데." 캐서린이 말했다.

"나도 스키 못 타요." 내가 말했다. "일단 당신이 아기를 낳으면 함께 배웁시다."

"하지만 당신은 지금도 배울 수 있어요."

"당신이 나와 같이 배울 수 있을 때까지 기다리고 싶어요."

"하지만 할 일이 아무것도 없어서 지루하지 않아요?"

"아니. 나는 당신과 함께 있는 것이 좋아요. 나는 스위스에서의 생활을 즐기고 있어요. 당신은 안 그래요?"

"나도 즐거운 생활을 하고 있다고 생각해요. 하지만 이제 내가 몸집이 커져서 당신을 지루하게 할까 봐 두려웠어요."

p.270 "오, 내가 얼마나 당신에게 미쳐 있는지 당신이 알면 좋을 텐데."

"알아요. 하지만 나는 당신이 때로는 불안해한다고 생각했어요."

"때로는 그렇지. 왜냐하면 전선과 내가 아는 사람들이 궁금하니까."

"무엇이 궁금해요?"

"리날디와 신부님과 다른 사람들에 관해서. 하지만 전쟁에 관해 생각하고 싶지 않아서 그들을 많이 생각하지는 않아."

"내가 당신을 처음 만났을 때 나는 정신 나간 어린 여자였어요. 하지만 지금은 제정신이에요. 나는 그냥 아주아주 행복해요."

"자러 갑시다, 내 사랑." 내가 말했다.

"좋아요. 정확히 같은 시간에 자러 가요."

"그래요."

우리는 동시에 잠이 들지 않았다. **p.271** 나는 잠이 들기 전에 이 일 저 일을 생각하고 캐서린이 자는 것을 지켜보며 오랜 시간 동안 깨어 있었다.

제39장

p.272 1월 중순에 나는 턱수염이 덥수룩하게 자랐고 겨울은 춥고 날씨가 맑은 낮과 혹독한 추운 밤으로 틀이 잡혔다.

"당신 수염이 아주 마음에 들어요." 캐서린이 말했다. "아주 뻣뻣하고 사나워 보이지만 만지면 아주 부드럽고 멋있어요."

"수염을 기른 내가 더 좋아요?"

p.273 "그런 것 같아요. 꼬마 캐서린이 태어난 후에 나는 다시 날씬해지겠죠. 내가 머리를 자르면 나는 당신에게 멋지고 새롭고 다른 아가씨가 될 거예요."

나는 아무 말도 하지 않았다.

"내가 머리를 잘라도 상관하지 않을 거죠, 그렇죠?"

"상관 안 해요. 재미있을 것 같아요."

"오, 당신은 아주 사랑스러워요. 그리고 아마도 나는 당신에게 달콤하게 보일 테고, 내 사랑, 아주 날씬하고 흥미로워져서 당신은 다시 나와 사랑에 빠질 거예요."

"참 내." 내가 말했다. "나는 이미 충분히 당신을 사랑해요. 무엇이 하고 싶어요? 나를 망치고 싶어요?"

"네. 당신을 망치고 싶어요."

"좋아요." 내가 말했다. "그것이 내가 원하는 거예요."

제40장

p.274 우리는 행복한 생활을 했다. 1월과 2월을 보내며 살았고 겨울은 아주 아름다웠으며 우리는 아주 행복했다. 그런 다음 3월, 즉 아기가 나오기 한 달 전에 우리는 병원이 있는 로잔으로 이사하기로 결정했다.

p.275 우리는 몽트뢰에서 로잔까지 기차를 탔다. 우리는 근사한 중간 크기의 호텔을 발견했다. 우리가 거리를 지나 호텔의 마차용 입구로 들어설 때는 비가 부슬부슬 내리고 있었다. 구팅겐 부부와 함께 지낸 후라 호텔의 모든 것이 호화로워 보였다. 객실의 창문들은 꼭대기에 철책이 달린 담장이 있는, 비에 젖은 정원이 내다보였다.

캐서린은 모든 불을 켜고 짐을 풀기 시작했다. 나는 위스키 한 병과 소다수를 주문하고 침대에 누워 역에서 사 온 신문을 읽었다. 1918년 3월이었고, 독일군의 공세가 프랑스에서 시작되었다.

마을은 근사했고 우리는 함께 가장 멋진 3주를 보냈다. 우리는 그 3주 동안 한 번도 안 좋은 시간을 보낸 적이 없었다. **p.276** 우리는 이제 출산이 아주 가까워졌다는 것을 알았고, 그것은 우리 둘 다 함께 있는 시간을 조금도 잃어버릴 수 없다는 느낌이 들게 했다.

제41장

p.277 캐서린이 새벽 3시 경에 진통을 겪었다.

"괜찮아요, 캐트?" 내가 공황 상태에 빠져 물었다.

"좀 아파요, 내 사랑."

p.278 나는 접대원에게 마차를 불러 달라고 요청했고 우리는 아래로

내려갔다. 밤은 청명했고 별들이 밝게 빛나고 있었다. 캐서린은 아주 흥분했다.

"진통이 시작되어서 아주 기뻐요." 캐서린이 말했다. "기다리는 것은 이제 곧 끝날 거예요."

"당신은 훌륭하고 용감한 여자예요."

병원에서 한 간호사가 우리를 맞이하고 우리를 병실로 안내해 주었다.

"여기가 환자분의 병실이에요." 여자가 말했다. "옷을 벗고 침대로 들어가세요. 여기, 환자분이 입으실 병원복이 있어요."

내가 무슨 말을 하기도 전에 캐서린은 분만실로 옮겨졌다. 나는 가운을 받았으므로 캐서린을 따라 안으로 들어갈 수 있었다.

"안녕, 내 사랑." 캐서린이 긴장된 목소리로 말했다. "긴장돼요."

"헨리 씨이십니까?" 의사가 물었다.

"네. 어떤가요, 의사 선생님?"

"아주 순조롭습니다." 의사가 말했다. p.279 "진통 때 마취를 시키기가 용이하기 때문에 이 안으로 들어온 것입니다."

"지금 마취하고 싶어요." 캐서린이 말했다. 의사는 캐서린의 얼굴에 고무 마스크를 착용시키고 다이얼을 돌렸으며, 나는 캐서린이 심호흡을 하고 있는 것을 지켜보았다.

"다시 하고 싶어요." 캐서린이 말했다. 캐서린은 고무 마스크를 자기 얼굴에 바짝 대고 가쁘게 숨을 쉬었다. 캐서린이 신음하는 소리가 들렸다. 그런 다음 캐서린은 마스크를 벗고 미소를 지었다.

"진통이 더 심해지고 있어요." 캐서린이 말했다. "하지만 걱정 마요, 내 사랑. 당신은 나가 계세요. 가서 아침 식사라도 좀 하세요."

나는 하라고 한 대로 했다. 내가 다시 돌아왔을 때, 의사는 나를 보고 안심하는 것 같았다.

"남편분이 오셨습니다." 의사가 말했다.

"오, 내 사랑, 이 의사 선생님은 훌륭하세요." 캐서린이 아주 낯선 목소리로 말했다.

p.280 "당신 마취제에 취했어요." 내가 말했다.

"알아요." 캐서린이 말했다. "조금 더 주세요. 조금 더 주세요." 캐서린은 마스크를 붙잡고 인공호흡기가 딸각딸각 소리가 나도록 짧고 깊게 숨을 쉬었다. 의사는 나에게 자기와 함께 밖으로 나가자고 몸짓했다.

“환자분이 아주 고통이 심합니다.” 의사가 말했다. “우리에게는 두 가지 선택권이 있습니다. 산모와 아기 둘 다에게 아주 위험할 수 있는 겸자 분만을 하거나 제왕 절개를 하는 것입니다.”

“제왕 절개를 하다가 죽으면 어떡해요?”

“제왕 절개는 정상 분만보다 조금도 위험하지 않습니다.”

“선생님이 직접 집도하실 거죠?”

“네.”

“그러면 어서 해 주십시오, 의사 선생님.”

분만실 안에서 나는 캐서린이 고통으로 비명을 지르는 소리를 들었다. 의사가 안으로 들어갔고 간호사들이 따라 들어가며 말했다. “제왕 절개를 할 거예요. p.281 제왕 절개를 할 거예요.”

약 한 시간쯤 후에 의사가 나오고 간호사가 따라 나왔다. 의사는 방금 막 껍질을 벗긴 토끼처럼 생긴 것을 두 손으로 들고 있었다. 의사는 그것을 들고 복도를 급히 가로질러 갔고 다른 문을 통과했다. 나는 의사를 따라갔고 그들이 방에서 갓난아이에게 어떤 조치를 하고 있는 것을 발견했다. 의사는 갓난아기의 발뒤꿈치를 잡아 들어 올리고 아기를 찰싹 때렸다.

“아기는 괜찮나요?”

“멋진 아들입니다. 적어도 5킬로그램은 나갈 겁니다.”

나는 아기에게는 별 감정이 없었다. 어쨌든 나와는 관련이 있는 것 같지 않았다. 나는 부성애가 전혀 느껴지지 않았다.

p.282 “아들이 자랑스럽지 않으세요?” 간호사가 물었다.

“자기 엄마를 거의 죽일 뻔했어요.” 내가 말했다. “그래서 자랑스럽지 않습니다!”

“아들이 생겨서 행복하지 않으세요?”

“우리는 아들을 원하지 않았어요.” 내가 말했다.

나는 복도를 달려 내려갔고 분만실 문으로 갔다. 캐서린은 죽은 것처럼 보였다. 캐서린의 얼굴은 잿빛이었다. 아래쪽 조명 밑에서 다른 의사가 캐서린을 봉합하고 있었다. 잠시 후 의사가 나왔다.

“환자는 어떤가요?”

“이제 들어가서 만나 보셔도 됩니다.”

나는 분만실로 들어갔고 캐서린은 손을 내밀었다.

“안녕, 내 사랑.” 캐서린이 말했다. 캐서린의 목소리는 아주 약했다.

"안녕."

"아들이에요, 딸이에요?"

p.283 "쉿. 말하지 마세요." 간호사가 말했다.

"아들이에요. 튼튼하고 건강해요."

간호사가 이상하게 나를 쳐다보았다.

"이제 나가 주세요." 간호사가 말했다. "헨리 부인은 휴식을 취하셔야 해요."

"바로 밖에 있을게요. 얘기 좀 할까요?" 내가 간호사에게 말했다. 간호사는 나를 따라 복도로 나왔다. 우리는 복도 아래쪽으로 조금 걸었다.

"아기가 잘못됐나요?" 내가 물었다.

"모르셨어요?"

"네."

"살지 못했어요."

"사산아였나요?"

"숨을 쉬지 않고 있었어요. 탯줄이 아기 목에 감겨 있었든지 그랬던 것 같아요."

"그래서 죽었나요?"

"네. 유감입니다. 참 예쁘고 몸집이 좋은 아들이었는데요."

p.284 나는 창밖이 내다보이는 복도에 있는 의자에 앉았다. 어두운 하늘과 창문에서 들어오는 빛을 가로질러 떨어지는 비 외에는 아무것도 보이지 않았다. 그랬던 것이다. 우리의 아기는 죽어 있었다. 그래서 의사가 그렇게 지쳐 보였던 것이었다. 하지만 그들이 처치실에서 왜 그렇게 아기에게 적극적으로 조치하고 있었을까? 그들은 아기가 의식을 회복하고 제대로 숨을 쉬기 시작할 거라고 생각했던 것이 분명하다.

그래서 이제 나는 복도 밖에 앉아서 캐서린이 어떤지 이야기를 들으려고 기다렸다. 간호사가 나오지 않았으므로 잠시 후 나는 문으로 다가가 문을 아주 가만히 열고 안을 들여다보았다. 복도는 불빛이 밝은데 방 안은 깜깜했기 때문에 처음에 나는 아무것도 볼 수 없었다. 그런 다음 나는 침대 옆에 앉아 있는 간호사와 베개를 벤 캐서린의 머리를 보았다. 간호사가 조용히 문으로 다가왔다.

p.285 "아내는 어때요?" 내가 물었다.

"환자분은 괜찮아요." 간호사가 말했다. "가서 저녁을 좀 드시고 그러고 나서 다시 오세요. 환자분은 쉬셔야 합니다."

나는 복도를 지나 계단을 내려가서 병원 문을 나섰다. 나는 빗속을 뚫고 어두운 거리를 내려가 카페로 갔다. 카페는 안이 환하게 불이 밝혀져 있었고 탁자에는 많은 사람들이 있었다.

나는 햄과 달걀을 먹고 맥주를 마셨다. 햄과 달걀은 둥근 접시에 담겨 있었는데, 햄이 밑에 있고 달걀이 위에 있었다. 그것은 아주 뜨거웠고 처음에 한 입 가득 먹고 나서 나는 내 입 안을 식히기 위해 맥주를 한 모금 들이켜야 했다. 나는 몹시 배가 고팠고 웨이터에게 한 접시를 더 주문했다. 나는 음식과 함께 넉 잔의 맥주를 마셨다. 나는 아무 생각도 할 수가 없었으나 내 맞은편 남자의 신문을 읽을 수는 있었다. 그것은 영국군 전선에서의 돌파 작전에 관한 기사였다.

p.286 내가 자기 신문의 뒷면을 읽고 있는 것을 보았을 때 그 남자는 신문을 접었다. 나는 웨이터에게 신문을 달라고 할 생각을 했지만, 집중할 수가 없었다. 카페 안은 더웠고 공기는 담배 연기가 자욱했다. 탁자에 앉아 있는 대부분의 사람들은 서로 알고 있었다. 카드 게임이 몇 개 진행되고 있었다. 웨이터들은 바에서 탁자로 술을 나르느라고 분주했다. 나는 일어나기 전에 맥주 두 잔을 더 시켰고 병원으로 돌아왔다.

병원에서 나는 복도로 내려오는 간호사를 만났다.

"호텔에 전화를 계속 드리고 있었어요." 간호사가 말했다. 나의 몸 안에서 심장이 덜컥 내려앉았다.

"뭐가 잘못됐나요?"

"부인께 출혈이 있습니다."

"제가 안에 들어가서 아내를 봐도 됩니까?"

"아니요, 죄송하지만 아직 안 됩니다. 의사 선생님이 부인과 함께 계세요."

p.287 "심각한가요?"

"아주 심각합니다." 간호사는 병실 안으로 들어가서 문을 닫았다. 나는 바깥 복도에 앉았다. 몸 안에서 모든 것이 완전히 빠져나갔다. 나는 생각하지 않았다. 생각할 수 없었다. 나는 그저 캐서린이 죽을 것임을 알았고, 그녀가 죽지 않게 해 달라고 기도했다. "캐서린이 죽지 않게 해 주세요. 오, 하느님, 제발 저에게서 캐서린을 데려가지 마세요. 캐서린이 죽지 않게 해 주신다면 무엇이든 하겠습니다. 제발, 제발, 제발요, 하느님, 캐서린이 죽게 두지 마세요. 하느님, 캐서린이 죽게 두지 마세요. 제발, 제발, 제발 캐서린이 죽게 두지 마세요. 하느님, 제발 캐서린을 데려가지 마세요. 캐서린이 죽게 놔두지 않으신다면 저는 당신께서 말씀하시는 무엇이든 하겠습니다. 이미 저희 아기를 데려가셨잖아요! 캐서린이 죽게 놔두지 마세요. 아기는 데려가셔도 되지만 캐서린이 죽게 두시면 안 됩니다. 제발, 제발, 제발요, 하느님, 캐서린이 죽게 놔두지 마세요."

간호사는 문을 열고 손가락으로 나에게 들어오라고 신호를 했다. **p.288** 나는 간호사를 따라 분만실로 들어갔다. 내가 들어갔을 때 캐서린은 위를 쳐다보지 않았다. 나는 침대 한옆으로 다가갔다. 의사가 침대 반대쪽 옆에 있었다. 캐서린은 나를 보고 미소를 지었다. 나는 침대에 몸을 숙이고 울기 시작했다.

"가여운 내 사랑." 캐서린이 아주 부드럽게 말했다. 캐서린은 완전히 잿빛이었다.

"당신은 괜찮아요, 캐트." 내가 말했다. "다 괜찮아질 거야."

"나는 죽어가고 있어요." 캐서린이 말했다. 캐서린은 잠시 기다렸다가 말했다. "죽기 싫어요."

나는 캐서린의 손을 잡았다.

"나를 만지지 마세요." 캐서린이 말했다. 나는 캐서린의 손을 놓아 주었다. 캐서린이 미소를 지었다. "가엾은 내 사랑. 나를 만지고 싶으면 실컷 만져도 돼요."

"당신은 괜찮을 거예요, 캐트. 우리는 이것을 이겨낼 거예요. 당신이 괜찮을 것이라는 것을 나는 알아요."

"만약 무슨 일이 일어난다면 당신에게 편지를 쓸 생각이었지만, 편지를 쓸 시간이 없었어요."

p.289 "신부님이든 누구든 와서 당신을 만나 봐 달라고 했으면 좋겠소?"

"당신만 있으면 돼요." 캐서린이 말했다. "나는 죽는 것이 두렵지 않아요. 다만 미울 뿐이에요."

"너무 많이 말씀하시지 마세요." 의사가 말했다.

"괜찮아요." 캐서린이 말했다.

"나에게 뭐 시키고 싶은 것이 있소, 캐트? 무엇을 가져다줄까요?"

"아니요." 캐서린이 미소를 지으며 말했다. 그런 다음 잠시 후 말했다. "다른 여자와 우리가 한 일을 하거나 다른 여자에게 당신이 나에게 했던 말을 하지 마세요, 그래 줄 거죠?"

“절대로 안 할게요.”

“그래도 여자들을 만나면 좋겠어요.”

“그러기 싫어요.”

“말씀을 너무 많이 하고 계세요.” 의사가 가로막았다. p.290 “헨리 씨는 이제 가셔야 합니다. 나중에 다시 오시면 돼요. 아무도 죽지 않을 것입니다. 어리석게 구시면 안 됩니다.”

“알았어요.” 캐서린이 말했다. 캐서린은 말하는 것이 몹시 힘들었다.

“이제 방을 나가 주세요.” 의사가 나에게 말했다. “말씀을 하시면 안 됩니다.” 의사가 캐서린에게 말했다.

캐서린은 나에게 윙크를 했고, 그녀의 얼굴은 전보다 더 잿빛이었다.

“문 밖에 있겠소.” 내가 말했다.

“내 걱정은 하지 마세요, 내 사랑.” 캐서린이 말했다. “나는 전혀 두렵지 않아요.”

나는 바깥 복도에서 기다렸다. 나는 아주 오랜 시간을 기다렸다. 간호사가 문으로 오더니 나에게 다가왔다.

“부인께서 매우 위독하신 것 같습니다, 헨리 씨.” 간호사가 말했다.

“죽었나요?”

“아니요, 하지만 의식 불명입니다.”

나는 캐서린이 연속으로 출혈을 일으켰다고 들었다. p.291 의사는 출혈을 멈출 수가 없었다. 나는 분만실로 들어가 그녀가 죽을 때까지 캐서린과 같이 있었다. 캐서린은 한 번도 의식을 회복하지 못했고, 그녀가 죽는 데는 그리 오래 걸리지 않았다.

분만실 밖의 복도에서 나는 의사에게 말을 건넸다.

“오늘 밤 제가 여기에서 해야 할 일이 있습니까?”

“아니요, 헨리 씨가 하실 일은 아무것도 없습니다. 제가 헨리 씨를 호텔까지 모셔다 드릴까요?”

“아니요, 고맙습니다. 잠깐 여기 있겠습니다.”

“제가 드릴 말씀이 아무것도 없다는 것은 압니다. 이런 말씀은 드릴 필요도 없지만 얼마나 유감인지…….”

“괜찮습니다.” 내가 말했다. “아무 말씀 안 하셔도 됩니다.”

“안녕히 가세요.” 의사가 말했다. “정말로 호텔까지 모셔다 드리지 않아도 됩니까?”

p.292 “네, 고맙습니다.”

“제왕 절개는 저희에게 남은 유일한 선택 사항이었습니다.” 의사가 말했다.

“괜찮습니다.” 내가 말했다. “그 일에 관해서는 말하고 싶지 않습니다.”

“제가 호텔까지 모셔다 드리게 해 주십시오.”

“아니요, 고맙습니다.

의사는 복도를 내려갔다. 나는 분만실 문으로 갔다.

“이제 들어오실 수 없습니다.” 간호사 한 명이 말했다.

“아니, 들어갈 수 있습니다.” 내가 말했다.

“헨리 씨, 아직 들어오시면 안 됩니다.”

“아니요. 당신이 나가시오.” 내가 말했다. “당신들 전부 다 나가란 말이야.”

나는 그들을 내보내고 문을 잠그고 불을 껐지만, 모두 소용없었다. 그것은 조각상에게 작별 인사를 하는 것 같았다. 잠시 후 나는 병원을 떠나 빗속을 뚫고 호텔로 걸어서 돌아갔다.

memo

memo